All-American Girl

All-American Girl

The Ideal of
Real Womanhood
in Mid-Nineteenth-
Century America

Frances B. Cogan

The University of Georgia Press

Athens and London

© 1989 by the University of Georgia Press
Athens, Georgia 30602
All rights reserved

Designed by Louise M. Jones
Set in 10/13 Meridien
The paper in this book meets the guidelines for
permanence and durability of the Committee on
Production Guidelines for Book Longevity of the
Council on Library Resources.

Printed in the United States of America

93 92 91 90 89   5 4 3 2 1

Library of Congress Cataloging in Publication Data

Cogan, Frances B.
  All-American girl.

  Bibliography: p.
  Includes index.
    1. Middle class women—United States—History—
19th century. 2. Middle class women—United States—
Social conditions. 3. Feminism—United States—
History—19th century. I. Title.
HQ1419.C64   1989   305.4′2′0973   88-8590
ISBN 0-8203-1062-X (alk. paper)
ISBN 0-8203-1063-8 (pbk.: alk. paper)

British Library Cataloging in Publication Data available.

Most of the *Harper's Weekly* illustrations in this book
are from the Hargrett Rare Book and Manuscript
Library, University of Georgia Libraries. The author
and the Press thank the library staff for their kind
assistance in gathering the illustrations.

To my husband, Dan

To my parents, George F. and Clarajane Browning

And most of all, to my daughter, Betsy—
my own modern version of a potential "Real Woman."

Contents

Acknowledgments

In large measure, this book was made possible by the generous and continuing research grant support I received from several agencies. I would like to thank the National Endowment for the Humanities for the summer stipend I received in 1985, the Oregon Committee for the Humanities for the summer research grant I received in 1984, and the University of Oregon Faculty Research Grant Committee for awarding me a summer research fellowship in 1983. Through all the years, however, my mainstay has been the Center for the Study of Women in Society, which not only provided me with research grants and funding in 1985 and 1986 but published an article of mine, provided typing, xeroxing, and postage money when my home department could not, and generally supported me in every way possible, including paying for a research assistant, Lynn Botelho, whose excellent services I would not otherwise have had in 1985.

Colleagues and other professionals have also been responsible in many ways for this book making its way to a publisher. I would like to thank Professor Stuart Levine especially for his kindness, understanding, and recommendations, through *American Studies;* he encouraged me in my earliest efforts and, without ever meeting me face to face, extended a helping hand. Professor Louise Westling, a longtime friend and associate at Oregon, not only provided me with a personal introduction to her editor but was supportive on all other fronts as well. This editor, Karen Orchard of the University of Georgia Press, deserves heartfelt thanks for her patience and hand-holding throughout this process. Copy editor Trudie Calvert should get a medal for her punctilious, thorough, and sensitive editing of the text, leaving it more graceful certainly than she found it.

Here at Oregon I could not have begun this effort without the very vital help of Professor Richard Maxwell Brown of the History Department, who reviewed my methodology, discussed the scope of my project, and vetted my first full grant application. Friends as well listened, commented, and encouraged me; I would like to thank Gloria Johnson, Charlene Gates, Aletta Biersack, Susan Bowers, and Fred Newberry. I would also like to thank my department chairman, Professor Richard Stevenson of the Honors College, for reading my introduction and suggesting some very useful revisions. I should also acknowledge the continuing and enthusiastic support I received from my wonderful Honors College students throughout this process. I would also like to thank my brother, Tom Browning; his wife, Susan; and my niece, Cassie, as well as my cousin, Steve Stivers, for continuing moral support.

Faculty services at Oregon were invaluable in helping me complete this project. Foremost among them was the excellent help I received from the University of Oregon Library—the library in which I did all of my research. Thanks to Librarian George Shipman and his staff, microfilm and a microfilm reader were made available to me on a continuing basis, as well as access to rare nineteenth-century periodicals and advice books and continual help in tracking down sources across the country.

My acknowledgments would not be complete without mentioning the vital support and care given me in more ways than the merely physiological by my family doctor, Dr. Peter Cary. Through flu and doubts about child rearing, through thyroid testing and my child's emergency appendectomy, he was always there. I was able to complete this work in large part because of his spirited, thoughtful, and humane treatment of all our family's ills.

In conclusion, I must acknowledge the central value and aid beyond the call of duty of my typist, Joann Brady, who squeezed four pages into two on grant applications, typed when applications were due in twenty-four hours, and always managed to present me with material that looked exquisite, despite the incomprehensible rough drafts I handed in. To her most of all, I owe my most sincere thanks.

All-American Girl

Introduction

While inferior status and oppressive restraints were no doubt aspects of women's historical experience . . . the limitation of this approach is that it makes it appear either that women were largely passive or that, at the most, they reacted to male pressures or to the restraints of patriarchal society. Such inquiry fails to elicit the positive and essential way in which women have functioned in history.

—Gerda Lerner,
The Majority Finds Its Past

G erda Lerner's warning rang out nearly ten years ago, but it went largely unheard and unheeded, judging from recent works of feminist history and women's social history and criticism. The result has been exactly what Professor Lerner predicted—most readers and critics now regard the majority of American women in the nineteenth century as mindless consumers and drudges of a male-dominated capitalist world. This picture includes few, with the obvious exception of a pioneering cadre of early feminist women's rights advocates, to whom a modern woman can look with pride or even minimal psychological comfort. Indeed, set like a black opal in a frame of wretched wages and conditions for working-class women is the mid-nineteenth-century concept of the middle-class "Lady of Leisure." She "toils not, neither does she spin," we are told; rather, she carefully dedicates her life to ladylike consumption of luxury goods and practices devotions at the shrine of fashion and beauty, the former in whose service she distorts her rib cage and internal organs with corsets, the latter for which she becomes a "delicate flower" and a passive parasite. This, according to historians and critics, is the quintessential ideal of mid-nineteenth-century middle-class women. The wrongs done to women themselves stand out clearly in this picture, but uneasily, not nearly so clearly as the apparently tremendous idiocy of women who held such values.

How could our great-grandmothers and great-great-grandmothers have ever been intellectually seduced by such vicious nonsense, we wonder—and on the apparently enormous scale indicated by eminent historians, feminists, and social critics such as Lois Banner, Carroll Smith-Rosenberg, Catherine Clinton, and particularly, Barbara Welter? How could vast numbers of American middle-class women have clutched to their healthy bosoms an ideal of the "submissive maiden" when that ideal was physically injurious, economically unworkable, legally contraindicated for survival within the restraints of marriage, and intellectually vacuous?[1] Some historians, Anne Douglas among them, in her landmark 1977 work *The Feminization of American Culture*, dispute the notion that women pursued this ideal wholeheartedly and suggest that they maintained such a steel-engraved image only superficially, covertly holding the reins of influence inside the family, the church, and the social world to achieve what slight protections and partial reforms such women felt were possible.

I wish to offer with this study an alternative explanation. Although many women possibly did adhere to the stereotype of the fragile maiden (and used it as a cover for covert action), I suggest that another, more open, completely autonomous and indigenous American popular ideal existed for them to emulate—one that stressed, in Lerner's words, "a more positive and essential way" for women to cope with the world around them. This popular ideal advocated intelligence, physical fitness and health, self-sufficiency, economic self-reliance, and careful marriage: it was, in other words, a survival ethic. Though the writers who propounded this image—men and women both—did not officially name their ideal, they did say that they advocated a pattern by which "real women" (as opposed to Welter's famous Cult of True Women) should guide their lives. Because of this reference, I have chosen to call this competing ideal the Ideal of the Real Woman or Real Womanhood. It is my intention not only to prove that such a healthy ideal existed independently and coherently apart from the better-known Cult of True Womanhood but to point out its autonomy from the thrust of nineteenth-century feminism as well. The ideal of the Real Woman was a popular, middle-of-the-road image that recognized the disparities and the dangers protested by early feminists but tried to deal with those ugly realities in what it saw as a "female" way. It placed itself, therefore, firmly in the "separate sphere" controversy by claiming a unique sphere of action and duty for women, but one vastly extended and magically swollen past the dimensions of anything meant by that term to devotees of competing True Womanhood.

Further, I will show that the Ideal of Real Womanhood based its advice not, as did the Cult of True Womanhood, on the physiological and biological interpretations of female inferiority offered by heroic medicine, but rather on the triple bases of absolute necessity, health reform precepts, and observable clinical reality. Far from assuming that women were nervous, hysterical, and biologically weak specimens from birth, easily subdued and dominated by male force, strong emotion, and male rationality, the Real Womanhood ideal offered American women a vision of themselves as biologically equal (rationally as well as emotionally) and in many cases markedly superior in intellect to what passed for male business sense, scholarship, and theological understanding. Moreover, the Ideal of Real Womanhood demanded that the woman's duty to herself and her loved ones was not, as True Womanhood seems to suggest, to die, but rather to live; not to sacrifice herself, but to survive.

Survival under the Ideal of Real Womanhood, however, demanded that one do so as a *woman*, not as an *androgyne* or "freak"; the advocates of Real Womanhood saw the latter as the degraded and unnatural province of feminism, from which they deliberately distinguished themselves. Real Women survived but remained good daughters, good sisters, wives, and mothers because in their own eyes they were important to family and to society; they did not survive merely because they owed it to themselves alone to do so.

Here, then, is the critical rub for many feminist historians: the sense of duty to others, especially duty defined by gender roles, destroys any interpretation of these Real Womanhood writers as feminist and, to the unwary critical eye, identifies them to some degree with the self-sacrific-ing, self-denying maidens of the steel-engraving stereotype. This limited degree, unfortunately, has often proved enough for critics to dismiss such writers' works from thorough analysis, and therefore the Ideal of Real Womanhood has been ignored in the past, relegated to the status of either a marginally more sensible version of True Womanhood or, con-versely, as evidence of certain unrelated "anomalies" (unimportant in themselves) that occasionally cropped up outside the boundaries of the Cult of True Womanhood and, in a hazy, timid way, predicted the rise of feminism.

A good indicator of this research confusion exists in the scholarly notes of many current works: recent critics and historians have tended to view the complexity of nineteenth-century popular ideals in terms provided by the work of Barbara Welter, whose classic study, *Dimity Convictions*, gave the world in 1976 the first articulated critical discussion and definition of the Cult of True Womanhood, as well as placing that phrase in the history books for the foreseeable future. Critic after critic seemingly ignores the evidence of her own eyes because it contradicts Welter's monolithic paradigm of True Womanhood.[2] My argument is not with Welter's excellent scholarship, which proves the existence of such an ideal, but with the assumption that True Womanhood was the *only* popular ideal.

I have, however, other methodological and historiographic questions about recent work in the field, and since these questions have an important bearing on the current neglect of the Ideal of Real Womanhood, they need to be explored fully before I provide extensive proof for that ideal. My objections can be summarized by identifying four broad areas of disagreement: (1) the theory of evolutionary feminism; (2) the viability of applying the techniques and foci of the New Social History to popular middle-class works; (3) the applicability of neo-Marxian approaches to sources; and, finally, (4) the "oppressed past" approach to women's history, with its devaluation of ideals and didactic literature as a field of study. The problems I have encountered in each of these areas result, I feel, from historical or critical assumptions that distort our picture of mid-nineteenth-century popular ideals, leaving a heavily and artificially polarized theoretical picture that pits the last century's women's rights movement against the Cult of True Womanhood and ignores any possible alternative or middle position philosophically.

Of these arguments, perhaps the current tendency to dismiss as naive and critically unsophisticated any straightforward reading of primary texts has the most distressing effect. This approach seems to result in a curious critical blindness about what nineteenth-century popular writers actually said and substitutes for primary source information a theoretical version of either what such writers *should* have said or what critics assume they *meant*.

An example can show the unhappy result of ignoring the words and import of primary sources. Lois Banner, for example, in her otherwise excellent book about the changing concepts of American beauty during the past century (*American Beauty*, 1983), quotes various "reformers," who openly despised "Fashion" and wrote voluminously about the evil effects of corsets, cosmetics, and languor on the health and character of female America; Banner further notes that widely circulated periodicals such as *Harper's New Monthly Magazine* went so far as to warn young women of the health dangers of cosmetics because of their lead and mercury components. These serious concerns hardly seem to be proof of a mindless and monolithic acceptance of fashion and beauty above health, especially given the popularity of the periodical, yet Banner continues to dismiss their significance because "many were written to spread the reputations of their authors, and to promote sales of their own products."[3] In addition to these apparently self-serving health reformers, however, Banner goes on to list popular support for advice books advocating dress reform, preventive versus "heroic" medicine, and exercise—all insisted upon by writers seemingly without a single product to sell. Despite the obvious and significant popularity of such reform works, Banner dismisses their authors as "isolated reformers,"[4] who should not be considered as purveying a competing ideal simply because they ultimately failed to change the mind of female America about its adherence to Fashion. Curiously, she continues to point to the wealth of "irregular" medical men and advice writers (homeopaths such as Dr. Dio Lewis) and physical exercise specialists (such as William Blaikie), who joined the hue and cry for sensible diet, exercise, and dress reform, thereby seemingly deserting almost every precept of True Womanhood and fashion by advocating their complete antithesis in the popular press. The notion of a uniform acceptance of the pale, delicate, invalided maiden so beloved of True Womanhood advocates, then, seems dangerously threatened by these various splinter groups, which, though not coordinated in their efforts, nonetheless assaulted many of the same targets—all of which were the underpinnings of the Cult of True Womanhood. Denunciations like the following by Dr. Dio Lewis are obviously aimed at that ideal: "The fragile, pale young woman with a lisp, is thought, by many silly people, to be more a *lady,* than another with ruddy cheeks, and vigorous health. . . . There exists, somehow in the fashionable world, the notion that a pale and sensitive woman is feminine and refined, while one in blooming health is masculine and coarse."[5]

I would find it easier, along with Banner, to discount the significance of this growing mob of anti–True Womanhood voices if their advocacy of ruddy cheeks and splendid health had not made its way into the popular literature of the day as well. Short stories in popular magazines like *Harper's New Monthly Magazine* and *Ladies' Repository*—in which the heroine flexes her biceps and engages in strenuous physical activity—demand that more careful consideration be given to reform writers such as Lewis and Blaikie because their arguments obviously helped shape the popular image of the heroine in these stories. In Nora Perry's *Harper's* short story "Rosalind Newcomb," for example, the heroine is tanned and strong in the best tradition of Dr. Lewis; moreover, she is proud of her pink cheeks and strong arms and attributes these points of female desirability to her daily exercise "grubbing" in the fresh air two hours a day: "Gardening is a great beautifier, because it is so healthful. It makes one plump, and hearty, and pretty."[6]

Nor is the periodical short story the only popular form of literature in which the frail maiden is dismissed and the little brown girl summoned to serve as heroine. Mary Jane Holmes's 'Lena in the novel *'Lena Rivers,* Holmes's extraordinary secondary heroine, Maude, appearing in buckskins and carrying guns in *Rose Mather,* as well as Marion Harland's "Frank" Berry in *Ruby's Husband* indicate the presence of healthy, desirable womanhood in wide-selling domestic fiction. Indeed, this notion of the heroine even migrates into didactic children's fiction with such heroines as Louisa May Alcott's Rose, who is restored to health, loveliness, and moral duty by cold water and daily exercise in *Eight Cousins.*

Even popular female iconographs of patriotic virtue find themselves imbued with healthy and physically strong characteristics, as an article of Centennial nostalgia, "A Revolutionary Girl's Pluck," makes evident in the July 1876 *Illustrated Christian Weekly.* The author eulogizes the bravery and physical endurance of eighteen-year-old Emily Geiger, who rode a "fleet" horse "under perilous circumstances" to carry important messages from General Green to General Sumler. To do so she had to race through lines of pursuing British soldiers and, when finally captured, eat the messages, break away, make a run for the Continental lines, and deliver the messages from memory.[7] This is clearly a model of traditional American female endurance, "pluck," and bravery meant by the author to be antithetical to the delicate maiden of the Cult of True Womanhood with her smelling salts in one hand and a French novel in the other! "Real" American women are capable of performing like Emily Geiger; *un*-American women are too timid and too weak, the article seems to suggest.

When not only "isolated reformers" but novelists, not only short-story writers but authors of advice and best-selling etiquette books, continue to denounce female fragility, pale thin faces, and listlessness in the strongest and most unambivalent terms, a critic must deliberately seek strained explanations for such uniformity of opinion over an extended period of time beyond the obvious one that another ideal than True Womanhood existed. Primary texts, then, when read carefully and critically, are an invaluable source for discovering the shape of popular ideals.

To give Lois Banner her due, however, she acknowledges that the "majority of writers of nineteenth century advice literature also scorned the woman of fashion";[8] obviously she recognizes the presence of other ideal attributes for women, though not of another coherent *ideal.* She fails, however, to attribute any significance to these specifications because she believes that they were not translated into actual historical practice on any widespread basis among actual women. If women continued to wear corsets, complain of illness, and use cosmetics to make them appear paler before 1860 (after which year Banner acknowledges the ascent of a healthier standard of beauty), then such isolated reform ideals must not have any significance worth studying. This argument, finally, seems to devolve from the difference between studying and analyzing prescriptive and descriptive literature; critics have recognized in the past that the first does not necessarily lead to the second, *even,* I would add, in the case of the supposedly uniformly worshiped Cult of True Womanhood. It seems clear, for example, that the middle-class women traveling by wagon train to California and Oregon, the female missionaries, the women working all over the nation as schoolteachers, the women attending both female and coeducational schools of higher education, and the women supporting families did not follow the dictates of passive, sheltered, and fragile True Womanhood very convincingly either. Although such "exceptions" to the ideal exist in the historical evidence,[9] no one would insist that fragility and illness were never part of *a* popular ideal. My point is simply to suggest that it is very likely, based on didactic literature and popular novels—primary sources both—that more than one popular ideal for middle-class American women existed and was embraced between 1840 and 1880. American women, dealing with the complexities of real (as opposed to advice book) life, probably followed *neither* ideal slavishly.

The picture of what women in the mid-nineteenth century *did* value is further complicated by preconceptions among some modern historians about what is worth studying—and for what purpose. In Carroll Smith-Rosenberg's latest compilation, *Disorderly Conduct* (1985), she, more than any other historian or critic, clearly states one of the critical assumptions I have felt shadowing much of modern women's historiography. "Women's history," she explains, "is the daughter of political feminism." In fact, the very field of women's history owes its existence to the feminist movement of this century with its thirst to uncover a specifically female past.[10] No one could dispute the enormous debt scholars today interested in a uniquely female social, political, and literary culture owe to historians like Professor Smith-Rosenberg. The close and natural alliance between feminism and women's history, however, spawns a possible perceptual problem, I think. What one sees in *Disorderly Conduct,* in Lois Banner's *American Beauty,* and in Catherine Clinton's *The Other Civil War* (all works of the mid-1980s) is a tendency to regard primary sources as evidence either for or against a concept of "progress" up an evolutionary slope toward the pinnacle of feminism and modern consciousness. Any source that fails to provide a crucial step in this evolutionary climb tends to be dismissed as either retrograde or unimportant—or worse, occasionally gets wrenched into feminist shape, against all the evidence.

This interpretive bias immediately presents problems to those of us who study primary sources that are distinctly not feminist but that share similar goals with nineteenth-century feminist writers. The sources I have cited—dealing with fitness, for example, as well as attacking fashion—parallel writings by both Elizabeth Cady Stanton and Amelia Bloomer on these subjects. The former sources, however, cannot be seen even remotely as evidence of widespread feminist thinking because their authors refused to abandon the concept of a separate sphere of duty and activity exclusive to women.[11] Such sources, when critics and historians study them at all, are often jettisoned as examples of failed or stunted gropings toward modern consciousness. Women's history has become, in practice, perhaps too often, a study of feminist history alone. Although such a central focus is understandable, it excludes a large and important body of evidence, which, given sufficient critical attention, reveals a much more interesting landscape of middle-class women's values in the last century than most readers have experienced thus far; such readings see traditional values in an unnatural light because the entire popular past has tended to be used as a whipping boy for present feminist history.

I intend in this study to show the fine discriminations, the ingenious accommodations, the rationales behind the reform movements in health care, higher education, marriage choice, and employment which the group of writers I have loosely dubbed the supporters of Real Womanhood used, thereby necessarily stretching the definition of "woman's sphere," a sphere they stubbornly refused to relinquish. I wish to examine as well why such writers felt they had to maintain the fairy tale of women's sphere when they patently could not continue within its traditional boundaries. I will explore also the philosophical accommodations they made in their attempts to balance the realities and necessities of employment and child care, higher education and marriage. I hope to provide by this exploration a historical model for modern women either to accept or to reject, as well as an illuminating example (from a safely remote past) that illustrates the possible double thinking often involved in such balancing acts.

Such illustrative historical examples, however, may be ruled out altogether if one uses, as some recent critics and historians have, the tools and methods of the New Social History. On the surface, this would not seem to be the case. As Carroll Smith-Rosenberg explains, the New Social History has rightly redirected much historical energy away from traditional sources of inquiry such as the letters, battles, and political fortunes of famous men and famous female "honorary men"; instead, it applies its scrutiny to the lives of those "outcast" groups not generally considered worthy of sustained study—blacks, immigrants, the working class, and the "inarticulate." It also, as Smith-Rosenberg notes, sheds new light on the domestic worlds of these outcast groups, thereby providing a fuller and more accurate context, with a focus appealingly female and officially valid.

Although I agree strongly with Smith-Rosenberg and especially with Gerda Lerner about the importance of such a general shift (from the public to the domestic, for example) and accept the validity of studying subjects so woefully neglected in the past, I wonder if there is not an unconscious bias inherent in an approach that becomes less useful in studying the works of nonoutcast groups such as those appealed to by middle-class popular women's literature and advice texts. Because the New Social History concentrates on extracting insight from generally inarticulate or unpublished rather than popular sources, it seems uneasy in addressing itself with sufficient critical stringency to highly articulate works squarely in the mainstream tradition. One does not, for example, need to speculate imaginatively using the skeletal remains of a personal account book or diary of expenditures (a source frequently studied by the New Social History) about what a *popular* advice writer felt was important. Didactic literature by its very nature evaluates the world and presents its message straightforwardly, even stridently.

One could make a case (and many have) that this direct didacticism, especially in the case of domestic novels, is simply a stalking-horse for darker, more rebellious and contradictory feelings. I acknowledge that such a subtext is indeed possible; that is the reason I use such a variety of genres, rather than focusing solely on domestic novels, which, as Nina Baym especially has pointed out, tend to reveal interesting contradictory attitudes underneath the apparent support for the traditional restrictions of women's sphere.[12] A variety of genres, by both male and female writers, however, tends to support on the surface the presence of a unified, articulated ideal, which agrees fundamentally on key specifications of conduct, belief, duty, and standard accomplishment—on the ideals of what I have called Real Womanhood. Uniformity of opinion on the surface, I would suggest, has significance, especially expressed in multiple genres over a period of forty years.

The apparent preference of the New Social historians for documents and literature of outcast groups allies itself with another historiographical approach, the neo-Marxian. Both approaches run into interpretive problems, I believe, with these same middle-class, popular texts. The crux of the analytical problem rests with the dogged way such historians cling to an interpretation of the Cult of True Womanhood and their deliberate dismissal of texts advocating any other popular ideal. The very existence of a popular Cult of True Womanhood, they feel, supports and underlies the basic economic divisions developed around 1840 and provides evidence of the self-serving philosophy capitalist forces attempted to inculcate in women through the publishing industry. Industrialization took the means of production out of the home and placed it in the factory, as Gerda Lerner explains;[13] as a result, the theory goes, middle-class women, metaphorically, stripped of their looms and their spinning wheels, were left with nothing to do but consume in leisure. How they consumed, why they should consume, the moral justifications for consumption, and the symbolic, status-related importance of both consumption and leisure, Marxian historians claim, were the bones and sinews of the Cult of True Womanhood advice books and domestic novels and the reason for those texts' existence. In other words, capitalistic forces were afoot, and the publishing industry and the coterie of popular advice writers were their willing accomplices in convincing one segment of the population to support these unnatural divisions by spending, consuming, and staying out of the labor market.

Again, anyone who has read even a few of the advice books promoting the Cult of True Womanhood or even considered carefully the fantastically uncomfortable and restrictive fashions of the period cannot deny the thrust of the Marxian argument, any more than he or she can deny the division of labor on a national scale. My disagreement comes with the accompanying assumption that such a division—middle-class woman as passive consumer, man as active breadwinner and entrepreneurial capitalist—was monolithic, rigidly bounded or long enduring in individual cases. The advice books and domestic novels I have consulted present a much less sanguine understanding of the economic realities of the day—a vision more than supported by business historians such as Thomas Cochran. As he points out, an enormous rate of growth between 1840 and 1890 meant that "no business system in any other leading nation faced as severe problems as in the United States. . . . Business men had to run fast merely to stand still." American business was plagued with problems unknown in Europe—the sheer geographical size of the country and attendant transportation problems, the absence of a bureaucratic middle-management class (or a tradition of one), and the lack of any government regulation. These flaws led in turn to a violently overheated economy, subject to periodic boom-bust cycles characterized by depressions, recessions, and periods of hectic growth because economic growth or failure was based on "a view of situations more focused on immediate competitive pressures and short-run tactics for meeting them than on perfecting orderly or routinized ways of doing things."[14]

A volatile national climate in which businesses formed, flourished, and frequently were ruined outside of any regulation meant that a man and his family could be hiring servants and building a new house from business profits one year and barely able, because of bankruptcy, to afford two rooms in a run-down boardinghouse the next. No woman's "leisured" status, either as wife or daughter, was inviolate or always clearly defined. However much bankruptcy threatened leisured status, I would agree with Burton Bledstein in *The Culture of Professionalism* that such tragedies did not of necessity threaten *middle-class* status. As Bledstein points out and Carl Degler concurs, the "middle-class" designation *in America* was enormous, blind, and shifting, embracing whole groups as long as they possessed certain values—thrift, industry, sensibility, education, and morality—and *thought* of themselves as middle class. It was not a definition centered, as European class distinctions were, on money, birth, or even profession necessarily, nor did it "refer to a person's confined position in the social structure." State of mind and commonly held values defined it.[15]

For advice books to teach women a rigid, Europeanized class definition requiring leisure and only ornamental skills with which to shine in that life, or flirting techniques by which to trap a "good prospect," often thought of as socially higher because of birth, was to offer readers in a shaky business climate a quick ticket to possible destitution. Whereas the Cult of True Womanhood promoted such short-range blindness, overwhelming evidence exists that the competing Ideal of Real Womanhood was based on a livelier awareness of long-term American economic realities and urged its young women to prepare accordingly. The Reverend George Burnap, a best-selling advice author of the 1840s, for example, urged all young women—even those with wealthy fathers— to "be prepared for the crisis" by learning job skills before marriage. Mrs. L. G. Abell, another prominent advice doyen, lauded the well-prepared working woman with a shiftless, bankrupt, or sick husband who could "place herself and family, by her own exertions, above want." The Reverend George Weaver added unequivocally that "no woman possessed of a genuine womanly character" would be without the skills in a crisis to supply "life's necessities" through "some livelihood."[16]

These are hardly the dictates of leisure or fashion; the popularity of the writers does suggest the presence of a widespread ideal in direct conflict with that of True Womanhood. Neo-Marxist historians do not tend to credit such concerns—or such responses in preparation for self-preservation—to their famous "ladies" of the mid-nineteenth-century middle class; rather, they maintain that a concern about job skills was the exclusive province of working-class women. Thus this approach fails to examine the fact or the significance of the appearance of working-class advice in a middle-class popular context and continues to analyze middle-class female American ideals inside a contextual bell jar sucked dry of anything but unlimited and unchallenged leisure status. Even Gerda Lerner slips occasionally into this trap; in her famous essay

"The Lady and the Millgirl," she insists that "the women of the upper and middle classes could use their newly gained time for leisure pursuits: they became ladies." She adds that "women's work outside the home no longer met with social approval" after 1840 except for "large numbers of women in low status, low pay and low skill industrial work." These "large numbers" who, according to Lerner, were "only a heartbeat away from insecurity, even poverty," she defines as strictly working-class housewives.[17] Unfortunately, this economic insecurity was a condition that was all too possible for the "leisured" as well, given the economic climate and the reality of multiple business failures.

One last central issue needs to be addressed, and, to a degree, it also uncovers a certain historical presumptuousness: the current devaluation of studying ideals, unless one studies the degree to which those ideals are translated into historical reality, especially a historical reality that might be called the "oppressed past." I have already begun to address this issue in my discussion of Lois Banner's work and in making a distinction between prescriptive and descriptive sources. The value of studying prescriptive sources themselves, however, remains undefended, especially in the face of some feminist critics' contention that emphasis on ideals does grave disservice to the multitude of injustices historically present in so many women's lives. To study an ideal, they seem to say, is to trivialize reality—a reality in which married women before the Civil War were "legally dead," as Helen Woodward points out. Since women were classed with minors, lunatics, and idiots, they had no legal control over their own money, property, children, or, to a large extent, lives. Primary sources reflect this fact. One has only to read Mrs. A. J. Graves's 1841 appeal for redress of working women whose wages have been snatched and spent by drunken husbands while the children are allowed to go hungry to feel the poignancy of women's legal and social plight and even now to experience a flare of anger at the injustices done them. Almost forty years after Mrs. Graves's appeal, an unsigned *Harper's New Monthly Magazine* article, "Working-Women in New York," elaborates grimly, despite a change in the legal status of women, on the pitfalls, hazards, and pain that await the ordinary middle-class woman driven by financial necessity into the work force. Why (the feminist argument against an exclusive study of didactic literature runs) should valuable scholarly time and intellectual energy be spent dealing with the "lies and evasions," as Barbara Ehrenreich and

Deirdre English put it, of advice book and domestic novel "reality" since to do so seems to validate and somehow countenance the poisonous marzipan version of women's lives and ignore the grim truth?[18]

My answer to this charge is twofold: first, any comprehensive and careful survey of didactic literature will reveal more truth about the actual conditions women faced than lies; and second, to question a study of the ideal is to question the value of studying the way women are taught by popularly held assumptions to think of themselves and their capabilities, duties, and just rewards in life. In regard to the latter, if, as Barbara Welter and others have so often pointed out in their attacks on the passive and ornamental Cult of True Womanhood, an ideal can justify, teach, and mold women into becoming perpetual children, bereft of self-worth, weak in body and mind, then surely an ideal that stresses the opposite set of values is equally worthy of study for exactly the same reason. Between 1820 and 1852, the *Bibliotheca Americana* listed more titles for advice books than for any other genre, and such books directed their advice to middle-class audiences who made up as much as three-fourths of the population and "set the cultural tone and level of society." Thus to ignore the ideals promulgated by such books is to ignore a set of American cultural *données* with tremendous possible impact, either in whole or in part. Barbara Welter's classic work, *Dimity Convictions*, outlines the impact of what is obviously one set of middle-class ideals—the Europeanized, aristocratic-leaning ones that denied women useful employment or adult status. The Ideal of Real Womanhood reflects yet another, competing set of middle-class values—ones, I would argue, more intrinsically republican and indigenous in their expression and attitudes, resulting in the active, intelligent, and self-sufficient portraits of women evident in many domestic novels. As Carl Bode has pointed out, the advice books and didactic fiction reflect both "a time of growing faith in the power of human nature to shape itself" and an American belief in human "progress" away from an original depravity.[19] Though this has become, in feminist critics' hands, a much discredited view at least of female attitudes during the period,[20] I contend that the Real Woman ideal continues by its very presence and widespread popularity to convey a pervasive sense of that progressive impulse and attitude of optimism that Bode insists existed.

Such optimism, however, was neither dewy-eyed nor unequivocal, and this brings me back to my earlier point: the Ideal of Real Womanhood accurately assessed the obstacles and dangers women faced both at home and in the larger male world. Optimism exists because the advocates of Real Womanhood felt such obstacles could be surmounted and the dangers craftily avoided, if readers followed their advice. Much of the material in advice books—and indeed, domestic novels—dealt with identifying these obstacles, charting their dimensions, indicating fruitless paths around them, and mapping out successful strategies and trails.

One of the common misconceptions about the nineteenth-century ideal woman, shared especially by Marxist historians, is that she could find refuge from the horrors and dangers of the economic world at home. As Nina Baym points out in her study of mid-nineteenth-century domestic fiction, nineteenth-century American domestic authors rarely present "Home" in uncritically glowing terms. "Home is more a detention camp than a 'walled garden,'" Baym explains, and the only similarity between the idyllic walled garden painted by both True Womanhood advocates and modern critics and the home is the presence of the walls. The true pattern of domestic novels, Baym explains, is for the heroine to escape trauma by *leaving* home—a home characterized by neglectful, cruel, or inadequate kinspeople. The heroine then goes on to succeed in the world on her own. Baym characterizes such heroines as "warm, generous, and good natured . . . [who achieve] happiness and success through self-discipline, with the aid of teachers and examples, and sometimes in the teeth of determined opposition." This is hardly the vision of the "escape from the world of market reality" into the home which Ehrenreich and English suggest is the popular ideal's flatulent answer to women's very real problems, especially when business problems in the form of bankruptcy and social disasters in the form of alcoholic husbands and fathers invade the home itself—plot complications that frequently occur in both domestic novels and short stories, as I have indicated in another place.[21]

The Ideal of Real Womanhood, then, with its emphasis on self-reliance and self-support, allowed the young woman to escape or avoid the inadequate or vicious homes Baym describes. A popular ideal indeed urged them to do so, as it would later urge the "occasional" unfortunate married woman with children to take them and flee a drunken or abusive husband; armed with the ability (ideally) to earn a living, she had no reason to stay. Far from feeling that she had to put up with near-homicidal treatment because she was too frail, untrained, and illogical to fend for herself (as the competing Cult of True Womanhood told her), the Real Womanhood heroine was determined to survive. She was also determined to give her children—if she had any—the best possible chance of survival. As a result of such didactic fiction and advice texts, during a forty-year period in the mid-nineteenth century, ideals of fragility clashed with ideals of competence, pious self-sacrifice with survival, and the popular middle-class reader was left with two countering class images of women's nature, capabilities, and goals to study and possibly emulate.

Although the Ideal of Real Womanhood has never before been clearly identified or isolated as a coherent popular theme, I would be remiss if I did not mention some of the scholars who have identified fragments of it and suggested the directions I eventually took. Nina Baym, perhaps more than anyone, has made highly significant contributions to a better understanding of the didactic domestic novel and the curious forms the female ideal takes in that context, but she understandably limits herself to the novel and does not explore the parallel reflection of many of those same ideals in advice literature of the period. Barbara Epstein touches the edge of the Ideal of Real Womanhood in her fine study *The Politics of Domesticity,* but she attributes traces of this ideal to the particular effect of both the temperance movement and evangelism rather than the reverse; in neither case does she recognize the larger preexisting presence of a coherent ideal competing with that of True Womanhood. Karen Halttunen's *Confidence Men and Painted Women* is yet another work whose thesis overlaps mine in several places for it provides solid insight into the philosophy of "sincerity" as it functioned in acquaintanceship and etiquette rules in an increasingly mobile American society, but the book is limited to those questions, rather than exploring the larger context of female competence and self-reliance—especially in marriage choice—such etiquette seems to suggest.[22]

Other scholars have done much to disinter the sharp-cornered historical realities of women's lives during the period, and their work further buttressed my sense of the widespread knowledge and probable impact of a second (and more realistic) ideal for women. Historians such as Page Smith and Ernest Earnest make distinctions (all too frequently ignored) between various periods of American social history, but their work is restricted to the historical reality of young women's lives and does not explore the ideals these same young women imbibed from advice books, novels, and short stories. The same is true of Erna Hellerstein, Leslie Hume, and Karen Offen's collection, *Victorian Women*, which includes documents from England and France as well as those from the United States. Although such historians show that, in some instances, the reality of women's lives and their assumptions do not match—and that tangible and bitter disappointment at this slippage is revealed in diaries—they do not explore the wealth of material existing in the form of popular didactic literature, other than those pieces clearly representing the Cult of True Womanhood. Only Carl Degler has hinted at the presence of a second and competing popular ideal such as that of Real Womanhood. In his study *At Odds: Women and Family in America from the Revolution to the Present,* however, he confines himself almost exclusively to the subject of married women with children, largely ignoring those young women who might eventually become wives and mothers. Finally, Rosalind Rosenberg's study of the intellectual roots of modern feminism, *Beyond Separate Spheres,* provides a valuable line of demarcation between feminism and the Ideal of Real Womanhood by discussing the centrality of the separate sphere issue to feminism's own definition and extended goals. This study does not deal extensively with those writers who insisted that they abhorred the tenets of early feminism and clung instead to some version of woman's sphere, however expanded and peculiar. It is, however, particularly Rosenberg's cogent emphasis on feminism's desire to free itself from the restrictions of woman's sphere that leads me to discount Jill Ker Conway's attempt to see Real Womanhood writers as "conservative-sentimental" feminists.[23]

In explaining my differences with other critics, I have in essence argued for the existence of the Ideal of Real Womanhood. In the chapters that follow I will illustrate various aspects of this contention by showing evidence of its tenets in various genres, by exploring how those tenets appeared, in what sense they seem to have been popularly understood, and what modifications genre itself seems to have imposed on the ways principles such as advanced education and physical fitness were presented. Domestic novels often present heroines of extraordinary intelligence, but such heroines frequently are "home educated" rather than matriculants of colleges such as Antioch. Part of the reason, I believe, rests in the requirement that a domestic novel have a particular setting, namely, the home (or the place where the heroine lives when she goes to work). Such novels explore the burden, the pain, and the occasional joy of relationships among family members and friends, as well as the acquisition of a salary, on occasion, to support selected family members. In neither case do the genre requirements allow for the heroine to go away to college and live in a dormitory. Rather, in her travail as a working girl, the heroine must face pressures on the job from wicked or unscrupulous employers, battle for economic security and moral purity, and in every way possible show her bravery and fortitude against a heavy storm of opposition. The considerations of genre, then, demand extended discussion of those principles of the Ideal of Real Womanhood which I consider universal among genres, though they appear in slightly different outward form depending on whether they occur in a novel by Augusta Evans, a novella by T. S. Arthur, an advice book by Mrs. L. G. Abell, or a short story by Mrs. H. C. Gardner. My task in the chapters that follow—discussing physical fitness and health, education, marriage, and employment—will be to examine these principles in a wide variety of circumstances and situations. It is analogous to examining a jewel's facets and then subjecting that jewel to a variety of tests to assure oneself of its true classification in general and its individual strengths and weaknesses in particular.

One important way by which prospectors, as well as jewelers, identify a rough gem is to examine the geological formation from which it came and the ore surrounding it. There is an analogous concern for those of us seeking to prove the existence of a popular ideal. Popular ideals, for example, do not usually emerge from the pages of scholarly textbooks or from private letters; their stratum is popular publications reaching the very broadest audience.

To test this hypothesis of a competing ideal, it was necessary to delve into the somewhat disreputable (in a scholarly sense) ground of popular didactic literature. Seemingly, an ideal would be promulgated through those media self-consciously offering either straightforward advice or, more indirectly, models of approved female behavior. Certain genres met these criteria: self-proclaimed female instruction books (labeled variously "Advice," "Guide," "Instruction," or "Etiquette") and, of course, female domestic novels that were written (unlike those of better-known standard authors such as Herman Melville and Nathaniel Hawthorne) for primarily female audiences and featured a heroine making her way in the world, dealing with immediate, realistic, and often domestic concerns as opposed to exotic adventures. In addition to these two sources, I include popular periodical fiction that features stories of exemplary *American* heroines of everyday life who illustrated themes of home, family, self-support, and marriage; as a corollary, I include editorials and articles in periodicals addressed specifically to women about "female" problems such as the concern over physical fitness for women, working conditions, health, or education. Such pieces, in their didactic discussion, obviously stress what their authors believe to be model female behavior based on assumptions about female abilities and inherent needs and thus would provide an illuminating cross-reference to those attributes I found stressed in other genres.

My initial survey of these sources indeed revealed the strong presence of a popular ideal other than the supposedly monolithic one of True Womanhood. It became clear that a body of evidence existed which historians of the True Womanhood cult had either overlooked or written off as anomalous.

The issue of the anomalousness of such evidence required careful attention if I were to prove my hypothesis about the presence of a competing popular ideal. To prove that the evidence was more than the ephemera of a temporal fad, or the product of a handful of eccentric individuals, or, indeed, the intrinsic by-product of the very genre I was examining—and thus limited to it, rather than evidence of a widespread popular ideal—I had to arrive at a methodology that would sternly eliminate any such distortions.

To eliminate any strong exploratory bias owing to genre (for example, etiquette books by their very nature might demand certain niceties of behavior which ordinary women never intended to embrace or practice, except on special occasions), I determined that I would demand, as evidence of this competing popular ideal, that its characteristics appear in a variety of genres: domestic novels, advice books, editorials, short stories in periodicals, and articles. Any characteristic I did not find reflected in more than one kind of source I would eliminate from the growing definition I was deriving of this competing Ideal of Real Womanhood.

To avoid mistaking a single, cranky individual's progressive ideals for evidence of popular values, I determined as well to accept no source unless it had had national publication—that is, I eliminated both regional publications outside of the eastern seaboard (the home of national publishing, for my purposes extending as far south as Baltimore) and eliminated as well any self-published books unless I could show a continuing demand for them as evidenced by years of publication extending well beyond a decade. Again, multigeneric agreement on characteristics also helped to exclude individual eccentrically directed sources.

Possible fads in advice were harder to rule out, though the presence of similar evidence multigenerically would at least guarantee that the fad was a national one, if only temporarily. Longevity of publication—as evidenced by publication and reissuance information—provided another helpful parameter to restrict bias in this regard. For all my sources (unless I noted otherwise and explained why), I insisted on more than a decade of constant publication; anything longer than ten years would hardly be classified as a "fad" because it suggests popular and continuing acceptance. Additionally, as a long-range check, I determined, based on my initial investigations from the bulk of the evidence I sampled, that any works I used should fall within the forty-year period 1840–80. Earlier advice books tended to support almost entirely the contentions of the historians of True Womanhood, and sources later than 1880 seemed to revert to True Womanhood, or the New Woman (of which more later), or to feminism itself. Therefore, to guard further against decade faddism, I demanded of my sources that the attitudes, characteristics, and values they promulgated for young women be consistent with other works within that forty-year period—even if the source in question was in publication no longer than fifteen years. Consistency of attitude and outlook among sources spanning forty years seemed clear proof of an integrated and independent ideal. Interestingly enough, the Civil War seems to have had only a marginal effect on attitudes toward employment, since the virtues of working find strong advocates twenty years before and fifteen years following the war.

Using this same logic of longevity, I also decided that I would not use only the number of editions as an indication of popularity. In nineteenth-century publication practices, a book could have a large number of editions that were issued within one decade or even a half-decade. A large number of editions would, then, provide proof only of a singular (but temporally limited) popularity that soon burned itself out—in other words, a fad.

Since I hypothesized that this competing ideal was undoubtedly a distinct product and reflection of American values, I was careful as well to use only sources originally published in the United States between

1840 and 1800, rather than any first published in England and later reprinted in America. I also eliminated books not published in the Northeast, not only to avoid any regional, rather than national, bias, but because, unlike New England, as William R. Taylor (*Cavalier and Yankee,* 1961) and Louise Westling (*Sacred Groves and Ravaged Gardens,* 1985) have pointed out, the South has been—and was in the nineteenth century—more culturally dependent on and more influenced by British ideals than was the rest of the United States. This was especially so in regard to its ideals for women. Several continuing scholarly practices which I feel have done much to obscure American ideals for women involve not making both these national and regional distinctions when citing sources. Books originating in England and reprinted in the United States for over a decade, or books originating in the South, may have attained popularity, but they cannot be said to express uniquely American values. My hypothesis was clearly that a *competing* popular ideal existed between 1840 and 1880, not that it was the *only* ideal for American women. Obviously, evidence exists for both the transatlantic (and southern) True Womanhood ideal and the more indigenous northern Ideal of Real Womanhood I hypothesized.

To determine a book's country of origin, length of publication, and general publication history, I had to rely on a variety of resources. I determined country of origin by finding out as much about the various authors as I could from both *Appleton's Cyclopaedia of American Biography* (1886–89) and Frances E. Willard and Mary A. Livermore's *American Women: A Comprehensive Encyclopedia* (1897), which I used to trace female authors not considered by male editors important enough to be included in *Appleton's Cyclopaedia.* Both encyclopedias frequently contained dates and country of publication for most of an author's important works and sometimes name changes and reissuance information as well. Additionally, I checked the publication history in both the *American Catalogue* and in the *National Union Catalog: Pre-1956 Imprints* (*NUC*). The latter lists for all editions the copyright, date, and place of publication and tells in many cases whether the book is the first American edition or simply an American book. Though the *NUC* only lists those books which participating libraries record (based on their holdings) and submit, the *NUC* can, in conjunction with the other resources I mentioned, narrow the field considerably on dates of publication and country of origin for those works it lists.

As a final resource, in regard to popularity, I made use of both of Frank L. Mott's excellent and standard reference works, *Golden Multitudes: The Story of Best Sellers in the United States* (1947) and *A History of American Magazines, 1850–1865,* Volume 2 (1957). In the first case, Mott not only listed the titles of best-selling novels for each year from 1830 to 1890 but defined the term "best seller" and "better sellers" and listed sales requirements for each decade for those terms to be applied. In his work on American magazines, his research provided me with publication history and name changes for national periodicals, as well as those periodicals' circulation figures, popularity, and impact. Although his survey in Volume 2 covers only to 1865, it does show the original date at which the periodical was founded and, if it lists ten years or more for publication, the periodical meets my methodological demands. In addition to the works by Frank L. Mott, Nina Baym's outstanding work allowed me to select which popular female authors I would read by giving me information on their popular reign in print, the themes that distinguish domestic novels from others, and how "typical" certain authors—and, most important, certain works by certain authors—were of both the genre and that author. For example, I chose to use Caroline Lee Hentz's *Linda* rather than her more infamous reply to Harriet Beecher Stowe's *Uncle Tom's Cabin, The Planter's Northern Bride,* not only because the *Northern Bride* was political rather than domestic in its intention but because *Linda* was more representative of Hentz's work. Nina Baym's groundbreaking scholarship made such distinctions possible. Similarly, Baym's work also made it possible to exclude novels primarily directed at juveniles (such as the incredibly popular *Elsie Dinsmore* by Martha Finney) from those novels primarily for young adult or adult audiences—those audiences to whom the advice books were directed and for whom the Ideal of Real Womanhood was articulated. Incidentally, although several of the best-selling authors I chose to use were originally from the South or neighboring border states (Augusta Evans and Mary Jane Holmes, for example), their works were nationally popular and published in the Northeast; these characteristics, as well as their intense popularity, were enough to allow them to be included under my methodology and show as well that mere geographic location of the author does not always guarantee adherence to a particular set of values; the presence of northeastern authors supporting the True Womanhood ideal shows the same thing. Geographical location for publishing houses does, however, show whether a novel has national or primarily regional exposure.

Poole's Index to Periodical Literature, especially its prefatory pages, provided me with valuable information about both the journals and periodicals in which articles appeared, the country of origin of those journals, and whether the articles had first appeared in foreign (specifically British) publications. Some articles, I found, had originally been printed in *Blackwood's* or the *Cornhill Review* and were, therefore, unusable for my purposes. *Poole's Index* also distinguished between magazines that were for a general, as opposed to a specialist or professional, audience— a particularly important distinction when one is attempting to define a popular ideal. By using both *Poole's Index* and Mott's *History*, I was able to eliminate articles written by specialists for specialists. The differences between what the public thinks and what professionals think about such subjects as female maturation, intelligence, growth, and intrinsic nature are frequently enormous—especially if one compares, for example, articles in periodicals for a general audience such as *Popular Science Monthly* with those intended for a community of specialists such as the *Journal of Social Sciences.* Certainly during the mid-nineteenth century, specialists and popular opinion did not consistently agree—and popular opinion was far less restrictive and sex-biased when compared with the dicta imparted to one another by obstetricians, gynecologists, and budding social scientists. As Burton Bledstein's work points out, the steadily increasing distance between the public and the specialist in the nineteenth century was a function of established professional principles regarding "professional knowledge" and a growing movement toward accreditation in a field—information that eventually would be available only to "professionals" with the proper degrees, not to the public.[24]

Modern critical and historical works that rely heavily or entirely on either specialist publications or medical school textbooks to tell us what "everybody thought" about women's inherent abilities or their biologically determined characteristics are, therefore, doomed to distortion. This becomes particularly clear when one considers the mid-to-late-nineteenth-century professional struggle between doctors practicing "heroic" medicine and other medical professionals defining themselves as homeopaths, hydropaths, or naturopaths. Significantly, nonheroic medical professionals tended to be less restrictive about women. As the struggle for professionalism grew, one group's "experts" became the opposing group's "quacks." Popular publications made no such distinctions until near the turn of the century; rather, they presented the public with a melee of medical opinions from professionals writing specifically for a popular audience—professionals from a variety of medical backgrounds. None of the medical interest groups (including the heroic) "had a monopoly on medical truth," as Mary Walsh points out.[25] More important, none of them was publicly *perceived* to have such a monopoly. This is why Real Womanhood writers could offer medical articles for a popular audience which insisted that women had no inherent biological weakness and no inherent mental limitations, whereas gynecology textbooks of the same period were describing just the opposite "scientific" facts.

An examination of the four definitive characteristics of Real Womanhood which distinguish it from both feminism and True Womanhood provides a fully articulated definition of that ideal. In the chapters that follow I will examine the ideal's stress on physical fitness and health for its models of young women with its concomitant belief in the spiritual dimensions of health (Chapter 1). In Chapter 2 I will outline its demands for extended or higher education beyond the "common school" level and its important (and somewhat inventive) rationales for such an education in terms of womanhood and the home. In Chapters 3–5 I will outline the various "right reasons" for marriage, the preparations for that momentous decision, the skeptical and cautious stages and requirements of courtship, and, finally, the use of the engagement period as a time to guard against marital disaster. Finally, I will outline Real Womanhood's attitudes toward employment in all its guises (domestic, philanthropic, and salaried) and where it fits in the ideal's insistence on woman's duties toward her home and family. As the number of chapters devoted to each subject indicates, marriage was the most common topic discussed by all genres because it was the norm for most women (although allowances are made for those "few" women who might choose, sensibly, to remain single); education, physical fitness, health, and economic self-reliance and career hinge to a large extent on that decision. This emphasis on marriage as the norm and active duties demanded of woman is perhaps why, ultimately, the Ideal of Real Womanhood both emerged and finally disappeared.

ONE

Muscles Like Harp-Strings

Physical Fitness, Health, and the Real Woman

With a flash of laughing defiance, the girl bares her wrist, throwing into relief muscles like harp-strings. "I can row six miles without fatigue," she says, "and walk ten. I can drive and swim, and ride twelve miles before breakfast on a trotting horse. I eat heartily three times a day, and sleep soundly for eight hours out of the twenty-four. . . . Do I ever have headaches? Once in a while, but not so often as do my collegian cousins. Hysterics? No; nor the blues!"

—Marion Harland,
"What Shall We Do with Our Daughters?"

The defiant young woman quoted on the previous page is more representative of a nineteenth-century American female ideal than many today would suppose, though she is perhaps a bit excessive in the catalog of her physical virtues. Excessive or not, she clearly illustrates the strong emphasis some northeastern midcentury American advice writers placed on health and physical fitness, not just for boys but for girls, as well as the basis for this fitness in sound dietary, health, and exercise habits. Indeed, judging from such advice books, as well as articles in popular magazines like *Harper's Weekly*, the *Illustrated Christian Weekly*, and the *Ladies' Repository*, and those somewhat misty mirrors of the ideal, magazine fiction and domestic novels, the ideal girl of this period was a stalwart specimen.

This "angelic Amazon," as Inez Irwin calls her, was not, however, the only model proposed for young American women. The competing ideal, the Cult of True Womanhood, also had some dicta to impart concerning health, physical fitness, and femininity. Under that ideal the young woman with muscles like harp-strings would have been considered a bad example of indelicacy; the muscles she was so proud of and her ability to walk or row for miles would have been a source of shame and embarrassment. As Barbara Welter (and, more thoroughly, Carroll Smith-Rosenberg and Charles Rosenberg) have pointed out, the Cult of True Womanhood not only deplored such expressions of "animal" good health and vitality but saw them as proof positive of a lack of "true" femininity, at least a femininity whose parameters were outlined by leading gynecologists at the time. According to popular tradition from earlier decades and from abroad, as well as "professional" medical opinion, women had a much more delicate nervous system than did men because of the peculiar function of their reproductive organs. Because of this, and a greater "natural" sensitivity, their fragile nervous systems were likely to be overstimulated or irritated, with disastrous results. As

Smith-Rosenberg and Rosenberg explain, "Physicians saw woman as the product and prisoner of her reproductive system. It was the ineluctable basis of her social role and behavior characteristics, the cause of her most common ailments; woman's uterus and ovaries controlled her body and behavior from puberty through menopause." As a result of this physiological "handicap," the authors claimed that *truly* feminine women ideally had certain natural characteristics such as "nurturance, intuitive morality, domesticity, passivity and affection."[1]

The "True" woman, therefore, was much too beset by her chronic biological indisposition to have the stout constitution, the fearless active life, and the steady nerves described in the epigraph to this chapter. As Carroll Smith-Rosenberg elucidates, such medical experts felt that a girl past the crucial age of puberty would have "increased bodily weakness, a new found and biologically rooted timidity and modesty, and the 'illness' of menstruation." She adds that "doctors" insisted that, "at the commencement of puberty . . . a girl should curtail all activity" lest it overstrain her nervous system.[2]

How is it, then, that in reviewing advice books of the mid-nineteenth century, in reading domestic novels, periodical short stories, and other evidences of popular culture in the United States, we are faced repeatedly with injunctions to young women to build up their muscles, to get more out-of-door exercise, and to cease "moping" and "pretending to be invalids"? Obviously, not *all* doctors agreed (nor, apparently, did most popular opinion) with those quoted by the two Rosenbergs.[3] Just as obviously, another ideal—that of Real Womanhood, using opposing medical opinion and speaking more clearly for the popular perception— saw women in an entirely different way biologically and demanded of them different ideal behavior in regard to health, fitness, beauty, and attitude. This chapter then, discusses the rationales and admonitions of Real Womanhood to health and fitness and the portrait of the girl of Real Womanhood who emerges in fiction as a result. Not surprisingly, since this ideal appeared later but still contemporary and competitive with the Cult of True Womanhood, Real Womanhood tends to rail against the poses and beliefs thought characteristic of its rival. We see True Womanhood's wan girls and their famous nervous sensitivity—but we see it mocked, scorned, and, indeed, castigated in works by writers advocating Real Womanhood. In many domestic novels as well, the True Wom-

anhood characteristics become the hallmarks not of delicate wom-
anliness but of fraudulence, deceit, and villainy, as well as selfishness.

A much more widely read doctor than the doyens cited by the Rosenbergs, Dr. Dio Lewis, claims that "sickness is selfish" and goes on to sneer
at the True Womanhood ideal: "The fragile, pale young woman with a
lisp, is thought by many silly people, to be more a *lady*, than another
with ruddy cheeks, and vigorous health . . . there exists, somehow, in
the fashionable world, the notion that a pale and sensitive woman
is feminine and refined, while one in blooming health is masculine
and coarse."[4] He obviously disagrees, as did many other writers, as we
shall see.

Many advice writers, in fact, offer more than the suggestion of a frown
to those young women who are "invalids," that is, either unable or
unwilling to walk two or three miles before breakfast, bowl, yacht, ice
skate, or ride a horse, or who complain of languidness and weakness.
Such "weakness," advice writers indicate, is probably the result of either
personal perversity or moral degeneracy. Some writers, in particularly
zealous moments, suggest that such delicacy is also the result, if not the
cause, of mental degeneracy as well. Emily Thornwell, whose staunch
views on cleanliness and exercise, expressed in 1856, are something of a
shock to the uninitiated modern reader, has some acerbic comments to
make about the state of "elegance" sought by middle- and upper-class
girls. She sniffs at the lady of fashion and "the pale, sickly, and languid
countenance of that female whose hours of leisure have been passed
without occupation within her own chamber, or in listlessly lounging
upon a sofa or a couch." The only men that sort of ennui-laden grace
will appeal to, Thornwell warns coldly, are those who "have selected
their standard of beauty from among the victims of a round of fashionable dissipation."[5]

Other advice writers take up the cudgels of public debate to drive
home their point that physical well-being, vigorous health, and physical
fitness are the source not of "commonness" but of *true* (as opposed to
false) beauty. One such admonisher, the renowned William Alcott, is
blunt about the errors concerning beauty which have crept into the public mind: "We have set up among us a wrong standard of beauty, not
only of feature, but of form. The human female frame should not differ
essentially from that of the male. Or, rather, it should never, in these

respects, come to imitate either the wasp or the white lily." "Beauty of form and feature," Alcott announces roundly, "depend very much on bodily health."[6]

Domestic novelists follow suit in their characterization of both heroines and their foils. In Mary Jane Holmes's *'Lena Rivers,* John, Jr.'s, affection for his cousin 'Lena and his initial dislike for Mabel Ross are both based on health. Mabel Ross, even though she is sweet, kind, and infatuated with John, Jr., is also sickly and, apparently, discusses her maladies in great detail. Grumbles the adolescent John, even if Mabel is sickly, "she can at least keep her *miserable feeling* to herself. Nobody wants to know how many times she's been blistered and bled."[7] He finds her invalidism "a bore" and 'Lena's skill on horseback, high color, and vigorous health vastly more attractive. Though John does not marry 'Lena, his good friend does, and John marries a girl of both vitality and fitness, who is, significantly, regarded as something of a hoyden. The point is clear. Invalidism, at least to those advice writers and novelists holding a vision of Real Womanhood, is neither attractive nor a proof of femininity.

Indeed, invalidism not only detracts from physical beauty, but it seems to carry with it as well the slightest suggestion of spiritual slovenliness. Girls who are sick, the implicit argument seems to run, are those who ignore their "duty" to stay healthy—and this is a moral shortcoming, as Edwin Chapin explains, noting that it is *"morally wrong* to neglect or violate the laws of our physical being . . . [because] the culture of our physical powers is a religious duty." As Chapin explains, when a young woman "allows herself" to become ill, through a distaste of exercise, a love for "fashionable" (and restrictive) clothing, and an indulgence in late hours and spicy foods, she impairs the functioning of her mind and, with it, her rational faculty. This in turn inhibits her ability to make careful moral choices. As he explains, "a sound mind depends upon a sound body"; without both, a young woman not only selfishly takes up the time of others tending to her various ills, but she also becomes peevish, petty, self-absorbed, self-centered, pleasure-oriented, and depressive. Moreover, she lacks the necessary strength to do her share of the work at hand, whether at home or among the poor, and her judgment becomes increasingly warped by her own concerns. She becomes, in short, immoral and a burden. His rhetorical call to arms to

"OH, MY GOD! AM I GOING TO BE ILL?"

Harper's Weekly, April 21, 1860

his young female readers deserves to be quoted: "Upon the young [woman] then, I would especially urge the duty of a diligent exercise, every limb and muscle and organ. Be not so afraid of cold, or heat, or damp, as of sedentary indolence, or noxious confinement." He suggests the following concrete steps toward better health: to avoid fashion if it violates "physical laws of nature," by which, among other things, he specifies the corset and inadequate shoes such as kid slippers worn out of doors in the winter; to avoid using or taking anything that produces "an arbitrary and artificial comeliness" at the expense of health such as cosmetics for the cheeks or, again, tight lacing; to avoid "rash exposures, or unrelieved exertions" even if they come from a "zeal for duty," thereby eliminating the excuse of physical martyrdom in serving the needs of others; finally, to avoid "the racked frame, the jaded spirit, the debased and tormented soul of the mere pleasure-seeker." Though this last warning is somewhat cryptic, he apparently regards late night suppers, dancing until dawn, dram-drinking, and such social activities among the "fast set" as the convulsive actions of persons void of true worth, seeking to fill their spiritual emptiness by constant recreational distractions. The woman interested in maintaining her health (and thereby fulfilling her moral duty) should "use" amusement such as the practice or appreciation of the arts, nature, literature, and the like as a temperate and balanced rest from physical exertion and work, not as ends in themselves or, as in the case of the "mere pleasure seeker," as a way to make empty hours pass more swiftly.[8]

Nor is Chapin alone in his insistence that health, especially for women, who bear the race and keep the domestic balance in a wicked world, is a moral obligation. Thunders T. S. Arthur, women "cannot but feel more deeply than ever the duty that rests on them to preserve their health for the sake of the happiness of others, and the general well-being of society." He points out that if a young woman ruins her health, by the time she is either a single adult or a wife and mother "she will be a burden to herself, and the source of anxiety and grief to her nearest and best friends," unable to perform any of her duties, or at least unable to perform them well and without pain and disability.[9]

We find the same link between illness, lack of exercise, and moral degeneracy in magazine fiction. One example, a touching little piece revolving around the nature of true friendship, "Winifred's Vow," illustrates the worst of the advice writers' fears vividly, though only in passing. Once again, readers encounter a description of "thin hands" that lie "listlessly" in a silken lap; the author describes as well a "pale," wan face and an air of "no energy, no life." This is a description of Grace, Winifred's dearest friend. Grace is not, though the description lends itself to such an assumption, a lady of fashion; she is a fallen woman, and one soon for the grave, we discover. The unnamed author points out that Grace "had not always been the broken-hearted creature she looked tonight"; she is ill—dying of consumption and pregnant with an illegitimate child in the bargain. Paleness and languidness stand in this story as objective correlatives for moral and physical malaise—a correlation that occurs in more than a few sources. Winifred, the heroine, also stands as a metaphor—her robust good health, denoted by rosy cheeks and a splendid energy, mark her immediately as a good woman, one able to carry the heavy load the vow she has taken imposes on her: to raise Grace's illegitimate child "as though her own" and silently accept the misplaced censure of the community while so doing. Grace naturally dies in childbed—an outcome neither Winifred nor, probably, the contemporary reader doubted, given the "listlessness" she exhibited.[10]

Other advice authors and columnists make the same assumption implicit in "Winifred's Vow": that lack of bracing exercise, a slavish adherence to disfiguring fashion in clothing and attitude, and disinclination to row or to run are all indicative of a female state of mind that hungers after cheap novels and fast men, is easily gulled, and is inevitably blandished into bed. One columnist, Virginia Penny, writing in 1865, explains the causal relationship somewhat murkily in a scathing article entitled "Poor Health of American Women." Like another author, Daniel Wise, she adheres to the concept of the development and interdependence of mind, body, and spirit. Inactivity of the body inevitably leads, she feels, to inactivity of the brain, which, in turn, results in spiritual stasis and, eventually, both madness and moral degeneracy. The body needs exercise, she explains, to allow the brain to receive the blood it requires to concentrate. Without concentration, the intellect finds it hard to deal with interests "outside of itself" and becomes diseased and ready for the blandishments of the unprincipled or the imaginary aches and pains of "hysteria, hypochondriasis, and other varieties of mental disease."[11]

Apparently because of this inevitable link between weakness and degeneracy, advice writers were firm enough and strident enough in their condemnation of physical inability to make others feel that *valid* (as opposed to fashionable) invalidism needed a defense, especially in a nation that was becoming obsessed with rounded limbs, a bold stride, and rosy cheeks. In the face of such attacks, Mrs. H. C. Gardner felt called upon to deliver a defense of these unfortunates entitled "Invalid Women." Prefatory to her arguments, Gardner presents a brief tableau of the true invalid's world, with the eternal sick couch invaded by hordes of "friends" insisting the sickly soul "get out" and see if she doesn't "feel better." These same friends announce that the invalid needs nothing more than additional exercise and fresh air and seem determined to drag the lady by her hair into some vigorous game or other. There is, Gardner mourns, no sympathy or understanding in the nation at large about illness. Indeed, she divines a sense among the invalid's friends that the invalid is merely being perverse or lazy. Faced with this lack of charity and understanding, as well as the disapproval of and disbelief in her physical complaints and the inevitable censure and chivying with which friends and family greet her pains, the invalid has only the Lord left to comfort her: "We can tell him everything. He won't tire of the subject. And after we have told him how weak, and sick, and miserable we are, we haven't got to *prove* it." How one goes about proving illness, Gardner implies caustically, is to die![12]

Obviously, *La dame aux camellias* was not a viable model for American women; if, for reasons of fashion or even necessity, one emulated her, it was at the risk of being subjected to long lectures on the importance of getting out in the woods or the positive and therapeutic value of heavy housework or boating.

The invalid was forced, then, to take a secondary or even tertiary place in the hearts of her countrymen; the Real Woman lived up to every physical and moral expectation. One particularly vivid portrait of that ideal emerges in an unattributed work of fiction, "Crofut on Skates," which appeared in *Harper's Weekly* in 1860. In the story, the young man, Charley Crofut, has decided to risk (he feels) both life and limb to go skating—which he does not know how to do—because the girl he loves (named Atalanta, significantly) is fond of the sport. Struggling to put on his skates, Charley pauses momentarily in his labors to watch Atalanta as she goes out on the ice. Here is a truly American ideal: "Erect, and with scarcely an effort, she glides along, skimming the surface like a yacht before the wind . . . now she increases the speed of her flight. Her skate-irons ring as she spurns the humming ice." Charley watches her as she swirls and dips, skates backward, and, in multiple turns, dazzles him with the sight of her trim white ankles rising out of stout boots. He is overwhelmed with her grace and coloring, her strength and skill. It is of secondary importance that, later on, she sprains her ankle and has to lean on his manly arm; it was the bird in flight, not the injured specimen, that lured him. What he saw on the ice was what he loved. Female health and strength apparently do not dampen male ardor, though it is also clear that ideal women are neither autonomous nor invincible.[13]

In this story and in a two-page engraving, *Skating on the Ladies' Skating Rink in the Central Park, New York* (published a few weeks earlier in the same magazine) we see the wind-blown beauty and vigor of an entirely different species of young woman than modern readers have been led to expect. The passionate arcs of the legs in the engravings, the zest on the faces, even the whipping hair and scarves suggest not only speed but a certain magnificent, albeit controlled, wildness. Here are no demure hands hugging tasteful muffs to waists carefully cinched in. Here, instead, is an exuberance and a magic, a healthy love of coldness and of movement.

But how did these midcentury all-American girls develop? The advice books and columns, with their dicta about proper nutrition, sensible clothing, attention to personal hygiene, and frequent and stipulated forms of exercise, were obviously defining steps to take to reach this pinnacle of strength and beauty. One major influence militating against such eventual development, claimed advice writers and (indirectly) domestic novelists, was a stupid prejudice among many parents against "hardening" young girls physically as they did young boys. Many little girls from their infancy on were sheltered, supposedly to help them maintain both their health and, not surprisingly, their growing femininity. The bombastic William Blaikie, among others, deplores this enforced delicacy and speaks disparagingly of its unfortunate results, noting (with some exaggeration, judging by comments of other writers) that "thoroughly healthy, hearty women are not common among us" and adding sarcastically that it would be "positively dangerous to very many" to walk the five or ten miles a day he recommends. He also points out that young women suffer from uneven and inferior muscular development because of a lifetime of constricting clothing, lack of exercise, and general lassitude toward even ordinary vigorous movement. He is joined in his concern—at least for married women—by no less an authority than Catharine Beecher, who notes in the Preface to the third edition of *A Treatise on Domestic Economy* "the deplorable sufferings of multitudes of young wives and mothers" from, among other things, poor health resulting from lack of sensible exercise, fitness, and diet.[14]

Mrs. L. G. Abell explains the process behind this exaggerated belief in the "decay" of American women by describing the restrictive cotton-wool-wrapped upbringing of many nice middle-class girls: "She may not, like her brother, spend her time out in play; it will tan her complex-

Harper's Weekly, January 28, 1860

ion, and make room for *critics* to call in question the mother's sense of *female propriety,* or of spoiling her by *indulgence,* or she will soil her pretty dresses, which are deemed of more worth than the health of the little one."[15] Such wrongheadedness is, to many of the Real Womanhood writers, at the root of the problem: their enemy, though they would call it "fashion," is in fact the competing Cult of True Womanhood with its insistence on the ideal biologically determined passivity, paleness, physical delicacy, and weakness of women, an ideal forced into existence rather than naturally present. Abell's scorn and the guidelines laid down by other advice writers and even novelists and periodical fiction writers are, collectively, the proverbial gauntlet thrown down in the long war against cream-puff ideals for American women. Every piece of dietary, sanitary, exercise, and health advice offered is, in effect, a missile launched against the ideological enemy from which they wish to save the American woman.

To such writers, True Womanhood's program of enforced inactivity and isolation had ramifications far beyond whether a young lady could walk five miles without experiencing heart failure: the emphasis on physical fitness and health was Real Womanhood's opening maneuver to improve the mental, vocational, and rational abilities of young American women. With a sound body and a healthy brain, education was possible; with properly ventilated schoolrooms, warm clothing, and an attention to dietary correctness, that schooling need not result, as the opposing ideal claimed, in illness, insanity, and death; with education came the ability of the young woman to earn a living for herself through a profession or a trade; the ability to earn a living, in turn, freed her forever from the curse of the marriage market and the degrading hunt for a rich suitor; finally, choice in marriage meant better, sounder marriages, healthier children with better values imparted by a wise mother, not hired help, and, ultimately, a stronger, happier, better balanced, and more civilized society. Barbells and a light breakfast, therefore, were the ultimate basis for a complete reformation of society.

But how could this be accomplished if, as Holmes shows us in novels like *Meadowbrook,* young girls were subject to severe reprimand and punishment for ordinary active childhood behavior? Holmes's heroine Rosa Lee, at age nine, is punished for appearing in the following manner at the end of a summer day of play: "I came in from a romp in the barn, with my yellow hair flying all over my face, my dress burst open, my pantalet split from the top downward and my sun-bonnet hanging down my back."[16] Rosa, we discover, likes to jump from the hayloft, to swing on gates, to climb trees, and to walk the beams in the barn. Drs. Lewis and Alcott, not to mention Blaikie, would approve of such exercise and muscular development; so, too, obviously, does Holmes because the girl grows up to become the heroine of the novel and the family's sole support as a schoolteacher at the tender age of thirteen. She then goes on to lead a successful life as an independent woman for most of the novel before she chooses to marry a refined, intelligent, and wealthy young man, who is also a "kindred spirit."

Novels that paint the heroine in vigorous colors, like those of Mary J. Holmes, Augusta Evans, Elizabeth Ward, Fanny Fern, and Marion Harland, presented the faceless mothers of the next female generation of America with a vision approving such activity; advice writers provided the rationale behind the vigorousness and the plans and concrete steps to take to realize it.

The first and most obvious demand the advice writers placed upon the young woman was for sheer physical exercise, preferably out of doors in the clean, fresh air. Exercise performed inside, especially in the form of heavy housework (though also through the practice of gymnastics and the use of workout equipment), would do, but it was not advised without qualification. Again, the strangely familiar concept of weakness and resulting degeneracy reared its head in the reasons the writers gave for this lack of exercise. In an article entitled whimsically "Benefit of Household Care," in the *Ladies' Repository*, the editor berated middle- and upper-middle-class women for complaining about their illnesses and weaknesses and then points to the culprit: servants and a "perfect idleness" have made these ladies "lose what little health they started life with," as they direct servants to turn mattresses, haul in coal, and do the thousand other chores that would make the blood circulate in a vigorous fashion. The author advises young ladies to dispense with servants and do the work themselves, thereby, in true Yankee fashion, saving the price of servants while maintaining decent health at the same time. Even the conservative *Peterson's Magazine*, which in 1858 devoted almost its entire space to directions for sedentary employments such as embroidery and knitting or to pious poetry, found time to insert short aphorisms suggesting more various, if not strenuous, employment. "Laziness," the magazine notes, "begins in cobwebs and ends in iron chains." It further reassures its readers that a "life of . . . elevated action" will augment beauty, not wear it down. What constitutes "elevated action" to the editors is not specified; the author of "Editorial Chitchat" does, however, expect it to be something that will give "expansion and symmetry to the body" even as it "expand[s] the capacities of the soul."[17]

Abell agrees with both *Peterson's Magazine* and the *Ladies' Repository*. Though she does not discount the value to both health and spirit (and, as a by-product, beauty) of other forms of exercise, she is particularly fulsome about the benefits of housework as exercise. Of such beneficial (and without a doubt strenuous) exertions as hauling coal and pumping water, she states enthusiastically that "nothing gives such elasticity to the limbs, and roundness to the form, ease and grace to the motion, as the bending, reaching, lifting, quick walking, and swift motions involved in domestic exercise; and nothing gives such a healthful glow to the cheek, luster to the eye, cheerfulness to the spirits, full and healthful play to the lungs and heart, invigorating the whole frame." She, too, makes the point that a relationship exists between physical activity and good health, noting that the "whole frame" needs exercise or the whole body gets sick, and the woman herself becomes depressed and miserable as well. The cure Abell suggests echoes Virginia Penny in its stern assumption that lifelong invalidism is merely shameful self-indulgence. Like Penny, Abell suggests that a sponge bath in cold water once a day, a series of warm-up exercises every morning, some fresh air, draughts of cold water, and daily heavy housework will "cure" any such condition.[18]

There is more than a suggestion that the young women of America had better seriously take themselves in hand if they are to be patriotic citizens. Beecher, Lewis, and especially Blaikie are obviously disgusted with the occasional crop of langorous bisque-headed dolls. Blaikie views young girls on the streets of a large American city, and his description is as devastating as it can be, coming as it does from a man who believes large muscles, not cleanliness, are next to godliness and who also has an exercise book to sell. He wails, "Instead of high chests, plump arms, comely figures, and a graceful and handsome mien, you constantly see flat chests, angular shoulders, often round and warped forward, with scrawny necks, pipe-stem arms, narrow backs and a weak walk." He bemoans the lack of strong, broad, and symmetrically developed hands among modern young ladies, as well as the presence of pale faces. It is not a lack of housework he blames but the curriculum of some popular girls' boarding schools. He points out that the tiny bit of exercise girls get in finishing schools involves only their feet. Indeed, the "correct" habit of holding the elbows close to the body while walking and keeping the hands and forearms almost motionless prevents those members from developing and results in "poor indifferent specimens," which are hardly able, we assume from his tone, to lift either a coffee cup or a barbell.[19]

As Eleanor Thompson points out in her work on midcentury female education, the idea of "physical education" to many magazine writers was "not a subject to be pursued but healthful living." Though after 1860, one notices more and more advertisements for schools offering gymnastics and boating as well as riding to assure anxious parents that physical exercise was part of the curriculum, earlier in the midcentury, the concern about exercise took the form of recommending that it be done extracurricularly or in the home or, if in school, by reforming the physical conditions for pupils rather than through a coordinated physical development program. Dr. Calvin Cutter, for example, in both of his short books of popular anatomy, stresses that both young men and young women should change sitting positions frequently during school hours and participate in an outdoor "recess" time to rest one set of muscles and exercise another. He also insists that stools at school be the right height or, even better, that chairs be substituted because they help posture by supporting the back.[20]

This is not to say that Dr. Cutter does not believe in the enormous value of exercise in the fresh, bracing air out of doors. He—and Abell to a limited degree—feel that the unique combination of fresh air, activity, and (perhaps) sunshine have an almost mystical ability to preserve the health and to lift one out of the megrims. Perhaps this is because, as Cutter insists, fresh air and vigorous exercise prevent "costiveness" or constipation—in the midcentury an established culprit, which many thought responsible in large degree for lethargy and depression.[21]

Emily Thornwell certainly agrees with Cutter. To Thornwell and that group of advice book authors (who might well be dubbed the "Fresh Air Club"), exercise was not exercise unless it was performed out of doors, preferably in brisk weather. Housework—however onerous and wearing—simply did not fill the bill, even though it required the lady "to bustle from garret to cellar." Thornwell attributes the preservation of beauty and even the reduction of the symptoms of old age to outdoor exercise. She also believed it to be the key to good health and therefore seriously instructs young ladies on how to exercise to reap the greatest benefits. Her suggested activities were not for the faint of heart, though she demanded no more severity than other writers. Thornwell's great panacea for all ills was walking—long, strenuous trips. For young ladies to maintain their health, she stipulates, they should walk "vigorously" in the open air for two to four miles. Thornwell deliberately nips in the bud any thoughts the young ladies might have of combining this somewhat muscular exercise with the pleasures of a promenade. She is adamant that girls should never hope "to combine in a walk . . . the luxury of inaction with the benefit of motion." She means that girls should stride firmly along the path and cover considerable ground, not dawdle along showing off their dresses and hats to languid and fashionable misses. If the thoughts of that form of walking are too horrible, Thornwell has a backup plan—young ladies can ride on horseback for an equal distance at a "stiff" canter early in the morning. She does clarify, however, lest the girls in their enthusiasm for physical exercise misunderstand, that she does *not* mean for them to attempt to show the ability of a professional equestrienne; rather, the young woman should simply ride her animal with "some portion of a similar enthusiasm." If riding is performed in this fashion, there will be no room for the hated languidness of "fashion." Thornwell intends for these rides to be no sedate amble in well-cut togs down a prim bridle path; rather, she expects the young women to experience the buffeting of a swift passage and the bracing effects of inhaling great lungfuls of fresh air.[22]

Thornwell is not alone either in her belief in walking or in her advocacy of horseback riding as forms of useful exercise. Issues of the *Ladies' Repository* for 1865 bristle with stories in which the most violent forms of both riding and walking are introduced in a completely casual way. One such story, "A Summer's Adventures," by Emily Huntington Miller, discusses the journey of four schoolteachers to a "nearby" war hospital to obtain summer employment. The story is intriguing for many reasons, but one of its most interesting aspects is the way the four go about getting to this hospital and their attitude as they do so. Because they are impoverished and cannot afford a speedier means of transportation, they decide to walk all the way and to make a ramble of sorts out of the trek. This journey, in its emotional closeness, general exuberance, and fun, would today warm feminist hearts. The dialogue is particularly revealing. One of the four teachers mentions that it is rather a long way to the hospital, and the other replies: " 'Not much over a hundred miles,' said Esther, 'and why can't we walk as well as men? Didn't we walk up and down Mount Washington last Summer, and didn't every gentleman in the party give out except Willits?' " Mount Washington is no mean climb (6,288 feet), nor is a hundred miles through natural elements (including both rain and dust) a "ramble" even for intrepid walkers today. In this story, however, all four regard the journey as a lark and sing along the way, gaily joking with one another about sun-burned noses and dusty hair.[23]

Magazine fiction continues to surprise a modern reader, not only in the amount of physical exertion casually involved in the plots but in its nature as well. We remember Atalanta on the ice, and other forms of exercise are mentioned that are equally vigorous and even more out of keeping with the stereotyped vision of the Victorian American girl. "Sister Anne," a story by an anonymous author, which appeared in the 1855 *Harper's New Monthly*, describes the heroine as one who, like a female Henry Thoreau, spends her time trekking through the woods, listening to birds, and climbing trees—the latter a habit that gets her in trouble with her mother because not only is it unladylike, but it also ruins her stockings. It is important that Sister Anne is eighteen when she does this. Sister Anne is also fond of running on the beach and climbing big rocks. Indeed, when her unfeeling mother "sneers savagely" at Sister Anne for her apparent inability to support herself, the girl runs away from home, deciding to go to the big city, where she intends to sell her poetry (which she does), thereby symbolically linking physical activity and self-reliance, a combination we shall see over and over again. The author punctuates the description of Anne's leave-taking with references to her running and skipping away, tossing her bundle of clothes and poems into the air, on her way to the train station.[24] Obviously Sister Anne is a force to be reckoned with on more counts than one.

Though Sister Anne and the four schoolteachers on their summer ramble are obviously in keeping with the "Fresh Air Club's" idea of the properly fit young woman, there were other authors of advice books and articles who did not insist that the necessary exercise be spontaneous. William Blaikie and Dr. Dio Lewis were two of these. Both viewed exercise as a solemn and determined act done to correct, with scientific precision, any physical limitation, disability, or general physical weakness. They did not see it as an entertainment done joyfully and with carefree abandon. Though Blaikie recognized the therapeutic value of walking in the fresh air (he set up a schedule, for example, for working girls so that they could integrate such walking into their dinner hour), he is much more convinced of the need for regular, daily calisthenics. Using working girls as his model, Blaikie points out that such girls can "certainly" find ten or fifteen minutes in the morning "upon arising" to do deep knee bends, toe-touches and such; he also points to the wasted "odd" moments at work, when, during lulls in the midafternoon or midmorning, one could practice stretching exercises and other quick forms of calisthenics. Lest such activity seem too onerous, Blaikie attempts to lure his potential victims with an announcement regarding the results of such a regular program. If Blaikie's regimen is followed to the letter, he insists, there will be "an increase of an inch in height, of one and a half around the upper arm, of three and a half inches in the girth of the chest, of fifteen pounds in weight." He points out, in an approving summary, that this would work "marked changes in any young woman," and, he notes without hesitation, these would certainly be changes for the better. What girl, he later demands rhetorically, would not see the value in such a change?[25] A modern reader, with visions of bulging biceps and the net accumulated strength of a draft horse, is probably tempted to answer "many." Obviously, Blaikie expects no such answer; his attitude again points out the very real presence of the Real Womanhood ideal, at least in advice books, if not in practice.

Though an advocate of home exercise, Blaikie seems almost lukewarm on the subject compared with his predecessor Dr. Dio Lewis, author of *New Gymnastics for Men, Women and Children* (1863). Dr. Lewis, a spokesman for what might be called the "evangelical" school of exercise and physical fitness, is a man with a calling: to supply not only men and boys but women and girls as well with the physical training they are "dying for"; if the woman or girl so marked for death is not aware of this need, Dr. Lewis will bring her around, if only through the eloquence of his prose and the piquant quality of his illustrations. Dr. Lewis's book attempts to provide a system of exercises and gymnastic stimuli that will build up the weak muscles in the poor specimens he sees around him. His range of exercises is mind-boggling, and the sheer physical aptitude with which he expects the exercises to be approached is even more so. He states, to avoid misunderstanding, "I will rest upon the general statement, that all persons of both sexes, and of every age, who are possessed of average vitality, would, in the department of physical education, employ light apparatus, and execute a great variety of feats, which require skill, accuracy, courage, dash, presence of mind, quick eye and hand." The specified qualities of "courage," "presence of mind," and "skill" are not to be taken lightly. In the first half of his exercise book, Dr. Lewis puts his hypothetical woman student through a multitude of exercises involving large bean bags (nine to ten inches across, three-quarters full), hoops, wooden exercise rings (six inches across, one inch thick), wands (four feet long, one inch thick), and finally (Lewis's particular favorite), the wooden dumbbells (two pounds each). He guarantees that each of these aids, when used properly, will tighten, strengthen, increase, and expand flabby muscles, and each, he notes solemnly, was favored by either the Greeks or the Romans of antiquity.[26]

Nor is his female victim to escape the required torture for a quarter of an hour daily with these instruments by pleading modesty, lack of facilities in which to perform, or the constraints of clothing. Lewis points out that any room with adequate floor space, a mat, and music will suffice; as far as clothing is concerned, Lewis has designed a suitable exercise outfit for young ladies which features a dress with "perfect liberty about the waist and shoulders" consisting of a thin overskirt, pantaloons, and a thicker underskirt to prevent the first and second from tantalizing onlookers by hugging the legs too closely. Moreover, he assures his female readers, "the present style of the Garibaldi waist is very beautiful" and "particularly appropriate for gymnastics." He illustrates this outfit with a simple drawing in his book; it is certainly tasteful but it does hang somewhat hugely on the Lilliputian model Lewis draws as an example of the "average" woman.

To a modern eye, she had better be more than average if she is to survive the regimen of gymnastic routines that Lewis has in store for her. These, he insists, can be done either in a special room in the house briefly fitted up or in the lady's bedroom before she starts the day. She can, in fact, do them on her new "PANGYMNASTIKON," an instrument of frightening possibilities developed by the Germans and somewhat resembling, though in a more menacing manner, the modern all-in-one home exerciser advertised on television late at night. This invention, Lewis claims, "possesses the advantages of all other gymnastic appara-

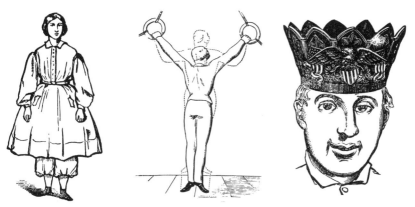

Left to right: the "Garibaldi waisted" gymnastic exercise dress for women; an illustration of exercise number 74, the "Stretched Angular Support Hang" on the Pangymnastikon; Lewis's invention, the iron "gymnastic crown," weighing one hundred pounds, worn fifteen minutes morning and evening to develop posture and balance. From Dr. Dio Lewis, *The New Gymnastics for Men, Women and Children,* 4th edition (Boston: Ticknor Fields, 1863).

tus" and is "the most complete *'multum in parvo'* in the gymnastic field." "Admirably adapted to the wants of those who cannot avail themselves of a gymnastic institution," it is, Lewis solemnly intones, "a God-send" to such people. Essentially, the contraption involves a set of gymnastic "hand" rings, which are to be set in the ceiling (minimum, twelve feet high); in addition, there are buckles and straps as well as a surprising number and variety of ropes. These can be combined ingeniously in a multitude of different ways so that the happy gymnast can practice as many as 107 different exercises. Of these, "not one," Lewis reassures his female readers, requires more strength than a woman possesses—and he includes exercises on the rings such as the iron cross and the one-armed lift (horizontal), as well as numerous somersaults, leaps, and swings. These are to be done on a daily basis in graduated stages of difficulty. (The iron cross occurs relatively early in the program.)[27]

The Pangymnastikon would certainly seem to be the very last (and certainly the most strenuous) word in the field of home self-improvement and exercise for women, but it is not. Dr. Lewis has one last device to offer to the habitually or congenitally weak among his readers: the "Gymnastick" crown—a piece of headgear worn in the manner of books on the head and for the same reason—to improve the carriage and the strength of the neck and spine. Unlike books, however, Lewis's crown (which, in his illustration is shaped like a real crown and tastefully decorated with an American eagle and crossed American flags) weighs between thirty and one hundred pounds and is made solidly of iron. The crown, too, can be graduated in weight as the sufferer after physical perfection develops stronger and stronger neck muscles. Exercises to be done while wearing this contraption include walking up and down stairs (good for the thighs), squatting, and duck-walking. Considering its heaviest possible weight (one hundred pounds), one can conclude that the thin, swanlike neck on a woman so prized in Sargent paintings and novels by Ouida was not an ideal, at least for Dio Lewis.[28]

Lest one assume that Lewis, Blaikie, and others were aberrant figures, I should note that for the entire year of 1876, the reserved *Illustrated Christian Weekly* carried a prominent advertisement for a product similar to the Pangymnastikon: "Goodyear's Pocket Gymnasium," which, according to the copy, was for "home, office, schools, hospitals" and was "endorsed by the most eminent physicians." There is no description of it, but the sobriquet "pocket" suggests the same ugly versatility possessed by the Pangymnastikon.

As if to underscore the importance of such significant muscular development, an occasional domestic novelist will have her heroine perform a saving and heroic act requiring just such enlarged biceps and triceps. Marion Harland's *Ruby's Husband* provides a vivid example of the sort of "all-American" heroine undoubtedly envisioned by Lewis and Blaikie. The heroine, "Frank" Berry, and her wretched and guilty suitor, Louis Suydam, are out for a drive in the pony cart at one point. Just after they have stopped to admire the view—and Louis is screwing up his courage to tell Frank that he is already married—they are attacked by a rabid dog. Harland's description suggests that the threat to life and limb is grave: "It was on the side nearest her, and Louis had but one glimpse of a huge head, black and shaggy, red eyes dropping a rheum, a double row of wolfish fangs, and a tongue flecked with blood and foam, when, with a smothered sound between a yell and a growl, the monster leaped." Louis, of course, though he is a potential bigamist, is only morally weak, not physically. Manfully he grapples with the beast, holding its "wolfish fangs" only barely away from his face, urging Frank to drive on—and save her life. Though gallant, Louis is obviously losing ground against the demonic strength and size of the beast. Frank refuses to desert Louis in his hour of need; she calmly climbs down from the cart on the side opposite the struggling pair. She takes off her shawl and does what any physically fit heroine of Real Womanhood would do: "In one corner [of the shawl] she had tied a loop, and drawn through it a running noose. Holding this open widely, she watched her opportunity to throw it over the dog's head, and, nothing intimidated by his bloody fangs and goggle eyes, drew it tight—tighter—the muscles of her wrist standing out tense and hard as steel, until, the strangled brute reeling to his death, Louis loosened his grip of the throat." Louis is both suitably impressed and grateful: he thanks Frank feverishly for saving his life and admits, with admiration at her strength, that the dog was "too many for me."[29]

Physical fitness in this heroic mode is not limited to works by Marion Harland, as Diana Reep notes in a critical work dealing with popular novels before World War I. Though, as Reep insists, rescue of a man by a woman is the "least consistent type," it is frequently the most interesting in its outcome. Reep divides such rescuers into two subtypes: the Indian woman and the white woman, noting that Indian women rescue white men "quite efficiently and quite consistently" but that the rescue of the hero by a white woman is often in a "far less dangerous situation" than that faced by the Indian woman and that the plot has a "strangely mixed" result. Although Harland's Frank Berry seems to have faced at least a moderately dangerous situation (rabid dogs, especially when attacking someone else, perhaps do not compare with cattle stampedes, bullet showers, or fire), Reep is correct that the outcome for the physically fit woman is not according to the plot pattern of "traditional male dominance and female submission." Though Reep suggests that such women are "not always immediately rewarded" by marriage to the rescued male, perhaps the presence or absence of such reward exists in the eyes of the female ideal dominating the story. Certainly in the Real Womanhood ideal, Frank Berry would not be "rewarded" with marriage to someone as morally seedy as Louis. Though later she *chooses* to marry him, it is only after he has purified his character, first by nursing his hateful wife, Ruby, for six years following a carriage accident that leaves her "simple" and raving, and then by becoming a free man—with outstanding moral character—following his wife's death, rather than following a divorce based on her adultery, which he could easily have procured. Frank lives a perfectly happy, fulfilled, and fulfilling life on her own, near enough to Louis to observe the changes in his character but not in a state even remotely resembling pining. Her physical strength and fitness are an index to her moral and spiritual fitness, and rewards are determined by the character of the suitor not the fact of one.[30]

Although in Reep's definition, Frank Berry's rescue of Louis Suydam is merely a curious plot with inconsistent results, it is hardly inconsistent with the general abilities and strengths, both moral and physical, displayed by the heroines of the Real Womanhood ideal of domestic novels—and these strengths often appear even when these girls are very young. Holmes's ten-year-old Yankee heroine, 'Lena, is a clear example: she defends herself brilliantly against a bullying fourteen-year-old southern male cousin when he continues, after being warned, to tease her, pull her hair, trip her, and slap her, as well as ridiculing her speech and her grandmother's lack of sophistication: "Feeling sure that not only herself but all her relations were included in this insult, 'Lena darted forward hitting him a blow in the face, which he returned by puffing smoke into hers, whereupon she snatched the cigar from his mouth and hurled it into the street, bidding him 'touch her again if he dared.' "[31] He doesn't—and eventually he comes to respect her highly.

So, too, years later, does the hero, Durward Bellmont, when, through a happenstance, he observes 'Lena's horsewomanship and that of her cousin Carrie, who, in True Womanhood fashion, is fluttery, fashionable, and dishonest, claiming to be afraid of horses and too nervous to ride. The contrast between both physical and moral characters darkens when the party mounts up. Durward, accustomed to southern ladies and True Women, ambles over to assist 'Lena in mounting her horse. She needs no help: "After bidding her good morning, he advanced to assist her in mounting, but declining his offer, she with one bound sprang onto the saddle." The slave attending notes (presumably as a compliment) that 'Lena " 'Jumps like a toad' " and " 'A'int stiff and clumsy like Miss Carrie, who allus has to be done sot on.' " On another occasion, after Carrie, squealing and pouting, is "done sot on" her horse, they proceed with their ride. 'Lena, a heroine of the Real Womanhood ideal and, obviously, a model of physical fitness, rides extremely well; Carrie, to impress Durward, the potential beau, "affect[s] so much fear of her pony that Durward at last politely offered to lead him a while." As

Holmes explains, this is indeed what Carrie hopes will happen because it "would of course bring him close to her side." Her eventual matrimonial hopes are dashed, however, in part because of the horseback riding: far from finding Carrie's helplessness appealing, he is bored with both her conversation and the bridal-path nature of their ride, much preferring 'Lena because she is not only intelligent and moral but needs no help managing her horse.[32] As usual in these stories, Carrie Livingston, in addition to being unable (or unwilling) to ride independently, also is cruel to 'Lena, openly attempts to marry for money, and is stupid as well.

Although vigorous riding, strangling rabid dogs, and exercising with the oddities of gymnastic crowns, pocket gymnasiums, and one-hundred-mile walks are, by themselves, sources of fascination, there was more to the ideal American girl's preoccupation with physical health than muscle expansion, body elasticity, and fresh air. The advice writers also stressed preventive medicine, including selected words of wisdom about diet, nutrition, personal hygiene, and the dangers of fashionable clothing.

The perfectly exercised body could not continue in the pink of that hard-won perfection if it were not taken care of properly in several basic ways. One of these was the necessity of eating "healthy" food. As Richard Cummings has shown in his fascinating work *The American and His Food*, eating healthy food such as fresh fruits and vegetables, fresh meat, and milk grew increasingly more possible as the decades passed. People began to eat more healthily, notes Cummings, when technology via modern means of transportation made it possible. As he points out, the twenty-three miles of railroad track in the United States in 1830 increased, by 1840, to two thousand miles, bringing fruit, milk, leafy vegetables, and meat speedily to cities such as Boston and New York.[33]

Popular cookbooks reflect the changes in northeastern eating habits through the recipes they include and the ingredients they demand. The 1852 *Ladies' Indispensable Assistant* (which is part cookbook, part advice book, and part pharmacopoeia), for example, has a recipe for cabbage soup, which is called both "valuable" and "healthful" and reflects the variety of vegetables presumed to be available. The base consists of boiled corned beef, but that is supplemented by "two small heads of cabbage," "a dozen or more potatoes peeled," "a cup of pearl-barley or rice," "two or three turnips," as well as fresh "sliced or grated carrots," and "an onion or two." This mixture, the recipe informs the reader, "makes a good family dinner."[34] The book also illustrates a shifting diet by its interesting mixture of easily preserved root vegetables (turnips, potatoes) and fresh vegetables (heads of cabbage, carrots, onions).

The advice books, especially those advocating Real Womanhood, reflect this health-based nutritional concern and the growing trend away from heavily salted and preserved foods toward a wider variety and fewer seasonings—"plainer" dishes. William Alcott, writing in 1850, is a thunderous advocate of the plainest of plain foods and insists that diets high in preserved or spice-laden foods cause poor health and nervousness in both sexes. According to Alcott, food should be "*simple*"; it should not ordinarily be mixed indiscernibly with other foods (he uses a minced pie as a negative example), nor should it be prepared "fancily" (that is puréed or mashed) or "overly seasoned." In this last case, one somewhat nerve-rackingly discovers that by "overly seasoned," Alcott refers to any use of salt, gravy, butter, pepper, vinegar, mustard, clove, cinnamon, nutmeg, turmeric, or ginger, and he forbids sugar, wine, syrup, marmalade, jam, and jelly as well. He rails additionally against "made" dishes that use seasonings, eggs, lard, and butter and combine foods unnecessarily, noting that these are hard to digest and cause a variety of health complaints. Among those made dishes he particularly forbids are mince pie, sausages, fritters, cake, and sweetmeats.[35]

Alcott is especially graphic in his warnings about preserved foods, noting that "the evil lies in the preservation from putrefaction, or decomposition, or decay, more than in the substance which accomplishes the object" because the substances that prevent decay also prevent or impede normal digestion. He singles out pickles, ham, salt meat, long-salted butter, and sausage in this regard. "Food," he notes with a peculiar emphasis, "*must not be too nutritious.*" He hastens to explain that he means that "a large amount of nutriment in a small space" (for example, foods that add fat, butter, eggs, cream, cheese, sugar, starch, tapioca, and the like) becomes too much for the digestive and circulatory system to absorb adequately and safely, thereby ironically echoing in part many killjoy modern cardiologists and nutritionists. Perhaps Alcott was less puritanical than he was conscientious—simply proscribing and prescribing in an attempt to cure the national epidemic of the midcentury: widespread chronic indigestion. For Alcott, the consumption of fresh foods, simply prepared with no condiments or spices, in their natural

shapes and unmixed with other foods, was a principle of good health—
if (and he is very stern in this regard) the young woman in question has
a "good appetite" not yet jaded by an overuse of spices and seasonings.
By a good appetite he means one that is neither too little (the young
woman merely picks at her food listlessly) nor too much (she eats everything in sight and has seconds). Alcott mourns that such extremes in
eating occur because, not surprisingly, no one "is willing to use plain
food." If a young woman could find plain food satisfying, it would prove
that she had a good appetite because she would not miss the "artificial
stimulation" of salt, butter, and pepper. For young women to possess or
cultivate such an appetite is Alcott's strongest recommendation. To keep
Dr. Alcott in perspective, however, we must remember that he considers
fresh, hot, homemade bread with butter "overly stimulating" and not
plain enough; unfortunately, home bakers and Alcott both realize that
part of bread's claim for fine taste is derived from its freshness, its heat,
and its crown of melted butter.[36]

Thornwell makes a substantial number of perspicacious comments
about food and its relation to complete health, though her rhapsodies
occur in the immediate context of attaining beauty. Her comments, which
eventually lead to a prescription for what we would recognize today is a
form of ova-vegetarian diet, are especially vivid: "A diet too rich or too
stimulating, commonly renders the skin coarse, and subject to pimples,
and gives it a thick, rough, and greasy appearance. Sometimes, however, it
renders it pale, sallow, and harsh." She goes on to note that though the
cheek in such a case may be red, it is not a "healthful" red but "more
resembles the flush of the dram-drinker, and arises from similar causes, viz.
too much stimulus." She does not specify what foods carry such stimulus
(Alcott's hot bread and butter perhaps), though another advice organ, the
Illustrated Christian Weekly, does list what it considers a "superbly healthy"
breakfast: lightly boiled eggs and chops "done rare" along with two-day-
old bread. Older bread, the article notes enigmatically, is "healthier." The
Ladies' Repository, on the other hand, does not mention specifically what
foods keep a person healthy, but it does construct a list of food habits that
will make one sick: drinking whiskey, drinking too many liquids with
meals, eating too fast, and not chewing adequately. It also directs its ire
against fashionable "dieting," as well as eating meals at odd times and
taking patent medicines.[37]

Food and food habits were not the only subjects that warranted the advice writers' concern. They mention personal hygiene even more frequently. Emily Thornwell is very specific about this delicate subject and seems intent on flogging her young readers into adopting more sanitary habits by offering them graphic descriptions of pimples being squeezed ("a [emerging] small white worm with a black head"), "scruff" on the scalp as a result of not brushing and washing the hair frequently, plaque on the teeth, and "rancid" sweat accumulating on unwashed under-linen. She even mentions the "parboiled" appearance of the feet, which develops if the stockings are not changed frequently enough.[38]

Nor is she alone in her insistence on cleanliness of person and garments. *The Ladies' Indispensable Assistant* felt so strongly both about changing clothes and bathing that each was mentioned in the section labeled "Etiquette"; the manual states that "cleanliness, absolute purity of person," was the first requirement of a lady—especially if she was to be healthy. The second was that she must wear clean clothes: "Better [to] wear course [sic] clothes with a clean skin, than silk stockings drawn over dirty feet," the entry warned. The *Ladies' Repository's* list of health rules notes that "neglecting to wash frequently" will make a young woman not only pimply, unpleasantly odoriferous, and less than a gentlewoman but sick as well.[39]

Like the wisdom-mongers of both the *Ladies' Repository* and *Illustrated Christian Weekly* editorial boards, Abell stresses the need to change clothes frequently and to keep the person clean if a young woman desires to maintain her health. Abell's program (which might be called a primitive "physics of health") stresses a new element of hygiene: she insists that fresh air is a cleansing agent. Fresh air is vital, she claims, because it "will remove much of the hurtful matter the skin is constantly throwing off, and the clothing should be often changed or aired on this account." Keeping oneself indoors, without exercise or fresh air, then, will bring on sickness, especially if the young woman is employed in continuous, close, and sedentary pursuits like sewing. Abell advises as well that one should not only change personal clothing and consume fresh air to maintain oneself but air bedding outdoors on a daily basis if possible and bathe frequently in cold water, not only to clean the skin but to strengthen the nerves.[40]

Washing frequently did not, in these advice books, mean only once a week—it meant every day and, in some cases, twice a day. "On no account neglect the daily matutinal bath," orders the *Illustrated Christian*

Weekly; young ladies should take a bath once or even twice a day, Thornwell advises. The baths, the writers insist, are most health-giving when they are cold—tepid baths are acceptable but only for invalids and babies. Obviously, given the spirit of the advice books and their distaste for anything even faintly suggestive of sybaritism, there is to be no "lolling" in the tub (even assuming one could do so in cold water). Once in the tub, writers agree, the young woman should make hearty use of a strong soap, applying it "vigorously" with a "rough" face cloth, a "flesh brush," or "horsehair gloves." The writers note as an inducement to the squeamish that this gives a "glow" to the skin, opens the pores, and makes the nerves "vibrate"—a description few would doubt. This form of bathing, Thornwell adds, is "the most effectual means of guarding against colds, and all the interruptions of the system."[41] Certainly if the body (and system) can survive the daily "matutinal" bath and treatment with horsehair gloves, such "interruption" does not seem a likely possibility.

Thornwell and her coterie are neither unusual nor sadistic in their injunctions concerning daily cold baths and vigorous scrubbings with abrasive instruments. William Alcott as well offers stern instructions, which concur with these ladies in both vigor and particulars. Alcott, however, suggests a reason behind the militant tone the writers take. Grimly he explains that, as a general rule, not one-fourth "of all the people of New England ever bathe their whole bodies in water of any temperature once a year. Many never bathe in their whole lives. And yet I know not but the people of these states are as careful in this particular as those of any other region this side of the Atlantic."[42]

Although the prospect of a bracing cold bath in Massachusetts in January would undoubtedly daunt even the stoutest heart, Alcott is adamant about both the practice and the need for his countrymen and women to participate in it to uphold the national health. Daily bathing in cold water, with strong soap and a friction brush, along with extensive exposure to sunlight, exercise, and fresh air, is an infallible prescription for continued health. He warns that for those who think they can trick the stern gods of health by going swimming in the summer instead of bathing, it is no substitute; swimming, he explains, does not really get the body clean—just wet.[43]

A peep into a "lady's traveling bag" of 1860, as itemized by etiquette author Florence Hartley, shows that Alcott's and Thornwell's injunctions of the 1850s apparently were widely accepted and carried into the next decade and thence through the 1880s. Hartley's list of items necessary for a "lady" to have with her when traveling is both numerous and familiar; the lady will maintain her health if she does not first succumb to the sheer weight of her baggage. First, she should have an "oil skin bag" in which she carries her sponge, friction, tooth, and nail brushes and personal soap; next she should have a calico bag containing her hairbrush and combs, a variety of pins (dressmaker) and hairpins, a mirror, a face rag, and an assortment of personal towels; if traveling overnight, she needs a carpetbag with her nightclothes, clean underwear, clean bed linen, a heavy shawl, a warm woolen hood, crackers, sandwiches, and a novel; finally, if she is traveling by sea or on water, she should add to this pile of "carry-on" luggage "a straw-covered bottle of brandy" and a vial of camphor in case of seasickness.[44] Armed with this mountain of equipment, Hartley's lady can eat healthily rather than be forced to partake of railroad or way-station food, sleep on spotless sheets free of any roving insect life, wash with indisputably clean materials, change into clean underwear, and take care of her health if she is cursed with seasickness; she is not only clean but self-sufficient about being so—two virtues for the price of one.

Although most advice writers concentrate on such obvious practices as bathing, exercise, and diet to maintain health, some address the amount of sleep a young woman should have each night and the conditions under which she should sleep. Generally speaking, advice writers suggest that a "full night's sleep" is necessary for continued health. They do not specify the number of hours, but they discuss the rhythm and pattern of that sleep. T. S. Arthur inveighs against keeping "irregular hours," as does Alcott; the *Illustrated Christian Weekly* and the *Ladies' Repository* are more specific. The *Ladies' Repository* in its list of ways people get sick notes that staying up late and sleeping in are surefire means of contracting illness, and its companion periodical insists that a young woman should get up in the mornings no later than 7:00 in summer or 7:30 in winter, lest the body's internal rhythms be disrupted and a slothful (and morally injurious) habit be commenced. As that periodical explains in its "Health Rule" 11, "Good rest at night is indispensible. Narcotics are medicated death. Earn your night's rest by plenty of exercise in the open air, by the magic of the matutinal tub, and by moderation and temperance in all things."[45]

For a strong negative example of the twin moral and physical results of keeping irregular hours and resorting to patent medicines or narcotics to restore the balance, one need look no further than the fictional character Mrs. Berry in Harland's *Ruby's Husband*. Mrs. Berry, mother (surprisingly) of the stalwart mad-dog-strangling Frank, is an aging coquette addicted to late hours, rich foods, an avoidance of bathing regularly in water of any temperature, with an enormous appetite for both narcotics and patent medicines. She powders, she paints, she laces to the point of internal injury in a vain attempt to maintain her youthful tiny waist; she flirts, she stays up past midnight socializing and sleeps in every morning dead to the world under the spell of narcotics; she is foolish, selfish, and shallow. Not unexpectedly, with the wheelbarrow load of physical fitness, health, and moral sins she trundles before her, she becomes ill— *really* ill. Mrs. Berry contracts cancer. Poor Frank is sworn to secrecy by her mother and on her own must sneak-read medical books in an attempt to help ease her mother's pain. This pain, we readers are obviously expected to agree, is no more than such an empty-headed and self-injurious person deserves.[46]

Daniel Wise seems to sum up all the advice about health maintenance best. In the following dictum, he also sounds the essentially pragmatic note that many people have come to regard as intrinsically American: he advises young women to "consult your common sense in relation to many popular injurious habits, and some simple work on physiology, that you may learn those laws of your physical organization, upon whose observance so much of the true pleasure of life depends."[47] His reference to "popular injurious habits" is indirect and somewhat obscure, but in context he seems to be referring to two popular targets of all the advice writers—tight lacing and neglecting to dress for the weather. Advice columnists and writers expend gallons of printers' ink on the subject of clothing and health in general and the horror of stays and tight laces in particular. From the length and virulence of the articles, one must assume that in real life (as opposed to the world envisioned by Real Womanhood advice writers) the despised fashion was a stronger force than good sense. Magazines like *Harper's, Godey's* and *Peterson's* devote a regular number of pages per issue to patterns for dresses, none of which seems to vary greatly from the fashionable corseted look, nor to make any marked bow to conditions of frigidity in the winter or humidity in the summer. Generally, dresses remained cumbersome and undergarments sheer, despite the presence in the same magazine of advice to dress for the weather. The problem was, in all probability significant—and one the advice writers saw as vitally connected with health concerns. Again, the villain seems to have been the "fashionable life." An editorial appearing in the April 1865 issue of the *Ladies' Repository* berates women for "complaining" about illness and then, the editor notes in scornful disbelief, going "into the streets or out to walk with only thin shoes and thin cotton stockings on their feet." This practice leads directly to disease, the editorial continues, and quotes the eminent Dr. Dio Lewis on the subject. When one remembers the high incidence of "putrid sore throat," pneumonia, and mastoid infections during the period, the concern the advice writers evince on this score seems a bit less hysterical, connected as these diseases were by physicians like Lewis with cold or damp feet and legs. So strongly does the author of this article feel about sensible clothing that he refers to the habit of sending children out with "thin" shoes and stockings as *"murder in the first degree."*[48]

Wise's admonition to dress sensibly appears to have fallen on deaf ears, however, especially when one considers the various magazines and books that insert warning notes like a rare string of black pearls through their texts. *Harper's Weekly* prints a warning in February 1860 in bold type to "lady skaters," pointing out that if, in the interest of fashionably trim ankles, they strap on their skates too tightly, the result will be a restriction of circulation, followed by frozen feet, and finally amputation. William Blaikie warns that restrictive clothing on young women, which "necessitates their avoiding all active, hearty play," produces slumped shoulders, crooked backs, and arms that are spindly, weak, and ugly.[49]

Even magazine fiction stresses dress indirectly, not only in regard to the moral fiber of the characters but to their health as well. The "Summer's Adventures" schoolteachers, for example, connect their excellent health and sunburned noses not only with vigorous exercise but also with the sensible clothing they adopt to protect themselves from the elements while allowing them a maximum of freedom. Their skirts are cut significantly higher than the tops of their boots to make walking along country lanes and through meadows easier and enterprises such as the hundred-mile ramble less hazardous in falls and sprained ankles. They wear stout boots with sensible heels and holland aprons over their dresses (to keep dust and briar damage to a minimum), as well as broad-brimmed hats. Many of the people they meet along the way comment on the girls' clothing, but none comment censoriously. In fact, the "fashionable" daughter of the landlady they stay with, with her teetering high heels and her tight lacing, is an object of private scorn to the wanderers, who view her as a fool and an unhappy (uncomfortable) slave of fashion. Significantly, she has a cold and sniffles as well.[50]

Abell would have approved thoroughly of the schoolteachers' choice of dress. In her own advice book she stresses the need to adapt clothing to weather, activity, and circumstance; as a guideline, she lays down her only rule: dress for "sufficiency" so that clothing is not excessive enough to provoke undue perspiration or light enough to bring on chills. She also has a word or two about the way clothing should fit—and those words are deliberately alarming: "Dress should fit without fettering the body. Fainting fits and death may be caused by tight dressing."[51]

Although Real Womanhood writers comment disapprovingly on the amount and suitability of clothing, their real hatred is reserved for the corset and the practice of tight lacing. Not one of the writers I have mentioned thus far has one good word to say about corsets—they see them as the fountain of an enormous number of diseases and deformities, with the usual secondary evil effects on character, intelligence, and morals. *The Ladies' Indispensable Assistant* not only lists the physical problems that accrue from tight lacing but categorically states that "no woman who laces tight can have good shoulders, a straight spine, good lungs, sweet breath, or is fit to be a wife and mother." The *Ladies' Repository*'s article "14 Ways by Which People Get Sick" lists tight lacing as "way number five" and informs the world that it leads to problems with circulation. The Reverend Bernard O'Reilly likens the "fatal passion" for "dress" (by which he means all fashionable dress but corseting in particular) as one with the desire to read "poisonous" novels and equally deadly.[52]

It is Emily Thornwell, however, with her love of graphic details and specifics, who denounces tight lacing most forcefully. Far from making a woman attractive, Thornwell sneers, "tight lacing . . . causes an extreme heaving of the bosom, resembling the panting of a dying bird," and this, as we have seen, is not the ideal image American girls should be taught to project. A "dying bird" appearance, unfortunately, is the very best image a young woman trapped in tight stays can have, according to Thornwell; she has worse descriptions to offer. Girls who lace tightly, she states, "present the appearance of a washerwoman actively engaged over a tub of hot suds" because of swelling of the neck and the red flush to the skin. Moreover, Thornwell notes, this physical appearance has a temperamental and moral reflection as well—girls so laced become "stiff, ungraceful, and ill-tempered."[53]

These effects, however, are basically cosmetic. Tight lacing has even more lasting anatomical ones, which Thornwell is quick to catalog: atrophied and "annihilated" chest muscles, restricted blood circulation, convulsive coughing, consumption, heart palpitations, excessive nervousness, cold hands, deformed ribs, bruised livers, improperly developed nipples, lateral curvature of the spine, displaced organs (liver, diaphragm, stomach, and spleen), and finally, displaced breasts. It is also "well-known," she adds, that the right shoulder "frequently becomes larger than the left," a fate she seems to feel will wreak the maximum amount of horror in feminine breasts and possibly convince young women to stop the practice.[54] Apparently, there was enough advice against the practice to have had some small effect—especially if we believe the evidence of advertising. Warner Brothers' advertisement in the 1876 *Illustrated Christian Weekly*'s numerous issues boldly meets the challenge set by the advice writers and attempts to overcome it with bald-faced effrontery—effrontery the company seemingly felt was necessary even in the delicate area of female hygiene to sell its product. "Dr. Warner's Sanitary Corset with skirt supporter and self-adjusting pads," the ad blares, "secures HEALTH and COMFORT of Body, with GRACE and BEAUTY of form," and is, moreover, "approved by all physicians." This little jewel was available for only $2—a price Thornwell, among others, would have thought 200 percent too high.

Grace and beauty, it seems, did not reside in corseting, frailness, feebleness, or pale faces and delicate hands. If Real Womanhood had its way, Amelia Sedley would not be the American model. That distinction would go to Sister Anne, the four young schoolteachers, Alcott's Josephine March, Harland's Frank Berry, Holmes's Rosa Lee and 'Lena, and Crofut's Atalanta. The ideal American girl was not a Pre-Raphelite beauty, at least to William Blaikie and others, but was better represented by classical statuary—Minervas, Niobes, and Helens with the "well-developed and shapely arm and shoulder, the high chest, the vigorous body, and the firm and erect carriage"[55]—as able to leap a fence as sew a seam, read an uplifting book as climb a tree or cook a meal. Such ideal

American girls would be the brands saved from the burning fires of fashion and the creeping illness of True Womanhood. They, in turn, the advice writers and novelists of Real Womanhood hoped, would raise future generations of healthy, fit, and sensibly clad young women who would reshape the moral character of the nation, exercising not only their physical and moral fitness for the greater good but being mentally fit enough to participate in the greater aims of society and find solutions to the problems of the century. To do so, however, required not only a physically fit body, a healthy outlook on life, and a well-balanced mind but the correct education to use each to its best advantage. The Real Womanhood girl had to be correctly educated, as the ideal built on its solid foundations of physical health and fitness by adding mental agility, acuteness, analytical ability, and knowledge to the edifice.

TWO

Education and Real Womanhood

Inactivity of intellect and of all the powers, will predispose to nervous disease and mental ailment.

—Mrs. L. G. Abell,
Woman in Her Various Relations

Critics have painted a dreary picture of the intellectual aspirations and ideals of nineteenth-century American women. Barbara Welter, for example, who says that the "four cardinal virtues" of piety, purity, submissiveness, and domesticity were the qualities most highly prized in women, suggests that American men—and indeed women themselves—never considered mental acuity or intellectual achievement to be virtues, or perhaps even possible for women. Both Carroll Smith-Rosenberg and Charles Rosenberg identify "the Victorian woman's ideal social characteristics" as "nurturance, intuitive morality, domesticity, passivity, and affection," noting that nineteenth-century scientists and physicians saw both her nature and her mentality rooted irrevocably in her biology. With a more delicate nervous system, one more likely to be overstimulated or irritated, woman had greater sensitivity and emotion than man but a constitution inherently less rational, less analytical, and more susceptible to dysfunction under mental strain.[1] Such an analysis hardly supports an ideal of the Victorian woman as a great thinker; how surprising it is, then, to find advice book after advice book, novel after domestic novel, and hosts of short fiction in popular periodicals that not only show ideal woman as rational creatures but laud education, scholarship, and intellectual background and discourse for them. Moreover, not only do the writers of these works seem to feel that women are as intellectually capable as men, but they insist that it is woman's God-given duty to develop her mind and her social and patriotic duty to put it to use. The result of denying the intellect, they note in complete contradiction to the Rosenbergs' findings, is illness and insanity. Obviously some evidence has either not been taken into account or has been included that should not have been.

As I have explained, two ideals coexisted in the United States between 1840 and 1880: the Cult of True Womanhood, which the Rosenberg articles and Welter suggest prevailed, and the Ideal of Real Womanhood, which both literary critics and historians ignore. Perhaps the diametric opposition of these two ideals is no more ideologically evident than in the differing views on the education and intellect of young women in which the nature of the vision of woman's inherent intellectual capability depends a great deal on the decade, the geographical region of publication, and the country. A close examination of both Welter's and the Rosenbergs' sources indicates that their primary evidence is derived from *both* English and American treatises by *gynecologists*, rather than by strictly American authors writing for popular audiences. Additionally, neither Welter nor the Rosenbergs make distinctions between decades, citing one report from the 1830s, another from the 1890s or late 1880s.[2] Between 1840 and 1880, however, there was considerable disagreement on the points the Rosenbergs and Welter claim were monolithically believed by American society: Real Womanhood, for example, flourished in the Northeast and was fiercely nationalistic; its proponents included medical men who told the popular audience that women's intellectual inactivity was one of the major causes of "nerves," narrow thought patterns, and general ill health, as well as depression. Although advice writers Drs. Dio Lewis, Calvin Cutter, William Alcott, and others were not gynecologists, they were trained doctors; Cutter was a surgeon with the Twenty-first Massachusetts Infantry; Alcott graduated from Yale College; Lewis attended Harvard Medical College.[3] They also disagreed with the gynecologists, as did physiologists, biologists, "physical culture" specialists, and "natural scientists" such as William Blaikie and Samuel Gregory. Gregory believed so strongly in women's intellectual abilities that he founded the New England Female Medical College in Boston in 1848—the first medical college for women in the world.[4] All of the men I have mentioned had the inestimable advantage of being widely read popular writers, unlike the sources used by the Rosenbergs, which include Drs. Thomas Emmett, J. Marion Sims, T. Gailliard Thomas, and Nathaniel Chapman, all of whom either published only in medical journals or wrote gynecology textbooks. Moreover, as I will show, the domestic novels of the same period tend to reflect a much more intellectual and well-read series of heroines than Welter and others would lead us to expect.

In this chapter I will examine the rationales behind specific requirements for education, how the Ideal of Real Womanhood fitted into the controversy over woman's sphere and female intelligence, and what part education played in the larger context of Real Womanhood, especially as education was understood by the literate public between 1840 and 1880. Before any fine distinctions between ideals of education can be made, however, it is necessary to place those conflicting definitions in context. What, in fact, did the popular mind mean by "education"? The definitions are as various as the writers who offer them. Eleanor Wolf Thompson, in an excellent study done in 1947, lists and discusses a variety of answers. Education could—and did, to some—mean simply experience with life and living; it could also mean academic training, which many understood to be no higher than the eighth grade. Another concept presupposed secondary work through high school, and still others believed women should pursue a course of "home study" completely outside school. Others meant vocational training when they referred to education, and for some spiritual or moral education through Christian instruction or training in citizenship and social responsibilities was the preferred course.[5] Whatever the definition, ladies' magazines (as Thompson shows), advice books, domestic novels, newspaper editorials, short stories, and essays all seemed to agree explicitly or implicitly that young American women should be educated. The problem for the critic, of course, is to sort out what subjects these writers considered necessary and the intellectual level at which they should be studied.

Here I will stress "academic" education—study in the classics, literature, history, philosophy, languages, mathematics, and the physical sciences. This is the educational ideal most visibly absent in the model of True Womanhood. Academic excellence was not only ignored but positively discouraged in all but the most superficial manner in the more famous ideal but was insisted upon in the Real Womanhood ideal, not as an end in itself or for personal fulfillment to any large degree, but rather as providing necessary knowledge for one to cope with the duties and obligations of a different kind of womanhood. This academic education should be undertaken to help fulfill woman's sphere, not for a career as such, as emphasized by feminist writers. Separating academic education from domestic, physical, or spiritual education is difficult because the writers I cite saw such subjects as interrelated. For example, Catharine Beecher and her sister Harriet Beecher Stowe, in their *New Housekeeper's Manual* (1873), indicate that the ability of the housekeeper to select "healthful foods" required some knowledge of nutrition, principles of digestion, and the nature of minerals, botany, and chemistry. Moreover, Beecher and Stowe indicate that this background knowledge, as well as that of "domestic economy," should be gained well before "a young girl has the heavy responsibilities of housekeeper, wife, mother, and nurse."[6]

Other advice writers such as the redoubtable William Blaikie in *How to Get Strong and How to Stay So* (1879) and Dr. Dio Lewis in *New Gymnastics for Men, Women and Children* (1863) see intimate connections between physical exercise and methods to increase intellectual acuity or inspire the imagination. To these gentlemen, to be physically fit is also to be intellectually alert—training in one aids the other.[7]

In the works advocating Real Womanhood, advice writers and domestic novelists through the traits they explicitly laud specify a variety, rigorousness, and academic quality of knowledge that young women must acquire to be "real" women. And they must acquire it either by schooling or by concentrated home study. These rigorous expectations are directly related to the advice writers' answers to key questions in the educational debate that raged throughout the midcentury: whether woman's mind was equal to that of man and whether it was capable of being educated in the same way (method) or in the same disciplines (subject) as man's.[8]

Before examining Real Womanhood's answers, for purposes of comparison, we need to examine True Womanhood's assumptions. The Cult of True Womanhood held that woman was to fulfill herself in the "instinctive" arts of child rearing, domestic pursuits, and spiritual comfort. Her natural genius lay in these areas, not among volumes of Euclid, Virgil, or Tacitus. The presence of a uterus and breasts was considered proof, along with "exquisite sensibilities," of the career the Lord had chosen for woman. Dr. Nathan Allen, in a paper presented to the Social Science Association of Boston, realizes that education *may* not be impossible for women but insists that it is detrimental to them and to the race. He notes, "They [American women] cultivate their minds . . . at the expense of their health and *legitimate* physical function" (italics mine). According to Dr. Edward Clarke, a writer of the late 1870s and the most famous of the True Womanhood opponents of female higher education, biology in the form of female physiological "organization" was, finally, destiny made manifest in regard to the question: "The problem of woman's sphere, to use the modern phrase, is not to be solved by applying to it abstract principles of right and wrong. Its solution must be obtained from physiology, not from ethics or metaphysics . . . without denying the self-evident proposition, that whatever a woman can do, she has a right to do, the question at once arises, what can she do? And this includes the further question, what can she best do? . . . The *quaestio vexata* of woman's sphere will be decided by her organization. This limits her power, and reveals her divinely-appointed tasks." Dr. Clarke's reasoning is somewhat complicated, however, and it takes a careful eye to unravel his true intention. He claims, somewhat surprisingly for example, that girls are intellectually capable of learning, organizing, and even outshining boys in any academic subject—he particularly mentions "unravelling the intricacies of Juvenal"—but that it is physically injurious for them to do so. To study these subjects in the "same way" as boys (that is, in college or advanced secondary school) is to ignore vital differences in physical organization that will inevitably result in a girl being cursed by "neuralgia, uterine disease, hysteria, and other derangements of the nervous system."[9]

Initially, Clarke does not seem to be advocating an ignorant existence for women; after all, he notes, "Women who choose to do so can master the humanities and the mathematics, encounter the labor of the law and the pulpit, endure the hardness of physic[s?] and the conflicts of politics." In the great educational debate, he would answer that, ostensibly, woman's brains are equally capable; her intelligence is sufficient to deal with typical academic curricula. But—and for Clarke this proviso in effect cancels out any true realization of female potential—she can do so only at great risk unless she does such intellectual work "in woman's way," not as a man would do it. To Clarke, this means that she must spend anywhere from seven to eight days a month before and during menstruation reclining and resting prone, not standing, studying, taxing her brain, or in any way being overstimulated. According to Clarke, any activity between the ages of fourteen and twenty-five (the "critical epoch," when sexual organs are supposedly formed) that requires energy—including working for a living as well as going to school—will draw necessary blood and vitality away from the forming sexual organs, causing malnourishment of ovaries and uterus and resulting in broken health, a lifetime of female trouble, and possible sterility or death. Activity before and during menstruation is particularly injurious in this regard.[10]

Clarke's ostensible answer to this dilemma is to make special arrangements at both work and school to provide the young woman (between the ages of fourteen and twenty-five) with a week and a half's excused absence as menstruation approaches; she should, he feels, be given special monthly dispensation from standing or sitting long hours (a common feature of school life). Given the nature of both the work world and that of college, however, both of which are loath to accept periodic absences, Clarke's plan effectively makes it impossible for young women either to receive a college education or to hold a job. He himself points out that impossibility by stating that Harvard cannot adjust its schedule to allow women to "keep up" if they follow this regimen, and he expresses regret that this is so. But these are the evils of coeducation: it takes no notice of women's organization and special needs. Even his system of periodic rest, however, is, in his own mind, merely a band-aid solution. He points out that college subjects—calculus, Latin, Greek, natural science, theology—all require an inordinate amount of sustained concentration, which, regardless of the time of the month, drains energy from the woman's body either as she is getting ready to enter the menstrual period or is trying to recover from it. Such an energy drain, it seems, can never truly be countenanced if a woman wishes to maintain her good health. Since the great evil is not only a regular school schedule of standing, sitting, and public recitation but the sustained attention to subject matter and memorizing, even home study can be deemed unhealthy. Basically, in Clarke's view, higher education in any form is dangerous to women's health. He backs up his arguments with two full chapters of case histories from his own practice, which show under a variety of conditions of work and study that women pay a heavy price for being educated, either academically or vocationally.[11]

Clarke, Dr. Charles Meigs, and others, then, insisted that by default True Women—that is, those patriotically able to bear the republic a healthy host of future citizens—remained virginally pure of any critical thinking, knowledge, or undue contemplation. Small wonder, then, that Barbara Welter, Carroll Smith-Rosenberg, Charles Rosenberg, and Anne Douglas Wood see in their writings the "scientific" basis for the fluffy-brained model of the True Woman; indeed it was—for that particular ideal. The Real Womanhood ideal spokespeople had their own set of doctors and considerably different answers to the question of woman's ability to conquer intellectual subjects or the ways in which she should do so.

One such advocate of women's education, Dr. Ely Van De Warker, in 1874, discussed the theory of energy deprivation and argued strenuously against it in a *Popular Science Monthly* article, insisting that "there is no such thing as one [health and growth] law for women and another for men" and that a healthy girlhood usually resulted in a healthy womanhood. Van De Warker's article is a direct refutation of the arguments of a British doctor, Dr. Henry Maudsley, as stated in a June 1874 issue of the *Fortnightly Review*. Maudsley's article, "Sex in Mind and Education," stresses the energy displacement theory and adds the observation that women are constitutionally "weak" as well. Much of this argument, like Dr. Edward Clarke's (given the similarity of titles, one wonders whether there was an influence), rests on the theory of the "critical epoch" when the sexual organs are formed. Dr. Van De Warker tackles the problem head-on: "My aim has been to fix, if possible, the actual value of the puberic [sic] age of woman as a crisis, so that there may be no fictitious bar to her progress to either a higher education, or to her training for any of the skilled labors suited to her strength." Van De Warker claims that if, in fact, any "crisis" exists, it does not occur between the ages of fourteen and twenty-five but, rather, between birth and the first ovulation. If ovulation occurs on schedule, then woman is "sexual perfection." Dysfunction later, he states, is caused by something that happened before the first ovulation. Given this chronology, Dr. Van De Warker states categorically that higher education could not possibly be the cause of later inability to have children or of any other of the hosts of sexual dysfunctions. Scathingly, he dismisses the Maudsley-Clarke obsession with "simple ovarian growth and function as a factor in the development of womanly mental and structural peculiarities" and instead grimly advises doctors and readers alike to pay more attention to general health and to a woman's intellectual and emotional needs in childhood, when the problems truly occur; his admonishments are stern: "Instead of curtailing her [a young woman's] opportunities for work and study, by throwing around her restraints, and, as it were, creating a disability out of a natural function," readers and doctors should instead try to arrange early on for young women to have healthy, active lives by following all the normal health procedures. His concluding remarks are particularly apt in regard to the question of comparative female intelligence, female health, and hurdles to achievement because of biological organization: "Let healthy ovulation be the natural outcome of a healthy childhood . . . all this time [during sexual maturity] the young woman is as able to sustain uninterrupted physical and intellectual work as the young man."[12]

Nor is Van De Warker the only doctor to see no contradiction between an erudite, intellectual female and a healthy, "womanly" one. Much earlier, in 1862, physiologist Samuel Gregory wrote an article that not only presupposed healthy, intelligent, and highly trained women but made a strenuous appeal for more female physicians. Far from being diseased, weak, insane, or hysterical victims, Gregory saw women physicians as particularly important because of their training: "The medical profession is incomplete and ineffective without female co-workers in promoting health and relieving sickness and suffering. While the doctor cannot be dispensed with, the doctoress is no less essential to the physical well-being of society."[13]

Gregory argues against the limitations of woman's sphere, which, through a narrow definition, includes no more than home and children. He stresses the need for women physicians *especially* (though not exclusively) in obstetrics and gynecology because of the woman physician's special ability to communicate with female patients about pressing but embarrassing concerns. In an aside, Gregory points out that nothing on earth can be considered more a matter of woman's sphere than delivering children and asks why this is somehow not considered "appropriate." His concluding argument has particular relevance for the debate over what constituted necessary or appropriate training for young women: "As a medical education would be a most valuable qualification for the maternal head of a family, suppose large numbers of young women should study medicine, commence practice, and then be diverted wholly or in part for a few years; they could then resume their vocation."[14] Several assumptions immediately catch the eye. First, there is no question in Gregory's mind that women are fully capable intellectually of undergoing and passing the curricular requirements of medical school. His entire argument is based on the belief that they are capable of such education and fully qualify as physicians. Second, he posits that those women who do become doctors will suffer from no unnatural or horrendous physical problems; indeed, he sees the results of such education as so entirely a part of a natural cycle that he presupposes a period of time during which they will have children and then return to work. One of his strongest appeals for more women doctors comes in the form of a suggestion that such training would prove valuable for someone who intended eventually to be a mother.

Gregory and Dr. Van De Warker were not alone in their insistence that efforts at higher education offered no threat to women's health. Other doctors concurred, stressing the beneficial nature of academic study to a woman's general health. Far from being deleterious, studying and advanced learning are over and over again cited by both Real Womanhood advice writers and doctors as absolutely necessary for general health maintenance. Even though Alcott, in his 1850 tome *The Young Woman's Book of Health*, does not recommend any particular routine of instruction, he insists that it be "extended and thorough" and states: "The higher and more harmonious the cultivation of the intellect, other things being equal, the better is the health." He excludes no woman from his program of "mental cultivation" and preventive medicine, going so far as to insist that every young woman "should have her mind well stored and disciplined, were it only for the sake of improving her own health . . . every faculty of the mind should be, in some way, highly developed, cultivated and disciplined." Alcott is apparently aware of some of the early arguments against rigorous education for women because he sets aside a page or two to deal with what he calls "prejudices in the vulgar popular mind against anything which, in a female, would approximate a liberal course of education." He takes his readers to task for allowing themselves to be swayed by such reasoning and labels it "ignorance"; he then points out that a strong education, especially involving such subjects as philosophy, theology, foreign languages, and mathematics, helps develop a woman's self-control and self-discipline. These subjects allow her to subdue negative thoughts, emotions, passions, and fears that are extremely threatening to good health and, instead, maintain a calm, balanced, and philosophical perspective, made up of even parts of rationality and sensibility along with a historical point of view that places the particular inside a more knowledgeable general context. This thinking eventually leads, through lack of these damaging emotions, to a healthier body. Dr. Dio Lewis also stressed the link between general health and both physical and mental exercise. In *Our Girls* (1871) Lewis listed a curriculum that would be most conducive to both mental cultivation and general health; he excludes French but strongly recommends natural sciences, history, mathematics, and "uplifting" literature.[15]

It would seem, then, that the *popular* mind did not speak out in one voice or accept only one view of woman's intelligence and the general physiological and medical effects of higher education. Far from unanimously embracing a vision of young women as hopelessly "diseased" and vulnerable because of their biological processes and therefore unable safely or intellectually to be educated or erudite, as Smith-Rosenberg, Rosenberg, and Welter claim, there was a marked difference of opinion on the subject. There is also considerable disagreement among mid-nineteenth-century advice writers concerning what a woman should know if she were to fulfill her obligations as wife, mother, sister, and daughter. Under the ideal of True Womanhood, these obligations almost entirely excluded education. Real Womanhood, however, made certain curious demands and posed even more curious and intricate rationales behind these demands for an academic education.

Whatever genre they used—short story, domestic novel, advice book, magazine article, or editorial—writers supporting the Ideal of Real Womanhood all seem to demand that young women have a rounded, fully developed liberal education with which to realize their feminine obligations. To a great extent, the stress on academic knowledge stretched the normal dimensions of the traditional woman's sphere considerably beyond anything the name now implies. The impulse to see the term "woman's sphere" as antithetical to education has, I think, blinded a number of critics and kept them from truly examining the stringent demands and the intellectually rigorous expectations that these writers outlined. This is not to say that writers of the Real Womanhood ideal advocated a cryptofeminism masquerading under safer colors, for they most certainly did not; rather, as Nina Baym has brilliantly pointed out in her study of women's fiction and the domestic novel, such writers advocated a philosophy that contained what we now recognize as several particularly feminist characteristics, but they are strictly confined within the larger framework of traditional values and an understanding of the role; they also deliberately eschewed feminism.[16] Most of all, this ideal was a matter of practicality, not ideology. Nothing makes one more acutely aware of this aspect than a review of the reasons given for the sort of education I will describe. Basically, these pragmatic rationales for extensive education fall into five groups in descending order of importance: (1) romance and marriage—to attract the right kind of man and to fulfill the duties of wife and companion; (2) domestic economy and child rearing—to be able to manage a household and raise children satisfactorily; (3) cultural atmosphere and morality—as mothers and teachers, guides to help transmit culture, gentleness, and morality to future generations, the immediate family, and society at large; (4) vocational—to be able, if the need arose, to support oneself, immediate or extended family, or to help financially in a marriage; (5) health and balance of self—to combat neurosis, depression, and mental illness and to widen one's horizons and enrich oneself as a person.

As the ranking suggests, self-enrichment was the least often reason given by the writers in their crusade for young women to gain an adequate academic education, and when it was mentioned, it was usually linked to a complex web of physical and mental health needs, which in turn would adversely affect the family if they were not met. It should be stressed, as Baym points out, that the female novelists of this period (under the Real Womanhood ideal, they were both female and male) accepted without serious question that men and women were different, that each had proscribed obligations to fulfill under God's laws, and that society was stratified and correct behavior was geared both to one's social level and one's divinely appointed sexual obligations.[17]

For a young woman to fulfill her obligations of gender in a family, however, she first had to find a suitable young man to marry. Once married, a young woman had to be prepared to function as a companion for her husband and a suitable hostess for his friends and business contacts if the family were to survive socially and financially. All three of these goals require, according to the writers advocating Real Womanhood, a liberal and well-rounded academic education. Obviously education in such skills as cooking, sewing, housekeeping, and etiquette was also required, but I am concerned here only with the uses of an academic education as these writers perceived it, though of course they would have expected young women to have learned, through a different kind of education, those other skills as well.

Both advice writers and novelists seem to agree, either explicitly or implicitly, that a liberal education and an ability to speak intelligently were necessary if one wanted to marry well—and all writers agree that "well" meant a man who was hardworking, compassionate, and moral rather than one who was merely wealthy or physically attractive.

Indeed, novels, essays, and short stories alike tell sad tales of women attracted to and carried away by wealth or looks, only to discover that the young man in question is at heart a brute and a drunkard and his wealth transitory or nonexistent. Marrying well also involved not only attracting and holding the affections of a young man but, of coequal importance, being able to distinguish the "right" sort of man from one who was basically a cad but *appeared* to be right. Education, then, served a double function: it made a girl able both to attract men and to make a discriminating choice among the suitors she did attract. T. S. Arthur insists that a young woman cannot make such a discriminating choice until at least two years after the end of her schooling because she lacks sufficient mental discipline, maturity, judgment, or thinking skills before then. He does not even consider that a young woman would dream of making a choice without having acquired some schooling. To Arthur and many other writers, education was so important in having a useful, happy life as a married woman that they predicted nothing but misery if a young woman should be foolish enough either to fail to educate herself or impulsively cease to finish her schooling and marry under the hypnotism of physical attraction. Arthur agrees with an earlier advice writer, Mrs. John Farrar, that the result of such impulsiveness will be the young woman's "mental degeneration" because she will go directly from "childhood" into motherhood and will have no time for her character to mature sufficiently or for her to gain the educated perspective and mental discipline required to survive in either marriage or the world. Mrs. L. G. Abell also counsels against early marriage when it precludes an adequate education, noting that a girl should have enough education and time for reflection to judge the "mind, temper, habits, and principles" of her suitor. Without an education, this frequently proves impossible.[18] The business of judging these qualities, as well as learning the procedure for judgment and the possible deceptions along the way, which the young woman should avoid, were matters needing both a well-stocked mind and a trained habit of clear thinking.

Fiction writers agree implicitly with advice writers concerning the value of a sound academic education, as brief examination of several heroines reveals. Each has a soundly bluestocking background, which enables her to make careful decisions about both careers and future suitors.

Augusta Evans's frighteningly erudite Edna Earl (from the 1866 bestseller *St. Elmo*) has command of several classical languages, higher mathematics, and comparative religion and theology. Far from being considered unwomanly or unattractive, Edna turns down proposals of

marriage from three different men during the novel, some of these proposals repeated more than once. She rejects them for various sensible
reasons and marries the rich title character only after having achieved
the self-supporting career and nationwide reputation her intellect told
her were both possible and prudent, in light of the suitors. Edna's education, incidentally, was of the home study variety; she was tutored by the
local pastor. *Some* of her favorite books, subjects, and authors, according
to her creator, include Burckhardt, Champollion, Lanyard, Belzoni, Ra-
cine, Zoroaster, Solon, and Lycurgus (the last two in Greek); Gnostic
doctrines, Talmudic questions (in Hebrew), the Koran, Egyptology, Des-
cartes (in French), and Plutarch. At least within the context of this
novel, a rigorous liberal education is truly rigorous and could hardly be
mentioned in the same breath with "fashionable" education, with its
emphasis on conversational French, watercoloring, and dancing.[19]

Another resolutely erudite heroine, Ellen Montgomery from Susan
Warner's wildly popular novel *The Wide, Wide World* (1851), finds true
happiness only in her books or in the immaculate company of her informal tutor, John Humphreys. Little Ellen's tutorials begin under John's
saintly sister Alice, who instructs the child in mathematics, biology, botany, English, history, and geography. Her home education continues under John, who instructs her throughout her adolescence in Latin, art,
architecture, political economy, philosophy, natural science, and theology as well as horseback riding. For outside expertise in a modern
language, Alice and Ellen both take French lessons from Mrs. Vawse, an
ancient Swiss émigré living in a tiny shack on a neighboring mountain.
Far from turning Ellen into a drab (as her long-lost Scottish relatives
claim), this healthy regimen makes her attractively well-spoken and
sweetly grave, in contrast to several vapid and poorly educated cousins,
the spoiled products of a fashionable education. John Humphreys's
marked preference for her also highlights Ellen's female excellencies, as
do admiring friends of her uncle. One such friend, M. Muller, whom the
author, Warner, refers to as "a Swiss gentleman and a noted man of
science," praises Ellen's extraordinary intelligence, character, and fluent
French and begs for her to be allowed to "read" science with him three
times a week—a great honor, Warner assures us.[20]

Other novelists, like Mary Jane Holmes, often show their commitment to the romantic importance of a solid education by thrusting the
poorly educated girl who chooses unwisely into the secondary role of

foil to the heroine. In *'Lena Rivers,* for example, Holmes offers us vacuous Carrie Livingston, who resigns herself to a wretched marriage with Captain Atherton in contrast to the more suitable match between her cousin heroine 'Lena (educated) and Durward Bellmont. In another novel, *Meadowbrook,* Holmes similarly gives the reader the character of disagreeable, fashionably finished Dell Thompson in her loveless marriage to Dr. Clayton to contemplate. Naturally, the heroine, Rosa (a former schoolteacher and governess), has found true happiness with the wise and genteel Richard.[21]

Other essayists and short-story writers simply use the silly girls of limited education who quit school as warnings and horrifying *exempla* to young women readers. Such is the case, for example, of Anna Wyman, the protagonist in T. S. Arthur's story "Engaged at Sixteen." Arthur's double description of Anna, before and after the fatal engagement, deserves to be quoted in full because it is perhaps one of the clearest examples of the thinking advice writers so despised—the frivolous short-sightedness and impatience to be grown up: "All at once, she Anna became restless, capricious, unhappy. She had been at school up to this period, but now insisted she was too old for that; her mother seconded this view of the matter." Later, thrown out by her brutal husband, Thomas Elliott, after he goes bankrupt, and with a baby in her arms, Anna drags herself home to her parents; Arthur apostrophizes, "Her ardent wish had been gratified. Anna was engaged at sixteen, and married soon after; but at eighteen, alas! She had come home a deserted wife and mother! And so she remained."[22] All this could have been avoided, Arthur suggests, through the comments of Anna's father, if she had finished school and learned how to judge both situations and men better.

This fiction illustrates how a sufficiently liberal education provides a girl with both the maturity and the judgment and critical ability to choose a husband wisely. Education, according to both advice writers and novelists, also can make the "right sort" of man present himself as a suitor, and such suitors are disgusted with girls who lack such education. Dr. Dio Lewis, for example, is adamant about his own male distaste for "silly" women of no education or judgment. He warns that sensible, sober, and upright men only toy with such women and states categorically that "nineteen times in twenty, sensible men choose sensible women." Lewis's portrait of such a woman is particularly revealing in light of what Welter and others claim was the ideal of True Womanhood: "I know a woman, twenty-five years old, and as big as both my grandmothers put together, who insists upon being called *Kittie,* and her real name is *Catherine;* and although her brain is big enough to conduct affairs of State, she does nothing but giggle, cover up her face with her fan, and exclaim, 'Don't now, you are real mean.' How can a sensible man propose a life partnership to such a silly goose?"[23] Far from being a model of what men supposedly want, Lewis, Arthur, Burnap, and others find such women revolting. Apparently writers advocating Real Womanhood sought women who could be helpmates and partners—educated, mature, sensible women—rather than child-women who would prove later to be weak and dependent as well as parasitic.

The Reverend George Burnap, in a series of printed lectures published in 1841, gives perhaps the most eloquent (but by no means the only) opinion on the positive, romantic value of a liberal and rigorous education. He speaks at length about "the beauties of a well-stored mind" and the attraction of such a mentality. He assures women that "a sensible and brilliant conversation will attract the notice of the well-educated of the other sex more than a coronet of jewels" and prophesizes both happy marriage and a full and fulfilling life for the woman who so prepares herself. He specifically mentions the "graver subjects" as a source of excellent study, especially mathematics, ancient languages, logic, and metaphysics, as well as literature, history, and science.[24] The assumption that the educated and well-versed young lady would prove most attractive to men is present in many magazine stories and more than a few domestic novels. Already we have seen the almost hypnotic allure both Evans's Edna Earl and Hentz's Linda Walton exert on the men around them; the same can be said for Holmes's various heroines as well. *Harper's Weekly Magazine,* for example, presents the heroine Mary Dashford's wit as the entire basis of her romance with equally witty and intelligent George Newberne. The two exist in a Beatrice and Benedict relationship, sparring and finally marrying at the story's end. Heroine Olive West in a story of the same name in *Harper's New Monthly Magazine* has a similar appeal. Olive is a poet, a doll dresser, and finally a publishing author, and she supports a bankrupt and mentally disturbed father. Her poetry and her education finally draw the wealthy and morally superior suitor to her. The heroine of "The School-Teacher at Bottle Flat," a short story in *Leslie's,* proves that education and a cultivated mind are not only romantically attractive but give women a powerful tool for moral influence even over men who ordinarily find schoolteachers, of either sex, lacking "the spunk of a coyote."[25]

Once she had selected and married a suitable young man, a young woman's liberal education made it possible for her to build a happy and stable home around the nucleus of shared interests and companionship. Advice writers, magazine article writers, and novelists all seemed to agree that intellectual and spiritual friendship between husband and wife were of paramount importance—and the range of subjects a young woman had studied contributed greatly to her success in achieving such a friendship.

Even the conservative Reverend Bernard O'Reilly notes that a young wife should be "able to converse with him [the husband] in his own language, or to discuss with him every favorite topic." Those topics, as outlined by O'Reilly, again seem to conform to the general notion of what constituted a liberal education among other, less denominational or dogmatic advice writers. O'Reilly specifically mentions languages, sciences, arts, and history, as well as mathematics, though in the Catholic tradition of woman's sphere within the Real Womanhood ideal, he stresses that though the woman's knowledge of such subjects should be "thorough" it should not represent "mastery," lest she prove herself "unfeminine." Clearly, for a young woman to know physics or algebra was no mark of a lack of femininity to either O'Reilly or, apparently, the American Catholic church. Indeed, O'Reilly specifically insists that a Catholic girl of thirteen should be "given the history of the heresies and schisms which still live and set themselves up against the authority of Christ's infallible church"; she should also have a full and thorough preparation in all Christian doctrines, biblical history, church architecture, religious painting, and sculpture.[26]

This call to a varied intellectual background as a necessary prerequisite for marital happiness is made repeatedly by writers of a variety of denominations, who show the young wife shining like an erudite jewel in conversation with her absorbed and adoring husband. Women, notes the *Illustrated Christian Weekly,* should not "prattle" but rather provide their husbands with conversation that is intelligent, stimulating, restful, cheerful, and kindly. The picture the magazine article paints is of a cozy fireside enlivened at the end of the day by shared experiences, shared enthusiasms on interesting subjects or hobbies, and "understanding."[27]

Husbands were more easily kept at home and away from rough companions, bars, or gambling halls if they could discuss their businesses, their problems, and their hobbies with a knowledgeable wife who was able to make an intelligent contribution to the conversation. As several writers point out, conversational subjects might range from merchandising to botany, from the stock market to archaeology; a young wife must be prepared to contribute despite the variety. A liberal education provided her with a background, but, more important, it gave her both the mental discipline and the understanding to find out more about a subject with which she was unfamiliar—and she was expected to do just that if the need arose.

The husband was not the only male exposed to the young wife's conversational charms. As Burnap, Harland, Arthur, and Lewis all point out, the husband's business associates and friends were also an audience. A wife's function as hostess was particularly important because it often was a means of aiding a husband in his climb up the career ladder, and it helped in making important contacts and impressing clients. The portrait of the liberally educated wife is also the portrait of the successful hostess, "toss[ing] the shuttlecock of repartee and discuss-[ing] *belles-lettres* with the scholars to the left and right." The advice writers continue to stress that the useful wife is not simply a creature of "accomplishments"; her educational needs go far beyond light conversational French, a few tunes on the piano, or singing. Indeed, these may even be a detriment. Dio Lewis, for example, states unequivocally that amateur piano playing is inevitably a "tiresome interruption" in an evening of interesting conversation, one that irritates rather than inspires, and that French as a conversational language has no "use" in polite society because there is "precious little in that language about science," and it would require "more than a Lamartine" to express ideas about current discoveries or government innovations. Surprisingly, he also strongly disapproves of girls studying Greek and Latin because such studies result in "a barbarism transmitted from the dark ages."[28]

It would be inaccurate, however, to leave this discussion without noting that, even under the criteria of the Real Womanhood ideal, the learned maiden or wife did operate under certain restrictions in regard to her conversation. She was expected to avoid the appearance of pedantry, for example, and cautioned against alluding excessively to the classics or "various departments of science" or making it painfully clear that she was better versed than her guests in any subject areas. She was not to lard her talk with Greek and Roman "tags" or discuss at length any subject with which her conversational partner was unfamiliar. Emily Thornwell, William Alcott, and Marion Harland stress repeatedly that knowledge must be combined with politeness and sensitivity toward the feelings of others.

Although Real Womanhood was primarily practical, it was also characterized by its balance—a hard-won balance between the demands of home, family, intellect, heart, and soul. One who was well rounded educationally had knowledge of feelings and manners as well as Egyptology and calculus, of child rearing as well as Cicero or Tacitus. Over and over again this ideal of education emphasizes the *wholeness* of character, life, and experience; absence of such wholeness because of an exclusive development of academic intelligence meant a poor education or the presence of disease. Alcott called such one-sided intellectual development in young women "precocity" and distinguished it from a state of active, strong-minded intellect. He saw it—and its outward manifestation, pedantry—as physically harmful and tied it directly to scrofula and related serious health problems. Burnap, though not so adamant on the physical effects of an exclusively academic education, still referred to its expression in the form of pedantic observations as "sure evidence of a defective one [education]." He did, however, state repeatedly that mental cultivation and education did not, by themselves, lead to pedantry; indeed, he presents his readers with a portrait of the truly educated woman against which they may measure their own behavior: "The thoroughly educated woman never tells you that she has studied Homer and read Faust, that she has made herself acquainted with the mysteries of Algebra and Conic Sections or labors by any indirection to lead you to infer that she has done so; but she gives you higher proof of her careful training, by the correctness, the elegance, and the knowledge with which she discusses every subject as it comes up." He soothes his readers, finally, by pointing out that those who accuse learned women of being pedants when they have not acted in such a manner are simply critics who have no mental accomplishments of their own. He dismisses such men as those who "fear" superior women.[29]

Other charges than that of pedantry could be—and were—made against learned women. One of the most common involved criticism of women who knew mathematics but could not prepare a simple meal or change a baby. As Marion Harland showed, burning the dinner while discussing the intricacies of *Rape of the Lock* with a husband's friends did not constitute "right" behavior. After all, these Real Womanhood writers agreed in this instance with those espousing the Cult of True Womanhood that women's main and primary profession was most often that of wife and mother. This belief is primarily what separates the Real Womanhood writers from avowed feminists. What critics such as Mary P. Ryan, Madonna Kolbenschlag, Page Smith, and Welter fail to see is that an academic education was not unanimously or necessarily considered inimical to being a good wife and mother—in fact, a great many of these writers saw such education as a requirement for fulfilling these duties.[30] The objection, it seems, was to an education that did not include as well training in the domestic arts. In support of this Thompson points out that the practical aspects of housewifery and child rearing were only two of the educational areas most editors of magazines deemed important; they were not the only ones.[31]

A certain poignant pragmatism about the subject wafts up from the pages of books by women such as Marion Harland and Abell as they explain that academic knowledge can in fact be useful in running a well-organized household and raising well-behaved children. Both ladies, despite their disclaimers concerning the primacy of domestic, marital, and maternal duties, point out wistfully that life would probably be much pleasanter for women with an intellectual bent if they could "live above the heat and odor" of housekeeping, cooking, and diapers, but economic constraints prevented most from doing so, and they must learn such skills as cooking and cleaning if only to prevent a lifetime of domestic chaos and mismanagement. A grim practicality intrudes here once more—and Real Womanhood was certainly practical. An education that contained no such instruction was dangerous. An editorial in *Peterson's Magazine,* after reviewing ideals of vocational and academic education, warns that society is "full" of "wives, who, having been intended for teachers, dressmakers, etc., and having capably discharged the calls of their profession, have, after marriage, proved utterly incompetent for their new vocation."[32]

Catharine Beecher (the "mother of home economics"), in the preface to the third edition of her *Treatise on Domestic Economy,* laments that there is mute evidence of "the deplorable sufferings of multitudes of young wives and mothers, from the combined influence of *poor health, poor domestics, and a defective domestic education.* The number of young women whose health is crushed, ere the first few years of married life are past, would seem incredible to one who has not investigated the subject."[33] Novelists as well join in the hue and cry over the lack of domestic accomplishments, though their criticism is more against a "fashionable" education than for domestic education per se. The domestic novelists rarely deal with the domestic sphere of married women; their heroines usually are academically trained young women who have, by reason of family tragedy or economic disaster, been forced to go life alone or serve as the sole financial support of aging parents or younger siblings. Yet even here, despite a much stronger emphasis on purely academic or vocational pursuits, there is great respect for those heroines who can "take over" domestically as well as work and bring home a salary, and there is censure for those who cannot. Mary Jane Holmes, for example, throws her title character, Rose Mather, into the home-front chaos of the Civil War and shows her to be inadequately trained and foolishly educated to survive the rigors of being a young wartime wife or a home-front nurse. Significantly, Rose is despised by other characters for the first sixty pages of the novel not only because she is unable to sew seams on shirts for the boys at the front or knit socks or cook, but also because she has no understanding, philosophical, political, or intellectual, of the issues about which the war is being fought. Rose is frivolous, foolish, "accomplished" in what the reader recognizes as a host of trivial finishing school subjects, and she is, finally, useless—a condition even she acknowledges. Her intellectual and domestic education is completed for her by other, better-qualified women she knows, and she emerges as a thoughtful, philosophical domestic mistress and mother by the novel's end.[34]

In another of her novels, *'Lena Rivers*, Holmes shows the title character, already imbued with domestic and intellectual virtues, performing an opposite literary function to that of Rose Mather. She is a model of competence and takes over when her foil, her cousin Annie Livingston, cannot either plan an elopement or cook the meal which her domestics have walked out on. Even Evans's highly scholarly Edna Earl proves herself a champion child rearer in one of her jobs as governess and is so sensible yet so compassionate in her handling of a spoiled, invalided boy that he soon prefers Edna to his mother, who is the product of a "fashionable" education. Other heroines—Mrs. A. D. T. Whitney's Leslie Goldthwaite, for

Harper's Weekly, February 3, 1866

example—often are shown performing intricate domestic tasks—sewing wedding dresses, cooking elaborate meals, filling out a hope chest with "dozens" of sets of homemade underwear—while discussing abstruse questions of metaphysics, poetry, and Christian theology.[35]

Domestic and academic education could, therefore, exist together, something which Cult of True Womanhood critics tend to ignore or flatly deny. The peaceful coexistence of two such different kinds of education was possible, I think, because advice writers were able to convince young female readers that an academic education could be the basis of a sound domestic education. Most prominent among such writers was Catharine Beecher. In her *Housekeeper's Manual* (which she coauthored with her sister Harriet Beecher Stowe) she explains that the aim of her book is to raise housekeeping to the status of a "profession" and to show "how many branches of science and training are included in woman's profession."[36] A quick look at the tables of contents of both the *Housekeeper's Manual* and Beecher's *Treatise* quickly convinces a modern reader that such academic subjects are required if one is to understand the advice Beecher offers. In her *Treatise,* for example, her chapters deal with the following subjects. Chapters I and II cover the foundations, "philosophically," of American institutions, especially democratic ones, and the basic principles of Christianity, along with selections from Alexis de Tocqueville. Chapter V discusses "the Laws of Health, and the Human system," including subsections on the bones ("Their structure, Design, and Use"), the spinal column, vertebrae, muscles and how they operate, the spine, blood vessels and the heart and circulatory system, organs of digestion and respiration, including an explanation of the process of digestion, and the process of lungs and respiration (all complete with elaborate diagrams and drawings). Chapter VI, on nutrition, discusses nutritional bases of disease and the physiological effects of certain foods on the stomach and digestive processes, compares "animal versus vegetable diets," and gives the chemical properties of food alone or in combination. Chapter XVI, on economics, examines income and expenditure of both time and money, practices of wholesale versus retail buying, and investments. A chapter on mental health treatment explains the brain and the nerves as they are affected by certain stimulants and the effect on brain function of a lack of oxygenated blood. Chapter XXI, on home nursing, involves "understanding the nature and operation of common medicines" as well as providing a pharmacopoeia of drugs and their uses. Chapter XXII is on first aid and how to deal with choking, "wounds of arteries," burns, poisons ("Corrosive Sublimate; Arsenic, or Cobalt; Opium, Acids; Alkalies"), bleeding from lungs, stomach, or throat, and how to deal with the effects of being struck by lightning. Chapter XXIV tells how to plan and construct a house, including "economy of labor." Chapter XXXV, on plants, tells how to take cuttings, to bud, to graft (whip, split, and stock grafting), to prune, thin, and transplant. Chapter XXXVII, titled "Miscellaneous Directions," offers helpful advice about the care of stock, including breeding and birthing for cattle, horses, and poultry, how to modify fireplaces structurally for more scientific ventilation, and how to waterproof shoes.[37] Lest anyone believe that Beecher was writing about these subjects in glittering generalities, a quick examination of passages in her *Housekeeper's Manual* reveals explanations full of such terms as "hydrostatics," "calorification," and "pneumatics," as well as references to "the first principles of animal and domestic chemistry," "hygiene and therapeutics," and "electricity."[38]

Chapter III in the *Housekeeper's Manual*, on the "Healthful Home," is clear proof of Beecher's belief that academic education was a necessary prerequisite to successful homemaking. The majority of the chapter is an explanation of how poor ventilation in the home results in illness for its inhabitants because of "oxygen starvation" and excess "carbonic acid" in the air. She goes into a lengthy explanation of the microscopic effects of "carbonic acid" on the blood supply to the brain, discusses the physical properties of warm and cold air and the circulation patterns in the room, and ends with a detailed discussion of structural modifications that could be made to the house or the ducts to provide better ventilation based on principles of physics.[39]

Although Catharine Beecher and Harriet Beecher Stowe are perhaps the most scientific about training in housekeeping and child care, other advice writers, among them Dr. Dio Lewis, Dr. Calvin Cutter, and T. S. Arthur, touch with less precise explanations on many of the same subjects and are advocates as well of a solid academic education. Arthur, for example, explains that a young lady must be adept in "bringing down her skill and information into every-day uses and pursuits" such as cooking, cleaning, and bookkeeping, and Lewis is adamant about the need for young ladies to understand the scientific principles involved in nutrition, ventilation, exercise, and home nursing.

Cutter, author of two popular gems on anatomy and physiology intended for young women's home study, notes that "a child should be taught to call each organ by its correct name" and adds that "education, to be complete, must be not only moral and intellectual but physical as well." How else can a young woman prepare herself with the information she needs to be a good wife, mother, and home nurse?[40]

In light of this concern, Cutter includes in his *First Book on Anatomy* a helpful appendix of questions and answers the home nurse might find useful; he also includes sample self-testing questions so that the potential sickroom attendant can check her knowledge to see if it is "up" to the rigors of the ordinary sickroom. Both the questions and answers as well as the self-testing section presuppose a high degree of memory if not knowledge; this presupposition is only partially offset by the gloss-ary of scientific terms he includes such as "acetabulum," "synovial membranes," and "periosteum." In the question and answer section, Cutter includes the following questions: "12. Describe the bones. 13. How many bones in the human body? 14. How are they divided? *Name them*" (italics mine). He also expects "educated" young women to know the names of over four hundred muscles and to be able to identify them on a chart, if asked. He hints, as well, that the thorough young woman who really values learning will spend time examining pigs', cats', and dogs' skeletons and corpses.[41]

Subjects both magazine article and advice book writers stress as important to explore academically and even "scientifically" involve child-rearing practices (Alcott's book, for example, includes sections on adolescence and childhood physiological and "moral" development), methods of discipline historically considered and evaluated, and home religious instruction (which requires background in theological contro-versies, biblical historical studies, and perhaps a sound grasp of the his-tory of the Reformation). Still others emphasize planning budgets, buy-ing food staples in bulk, the chemical actions of certain solvents on certain fabrics, and investments. Understanding these subjects de-manded a sound academic education—and does even today.

To see education as simply training young wives to run "scientific" households or participate in intellectual repartee with guests or a hus-band, however, is to fail to acknowledge yet another, perhaps more transcendent, use of education evident to advice writers, novelists, and essayists: education was the necessary prerequisite for the spread of culture and morality in a wicked, brutal, and materialistic world. As Anne Douglas points out, such writers sought to make a difference in society by exerting a discreet, omnipresent influence for "good" via magazines, domestic novels, and manuals of advice.[42] Their audience was primarily female—and they saw peculiar "female virtues" as vital to the reformation of society. Douglas regards this attempt as somewhat reactionary, self-serving, and even materialistic, but the sources them-selves seem not so conservative or coldly self-glorifying as she indicates, but rather progressive and even idealistic—at least in their own terms.

Most advice writers and other writers of didactic intent, whatever the later differences in their ideas concerning the extent of woman's sphere, would agree that woman's influence in the home on the moral develop-

ment of the men around her—or potential men, in the form of sons—
was enormous. Her influence in training a future generation of girls to
become carriers of either the flame or the disease of "softer values" (depending on one's perspective) is also not in dispute. What apparently is
in dispute is the extent to which these values served to "keep women in
their place" or to exercise a "pink and white tyranny," to quote Stowe,
over the gradual development of women as a group.[43]

Central to this discussion is the place of an academic education in the
process and an examination of the values such an education helped
transmit. If Welter and the other critics castigating the Cult of True
Womanhood ideal are correct, the values transmitted would have been
reactionary and, in the sense of modern "fascinating femininity," a self-
conscious, self-serving attempt to maintain the status quo. Even a brief
examination of some of the primary sources cited by such critics would
lead one to believe this was indeed the case. But the Cult of True Womanhood with its saccharine religiosity, its clinging to domesticated (and
by that definition, ignorant) virtues is, as I have shown, only one of two
ideals present in the writings of the period. The Ideal of Real Womanhood, with a different set of educational requirements and a different
(and vastly extended) definition of woman's sphere, was transmitting
quite a different culture and, I think, for a different reason. Writers such
as the Reverend George Burnap saw liberally educated women as the
main means of promulgating a "moral, intellectual and literary culture"
in a United States that, even in the eyes of some of its more thoughtful
citizens, was raw, culturally semiliterate, and harsh in its economic and
social policies. The boom-bust cycles of its overheated economy, the
crassness of its definitions of success, its cutthroat business practices,
and the very wildness and amorphousness of its standards of right and
wrong have been commented upon by both historians and literary critics.[44] Writers of Real Womanhood saw one of woman's most important
natural goals as the softening and refining of the society around her,
making it temperate, stable, thoughtful, literate, and humane, not only
through literary and journalistic works but more commonly through
direct instruction of the next generation. Women could make a direct
appeal to—and have a direct influence on—husbands, sons, and brothers. Women were in a uniquely powerful position to influence men because of the pervasiveness of their presence in men's lives as mothers,
sisters, sweethearts, wives, and daughters. Their direct influence in what

they considered proper actions, their promulgation of literary and artistic culture, their decisions on furnishings, family habits, and family religiosity all were tools that could improve society in the future, making it less a jungle of competition and more a garden of harmony and shared values and ameliorating its harshness to some extent in the present.

Some writers believed women had a wider scope of influence. Abell insisted that women's immediate influence on society was all-pervasive and that it had controlling power over customs and laws. She called this influence "a more *sacred appointment, a higher and holier work*" than anything a man did. To the Real Womanhood writers, this higher work required the transmission of subject matter that was more erudite than the intricacies of various tatting stitches or the sugary sentiments of Sunday school texts; it included philosophy, ethics, "affecting" literature, and human sentiments. Academic education with its firm emphasis on humanistic values, its accumulated insights from centuries, and its insistence on rationality rather than violence or passion as a guiding force was the perfect vehicle for the values such writers wished to promulgate. Women, therefore, had to receive such an education to improve their society. The Reverend George Burnap both explains the connection and stresses its importance: "We do not flatter her [the woman citizen] when we remind her how much influence she has in forming the taste and directing the pursuits of the other sex, how far the hope of her favor determines the aspirations and the efforts of those who are forming characters for life . . . there is nothing to which the human heart more involuntarily bows down than to woman when she adds to the natural charms and loveliness of her sex, the crowning glory of a vigorous, a refined, and cultivated intellect."[45] Such an influence could reform society intrinsically through the formation of better individual characters with higher, more judicious, and more humane values. Says Abell, "Knowledge and enlightened culture are the only basis of character. Withhold from the mind intellectual discipline, books, and intelligent society and fill it with a succession of trifles, and how can it be otherwise than empty and frivolous?" If the values the Real Womanhood ideal was promulgating included "sensibility" and "piety," they also included compassion, a love of beauty, respect for others, and literacy, as Alcott himself would admit. In a society in which businessmen and their families were ruined overnight, in which hurrying was a way of life, alcoholism a national epidemic, the social avoidance of the less fortunate a habit, and "culture" all too frequently represented by books by the yard in a "library," perhaps the values these writers sought to instill were needed. As Nina Baym points out acutely, although the values being promoted were those of a "cult of domesticity," it was definitely more reformation-minded than either conservative or traditional—it was, in fact, an all-out attempt to reform what the writers saw as the brutal world of values alive at the time and to make that world more bearable for the women, children, and other helpless dependents who were forced to live in it.[46]

If one doubts this interpretation, a careful reading of short stories and domestic novels written between 1840 and 1880 should convince even the most recalcitrant. Short stories such as T. S. Arthur's gem "Taking Boarders" (1851) or *Harper's* "Olive West" (1866) and "Winifred's Vow" (1855) paint a vivid picture of a world in savage economic flux and the terrible cost, both mental and financial, paid by women for the success ethic, the male indulgence in alcoholism, and general contempt for the gentler virtues. The portrait of the men involved is one of viciousness, weakness, or alcohol-induced violence, and the shape of their "values" is hellish.[47]

The sense of urgency such writers impart concerning the need to improve current society, as well as future generations, suggests still another use for academic education: to teach women to earn a living. Although this is among the less frequently mentioned of the rationales for obtaining an academic education, it is stated explicitly by a handful of advice writers, and it forms the basis of the heroines' actions in both the short stories and domestic novels I have noted, indicating the novelists' implicit approval. As we have seen, the economic conditions of the world in which the Real Womanhood writers lived seemed to demand some preparation for self-preservation. In the case of Real Womanhood, this meant both academic and vocational education before marriage to assure the young woman of food and shelter should a father "break up," a husband desert, go bankrupt, turn brutal, or be inconsiderate enough to die, or a guardian prove incompetent. The pragmatic strain in this ideal is strongly evident in this rationale. Although the ideal has much to say about the need for training in a "trade" or "vocation," that is not the main focus of this chapter, though it is the subject of a future one. Here I am concerned with the way writers of the Real Womanhood ideal saw academic education as a means of obtaining employment either for the young woman alone, the young woman as a member of a family, or (in some sad cases) the ex post facto head of one. The Cult of True Womanhood naturally made as little provision among its virtues for self-reliance as it did for education; according to both Barbara Welter and Ernest Earnest, its primary characteristic was one of endless, sweetly smiling passivity. Both Herbert Brown and Earnest refer to the True Woman as a "modern Griselda," and members of her species were, says Earnest, "delicate flowers, emotional rather than intellectual, given to fainting and to moral and religious preachments, and, of course, chaste in thought and deed." Such a woman, "a lady in the tower, weaving her tapestry and gazing into the mirror for reflections of her own life," could hardly be expected to go to work if her husband lost his job or to help out a bankrupt father.[48] Nor does True Womanhood presume to suggest what she should do. A review of the competing Real Womanhood advice books, especially during this period, shows startlingly an entirely opposite stance: women were expected to take over and keep a family from ruin, they were sternly told to prepare themselves for the single life thrust on them by necessity or taken by choice as preferable to a "loveless marriage," and, most of all, they were admonished that the ability to aid financially in family life if the need arose was part of woman's sphere. Occasionally this aid was in the form of piecework jobs like sewing, but more often young women are urged to obtain jobs making use of the knowledge derived from a "fine" education. There is little pity in the hearts of these writers for the woman who faints and whines in the face of family economic disaster; indeed, there is nothing less than searing and disgusted scorn. Such weaklings figure as either villainesses or foils to the heroine in the domestic novels to highlight the heroine's virtuous desire and ability to knuckle down and support children or siblings as well as herself rather than crumble under the pressure of economic adversity.

Heroine Olive West, in the *Harper's* story, entirely supported her father when he went bankrupt, not only by dressing dolls but by publishing her poetry, and Holmes's Rosa Lee teaches school to help out at home financially and becomes a governess when her father dies. Dio Lewis risks tedium on the part of readers of his advice books by delivering a series of little exempla which illustrate the value of a "real" as opposed to a "finishing school" education for young women when fathers break up and need the help of daughters for the family to survive financially.

Some of the occupations Lewis lists which are "suitable" for women include several that require not a little academic education, among them stockbroker, dentist, lawyer, lecturer, doctor, and minister, as well as the more common occupation of teacher.[49]

The Reverends Daniel Wise and George Burnap both suggest that an academic background might prove appropriate as a qualification for employment if necessary, and Wise especially warns young women about life as unemployed dependents and urges them to prepare themselves by obtaining well-rounded educations.[50]

If a young woman, however well she married, however astute and practiced in the womanly arts she was, could not avoid what the writers of the Cult of True Womanhood considered her natural propensity to depression, illness, and mental derangement, all her attempts to be a well-rounded, articulate, intelligent, and competent helpmate and mother would come to naught. To avoid such problems, Real Womanhood advocates again recommend education. Carroll Smith-Rosenberg, Anne Douglas Wood, and Barbara Welter, citing the advice writers and doctors of the opposing Cult of True Womanhood, not only ignore the value of education in this regard but point out that women were generally considered by such writers to be constitutionally "diseased" (both mentally and physically) from the onset of menstruation until after menopause—most of their life cycle. Menstruation, according to some advice writers and doctors of the period, brought "increased bodily weakness, a new found and biologically rooted timidity and modesty"; pregnancy and childbirth could drive a woman insane or break her health for the rest of her life; and menopause carried with it an entire train of mental and physical illnesses. Anne Douglas Wood, for example, cites William Alcott's comments on the " 'real disease' of nervousness" among American women as well as the views of the famous Dr. Clarke.[51]

Whereas Clarke and a variety of British doctors cited by Clarke, Wood, Welter, and Smith-Rosenberg point to both loss of virtue and excessive intellectual stimulation as irritating factors in this alarming biological state of affairs, the Real Womanhood writers saw the cause as something remarkably different. To such advice writers and novelists as William Blaikie, Dr. Dio Lewis, Dr. William Alcott, Augusta Evans, Mary Jane Holmes, Mrs. A. D. T. Whitney, Ada Badger, Mrs. L. G. Abell, and T. S. Arthur, such illnesses were not intrinsic to female biology but rather were the result of a poor mental and physical education, which in turn led to an indolent, aimless, and "fashionable" life lacking in both regular physical exercise and habitual intellectual stimulation. Far from regarding the fainting woman with myriad health complaints as the epitome of the "natural" woman, these writers despised and castigated such creatures, calling them "selfish," "soft," and "lazy."[52] Writers of Real Womanhood especially thought of both mental and physical health as conditions over which young women (and older women as well) had control; illness, therefore, was the result of having been slack and lazy in performing one's duties, which included not only getting regular exercise but, more important, educating oneself to maintain health, both mental and physical. In addition to seeing physical health problems as accruing, like an evil debt, from lack of exercise and inadequate understanding of nutrition and habits of cleanliness, such writers believed an academic education was useful in staving off depression, hysteria, and "unhealthy thoughts." These writers also believed there were corollary benefits for self-fulfillment and character growth in an academic education.

Real Womanhood writers saw depression and a variety of nervous diseases as linked to the lack of academic education and resulting lack of mental enrichment. The rationale behind such a seemingly remote connection was that lack of mental resources, inability to find a way to fill hours of ennui at home, and, most of all, lack of discipline over the thought processes were contributory to depression. An academic education, with its training in mental discipline, its humanities-stocked intellectual warehouse of interests, and its uplifting philosophies prevented a mild depression from progressing into a psychosis. As Abell notes, regarding both the cause and prevention of "mental suffering," "Great and noble powers bereft of their appropriate and needful exercise, become, in consequence, the sure sources of the keenest suffering. Constituted as we are, with sympathies, affections, and intellectual endowments, they must have scope for natural growth, and if circumstances forbid their development, then let circumstances be made where each power of the body and the soul shall be called into active exercise." She adds, "*Inactivity* of intellect and of all the powers, will predispose to nervous disease and mental ailment!" Nor is Abell alone in her regard for mental exercise; in rebuttal to Dr. Clarke's attack on higher education for women, Thomas Wentworth Higginson snorts that such education produces health because it keeps minds "happily occupied" and prevents brooding while it strengthens both judgment and self-control. Far from being a source of mental illness, Higginson sees an academically geared education, as so many of the advice writers do, as a means of combating any tendency toward depression or "nervousness."[53]

Higginson is not the only one to attack Clarke's "scientific" contention that an academic education led directly to mental illness or physical breakdown. In the collection of essays gathered by Julie Ward Howe to refute Clarke, Ada Badger, a schoolteacher, presents some cogent arguments drawn from her experience as an educator. She is, for example, more than passingly acquainted with Antioch College and denies hotly that the twenty-seven women graduates of that institution from 1857 to 1863 had either failed to produce children or gone mad following their graduation. She claims to have been personally acquainted with one of the women cited by Clarke in his case histories (probably "Miss G," who supposedly died from "brain deterioration") and says contemptuously that the woman's mental illness and death were not caused by higher education at a coeducational college; rather, four years of academic education was only a "slight cause among the many that converged to menace, and finally to overcome, that rarely endowed but perilously poised organization." Indeed, says Badger, studying and academic accomplishment probably delayed that student's breakdown and death.[54]

Academic education not only helped prevent mental illness, but it provided inexhaustible entertainment to the woman at home, as many of the Real Womanhood writers note. George Burnap points out that the interests and tastes encouraged and actively sown by such an education provided escape from "heavy-hanging" hours at home and dispelled boredom as well. As he tells women, "The great entertainments of all ages are reading, conversation and thought." He adds, eloquently, that a woman "needs not be assured, that it is for her own sake that we invite her into the pleasant walks of letters, that there is nothing more congenial with her retired and quiet occupations, no better solace for her solitary hours, no better resource against ennui and depression, nothing which so prepares her to adorn and enjoy society, nothing except piety, which can so arm her against those troubles which are the lot of all."[55]

Lest anyone assume that simple recreational reading was the solace referred to, the advice writers specifically forbade "light novels" as the source of such entertainment. Burnap, Abell, Arthur, and others speak of entertainment and fulfillment derived from reading and reflecting not on fiction but on history, philosophy, art, religion, natural sciences, and language. Arthur particularly despises romantic novels, which are "highly-wrought and unnatural," saying they are the products of "perverted and impure minds" and teach women to seek the wrong kind of love and the wrong kind of suitor, one whose "life is little else than one act after another of vice, brutality, and crime." Such a "hero," Arthur sneers, becomes an integral part of the so-called "happy ending" in these novels when the heroine marries him. Concludes Arthur, "The writer has the unblushing effrontery to tell us she is supremely happy. . . . It is all false!" In direct opposition to such a reading list, Arthur offers as suitable for study works of history that teach girls to admire leaders and to sympathize with the masses of common people. He also suggests works of philosophy because they lift the mind into the realms of abstraction, or poetry, which "warms, inspires and delights the imagination" and "purifies and refines the taste."[56]

Finally, beyond their therapeutic value as means of preventing mental illness or their recreational aspects, academic tastes and interests gave a woman breadth of vision and helped develop character. Abell, among others, deplored the "narrow" feelings and thoughts that she felt came from an exclusive concern with fashion and housework. She pointed out that such mental starvation made a woman gradually more antisocial, more selfish, more tasteless, more insensitive, and certainly more ignorant. She asked that both unmarried and married women seek to widen the scope of both their interests and their conversation and suggested that they continue the study of history, biography, travel essays, and theological works as well as make a lifelong study of art, music, politics, literature, and science so that they could talk and think about more than local gossip or domestic concerns.[57]

Daniel Wise strikes much the same note, expounding on what seems to be a common tripartite developmental ideal among the Real Womanhood writers. The most appropriate of "all aims at self cultivation," Wise tells his female reader, is the "highest and most harmonious development of your entire being, physical, intellectual and moral," because it directly affects not only the physical health but the growth of the soul as well. To Arthur and Alcott, not only were academic development and intellectual pursuits fulfilling for a woman, they were part of her duty to

God, who required this development from her if she was to be a true Christian and a thinking human being.[58]

Certainly the oblique reflections of the importance of personal and spiritual development as a result of education are apparent in several of the domestic novels. Edna Earl, heroine of Augusta Evans's *St. Elmo*, was not only educationally but morally superior to the book's antihero; indeed, when he tells Edna that she will have to put up her studies and her scholarship after marriage, she precipitously sickens following the ceremony.

Though Evans has carefully developed the proof of Edna's ill health before the wedding, her illness does follow close upon St. Elmo's announcement that she will study and write no more and is deliberately jarring. The connection between the two—the threat and her sudden poor health—is too carefully juxtaposed not to suggest that a life without academic or intellectual interests is diseased. Nor is Evans the only domestic novel author to suggest such an idea. Holmes in both *'Lena Rivers* and *Meadowbrook* draws heroines who are intellectually hungry, and it is because of, rather than despite, their wider mental vision and interests that the heroes fall in love with them and agree to lives surrounded by the accoutrements necessary to continuance of such tastes. Both refuse other suitors with less intellectual sympathy and more money.

The value of an academic education for any young woman was, then, for any number of reasons, considered enormous by writers espousing Real Womanhood. Not only did it help her attract the right man, but it gave her the judgment to choose him instead of his flashier but less trustworthy counterpart, the wrong kind of man. After marriage, it guaranteed a community of interests and pleasant (and useful) social relations with both friends and business associates. Moreover, to a woman committed to being the best possible wife and mother, academic education offered valuable background to the domestic arts and the running of a household, as well as insight into the eternally difficult process of rearing children. By studying such subjects as Latin and chemistry, stoicism and Wordsworth, that same excellent wife and mother could create a home environment in keeping with the highest cultural and moral standards and have a minute but important effect, through her sons and daughters, on the cultural and moral atmosphere of the future.

Such an education also enabled the American woman defined by the Real Womanhood ideal to preserve her health and fight off depression, hysteria, and general illness, not only through better knowledge of the causes of disease but through the therapeutic effects of a "mind well-stocked," as Alcott called it. Calmer, more logical, and less prone to debilitating invalidism than her counterpart—the figure called up by the True Womanhood ideal—this American woman had the strength to deal with adversity and, if necessary, to support herself or aid in supporting a family. If, as historians and critics alike claim, the nineteenth-century ideal for women was that of an angel, that of Real Womanhood was an amazon—to use Inez Irwin's term—strong, direct, clearheaded, self-assured, and physically healthy. The angel and the amazon, these writers assure us, were the result, as Wise points out, of "the highest and most harmonious development" of all the woman's capacities—especially the intellect, which these writers saw as the source of and the organizing agent that developed all the others.

Perhaps the ideal in its entirety can best be seen in the "beau ideal" given form by P. Thorne in his article "The Coming Woman": "She stands before us erect, supple, bright-eyed, alert. Perfect health shines in her eyes, glows in her cheeks, gives elasticity to her walk, a radiant cheerfulness to her face. Now what will she do with herself? Sit meekly down, a nonentity, a mere consumer of bread and butter, sighing, like 'Mariana in the Moated Grange.' . . . Not she. She will have some plan for her life—some real business in the world, some special work."[59]

Thorne's vision is particularly apt because, in addition to showing the variety of attributes acquired from a strong "liberal" education, it strikes a note any reader studying the subjects becomes gradually more and more aware of: tension of definition. Despite a careful acknowledgment of woman's sphere and the value and virtue of motherhood and wifedom that the Real Womanhood writers (both male and female) inevitably give, the reader is not wholly convinced that the writers completely believe in these vaunted absolutes. As we watch them stretch, widen, and pull the parameters of woman's sphere into increasingly more accommodating shapes, we might well wonder how much elasticity can remain in the old definition. How much farther can it be stretched and pulled before it breaks? With the implicit or explicit devaluation of man as superior made by Dio Lewis, Augusta Evans, Mary Jane Holmes, Elizabeth Ward, and especially T. S. Arthur, how long can the Real Woman remain satisfied with manifesting such limitations? How can she find pleasure in the domestic sphere, however scientifically or academically she approaches it? How long will she take up the burden of employment only under economic necessity or, in fact, continue to see it as a burden? There is an uneasiness here—an attempt to give a traditional, safe structure to a view that has very nontraditional implications, as if by showing in myriad ways the value to woman's sphere of an academic education, its implications would stop there. Writers of the Real Womanhood ideal seem deliberately, even rigidly and stridently, to separate themselves from "feminism" and those few women writers who labeled themselves as "feminist"; yet the fact remains that the Ideal of Real Womanhood is only a very short step away from the aftermath of Seneca Falls. How far, for example, is Ward's theological reconstructionist, Aunt Winifred, from Elizabeth Cady Stanton and her *Woman's Bible?* How far is Edna Earl from Emma Willard and others who set up female seminaries and taught as faculty members at universities? The alliance between woman's sphere and an academic education seems uneasy at best, and if we listen to those writers carefully, the strain is evident. It is particularly loud in Marion Harland's preface to her advice book *Common Sense in the Household* in what she calls her "familiar talk with my fellow-Housekeeper and Reader." She speaks of having a "cosy conference" with that individual, noting:

> I should perhaps summon . . . a very weary companion—weary of foot, of hand—and I should not deserve to be your confidant did I not know [myself] how often heart-weary with discouragement; with much producing of ways and means; and with a certain despondent looking forward to the monotonous grinding of the household machine; to the certainty, proved by past experience, that toilsome as has been this day, the morrow will prove yet more abundant in labors, in trials of strength, and nerves, and temper. You would tell me what a dreary problem this of 'woman's work that is never done' is to your fainting soul; how, try, as you may and as you do to be systematic and diligent, something is always 'turning up' in the treadmill to keep you on the strain; how you often say to yourself, in bitterness of spirit, that it is a mistake of Christian civilization to educate girls into a love of science and literature and then condemn them to the routine of a domestic drudge.[60]

As though her picture is too accurate and too convincing to let stand— and the "mistake of Christian civilization" too obvious—she struggles to reassure her reader that, in fact, academic education is not a mistake for a woman living within the domestic sphere: "Have faith in your own abilities. You *will* be a better cook for the mental training you received at school and from books. Brains tell everywhere, to say nothing of intelligent observation, just judgment, a faithful memory, and orderly habits. Consider that you have a profession, as I said just now, and resolve to understand it in all branches."[61] Somehow, these consolations seem inferior, if not bitter, fruit to a woman who has, as so many were encouraged to, spent time "with the immortals."

The Ideal of Real Womanhood faded away around 1880, and the Cult of True Womanhood prevailed until well into the twentieth century; perhaps the reason for the former's demise lies in this tension. Perhaps the strain could not be stood—the woman of academic background, mental discipline, and the ability to earn her own living may, finally, have found herself no longer able to fit inside woman's sphere despite the accommodations the Real Womanhood writers made. Giving up the struggle to consider chemistry a necessary and natural preparation for cooking, she may have seen it for what it was—the beginning of a professional career as a chemist. The beauty of Euclid perhaps began to suggest not the usefulness of the acquired mental discipline to plan menus and budgets but to further studies in mathematics. Finally, the Real Womanhood ideal may have trembled, then dissolved under the strain, leaving its followers reluctant but necessary followers of turn-of-the-century feminism.

THREE

Preparation for the Marriage Choice

She is responsible if she does not prudently consider her *choice*— not deciding hastily, or upon the dictates of mere sentiment or selfishness. If she will look closely, she may detect already, in the character of the unaffianced admirer, the lineaments of the unfaithful and dissipated husband.

—Edwin H. Chapin,
Duties of Young Women

To the writers advocating Real Womanhood, marriage was the central act of most women's lives, and it was one to be undertaken with the utmost seriousness. Far from being the crowning and unavoidable result of nights of moonlight (as many modern critics suggest was popular literature's set expectation), the choice to marry and of a partner was the result, these writers hoped, of a surgical, hardheaded, and even cold-blooded investigation and assessment. It was the result of a painstaking attempt to avoid disaster, rather than to assure bliss. As the Reverend Chapin indicates, "mere sentiment" had no part to play in a decision of such magnitude. Unlike their counterparts of the True Womanhood school, who wrote of feelings of inescapable passions, conjunctions of stars, and melting oneness, the Real Womanhood writers and many domestic novelists of similar kidney grimly set about giving advice to help secure a bearable future for those girls wise enough to listen. Romance, though not completely excluded, was restrained and occurred ideally only after the careful assessment of the potential mate.

The advice books I consulted and the domestic fiction I read tend not to deal with the actual mechanics of marital life, probably because their advice is preventive rather than analgesic. Once the marriage was made, the rarity and difficulty of divorce—even for physical abuse[1]—meant that there was little woman could do to change her marital situation. To Real Womanhood writers, "reform" was a cruel chimera in everyday life: one rarely managed to reform an alcoholic, a compulsive gambler, a chronic philanderer, or a wastrel; the behaviors usually continued, despite tears and promises to the contrary. Better, then, Real Womanhood writers seem to feel, to choose someone without such tendencies than to try later to employ clever strategies for making a "happy home" with a chronic drunk. Therefore, the advice writers devote much ink and energy to means by which a young woman can "winnow" suitors and examine a fiancé's behavior, rather than teaching her flirting techniques and "womanly wiles" guaranteed to bring her romance and later how to decorate the table charmingly and "manage" a suddenly nasty-tempered husband after the marriage.

This preventive emphasis is particularly obvious in the domestic novel's treatment of "romance." Despite John Cawelti's insistence that "proper sexuality" was one of the three basic "myths" informing popular domestic fiction of the nineteenth century, with its concomitant emphasis on the romantic trials and emotional tribulations of women striving to find "complete fulfillment" through marriage,[2] domestic novelists who support the Ideal of Real Womanhood were considerably less sanguine about romance than he indicates. As Mary Kelley suggests, and any close reading of the novels cited shows, the Eden of "domestic bliss" Cawelti and Henry Nash Smith presuppose is a paradise containing a snake—and that snake is clearly the male romantic lead. Novel after novel suggests, in concert with the more strident advice books, that heroines inevitably find to their dismay that they are morally superior to their suitors. Novelists also insist that, if a heroine is not extremely clever in her selection and self-control, she will end her days chained by matrimony to a man who is inferior to her in both morality and sense and will be forced by both law and convention to rely on him.[3] Despite Cawelti's firm belief that novelists subtly reprove heroines who take aggressive action against men who drink or otherwise misbehave, domestic novelists supporting the Ideal of Real Womanhood lionize such heroines and make them models for young female readers to emulate.

This is not to say that all males in domestic novels carry the mark of Cain on their brows, though as I have indicated in another work, the majority do. Rather, "good men" (by which domestic novelists mean those who are moral, intelligent, and trustworthy) appear only infrequently, and, suggests Kelley, their portraits amount to "a study in the feminization of the male" since they seek "above all to serve the needs of others, particularly women."[4] As a critic I remain less convinced about the good qualities of these ideal men than does Kelley. In novels such as Hentz's *Linda* and Marion Harland's *Ruby's Husband*, for example, not to mention Mary Jane Holmes's *Meadowbrook* and *'Lena Rivers*, the ostensible hero is so wooden-headed and credulous that either the arch-villainess of the piece easily draws him in emotionally or she convinces him of any number of false enormities supposedly committed by the heroine. The hero, in short, is frequently a fool—a quality that does not, at least to me, say a great deal about the esteem in which American men—even "good" men—were held and certainly casts a suspicious shadow over the myth of domestic bliss. Obviously, if even heroes needed constant watching lest they fall into error or misguided affection or pity, then a young woman modeling herself upon the heroine of a domestic novel and reading the straightforward counsel of the advice authors needed some program for coping with the emotional strains and strong natural magnetism incurred in courting. Both novelists (indirectly through the use of negative foils to their heroines) and advice writers (directly) provided sensible young women, before they reached the romantic stage, with a series of pragmatic guidelines by which to decide how to prepare for marriage, what age was the most auspicious for marrying, what distinguished "true" from "false" love, what situations were best for meeting the "right" suitor, and what scrutiny and analyses the girl should apply to those suitors to assure herself of their suitability. Finally, such writers explained in lurid detail why any number of traits, behaviors, or failings on the part of suitors would lead the girl to a domestic hell, rather than the romance she craved, following marriage. Interestingly, the Real Womanhood writers did not see marriage as the only way for a woman to find meaning in her life; under a variety of carefully delineated circumstances they insisted that no marriage was preferable to a bad marriage and that not all women were meant to marry.[5] Indeed, if those negative circumstances occurred, these writers insisted that the girl not marry.

Before examining advice for the first stages of courtship, it is necessary to understand that the Real Womanhood writers, both male and female, conceived of marriage as a risky and highly dangerous operation. None believed fully in married "bliss"; few believed that more than "spots" of companionship and contentment were possible in even the best of circumstances; all saw the state of matrimony even between well-suited partners as a thorny path strewn with boulders and pitfalls which one traversed safely only with the utmost care, dedication, self-control, and stamina. As Chapin notes solemnly, "Marriage will not be a perpetual service of affection for her, or a constant offering of admiration. But there will open before her occasions of trial, in which she must do, and endure, and sacrifice. And she only can insure a happy marriage who enters upon that state, with a mind prudently forecasting its contingencies, and a heart consecrated to all its obligations."[6]

The Reverend George Weaver adds his voice to the warning chorus, noting that many hapless young women go into marriage "blindly" and marry "whoever offers"; this, to him, is the stuff of tragedy. Weaver stresses that, not unlike a classical hero of old setting out on a perilous adventure against monsters and unknown dangers, the young woman must use every rational and intuitive skill in finding a suitable partner. No intellectual or emotional equipment should remain behind in the castle: "If there is any period in a woman's whole life when her sharpest eye, her keenest apprehension, her soundest judgment, and her most religious seriousness are needed, it is when she proposes to herself the question, 'Shall I accept in marriage the hand that is offered me?'"[7]

To carry the analogy further, writers of Real Womanhood felt that, like the epic or chivalric hero, the young woman must be mentally, spiritually, and practically prepared for the quest before she embarked upon it, or she would surely miscalculate and fall prey to monsters whose brutal magic or deceitful ways would easily overcome her slender defenses and her underdeveloped and incomplete understanding.

What, then, were the preparations a young woman should make before setting out on the matrimonial quest? Advice writers all agreed that mental and physical maturity were necessary. Unlike their opposite numbers supporting the ideal of True Womanhood, writers advocating Real Womanhood did not view a sixteen- or eighteen-year-old of either sex as ready for marriage. To them, this would be the marriage of "boys and girls," not "men and women," and would inevitably result in disaster. They referred to the "curse" of early marriage and demanded (especially for girls) that full education, physical growth, and mature judgment be acquired before girls considered the subject seriously. Given the years of schooling and private study involved in an ideal girl's "complete" education (academic, vocational, domestic) and the degree of physical fitness and health insisted upon for her, it is not surprising that advice writers considered "early" marriage to be one occurring "before twenty" and "very early marriage" as one "before eighteen." True or "timely" marriages occurred when the girl was between twenty and twenty-five—or even after twenty-five, according to some writers.[8]

Writers felt that girls under twenty lacked the judgment necessary to scrutinize and analyze a suitor with any degree of safety or sagacity. Without a mind trained and honed by wide reading in the liberal arts, by years of observation and experience with different men, by hundreds of hours of reflection and intellectual discussion and analysis, how was a girl to tell the false from the true, pyrite from gold, bigamists, con men, or fortune hunters from trustworthy, sensitive, and industrious lovers? Susceptible to flattery, their heads filled with the nonsense and "romantic" gibberish common to immature and uneducated girlhood, young women would quickly find themselves entranced by the superficial and encouraged into ill-considered intimacy or involvement. Without sufficient intellectual maturity, they would become that very vision so beloved of the True Womanhood school—passive, acted-upon maidens waiting to be rescued from monsters or towers by knights, rather than questioning, active participants destined to find and secure a decent life by their own efforts.[9]

Physical and mental maturity were not the only preparation, however, for making a sensible marital choice. For writers advocating Real Womanhood, the value of both academic and vocational education was beyond measure. A young woman trained in her judgment and thinking by a liberal arts education and prepared to earn a living to support herself through vocational training was at no one's mercy and need never submit to ill treatment or beg for the necessities of life from the hands of a penurious and selfish husband. A woman who, as a variety of advice writers pointed out and as I will discuss later, could be a bank clerk, a dressmaker, a doctor, a milliner, a missionary, a nurse, a teacher, or a writer could avoid both the "false reasons" for which many women felt compelled to marry "just anybody" and equally false reasons for staying with a man who might treat her poorly after marriage.[10]

The false reasons that lured women into brutal or faithless marriages were numerous if advice writers are to be believed. One that they frequently attacked was marrying to "acquire a home." Advice writers felt that a man worthy of a young woman's respect and admiration could provide a good home for her and subsequent children, but they insisted that affection and respect for the man were absolute prerequisites for marriage and that getting a home was a side benefit, not an acceptable primary reason for marriage. An editorial in *Peterson's Magazine*, tellingly titled "Honorable Often to Be an Old Maid," states the majority of advice writers' feelings straightforwardly: "*Marry for a home!* Marry to escape the ridicule of being called an old maid! How *dare* you, then, pervert the most sacred institution of the Almighty, by becoming the wife of a man for whom you can feel no emotions of love, or respect even?"[11]

All the Real Womanhood writers agreed that marriage without love, respect, and the possibility of mutual companionship was not only a desecration but unthinkable in practical terms. Frequently, as pointed out by T. S. Arthur and Mrs. A. J. Graves, as well as a host of novelists, the man with a home might lose it shortly after marriage. Unless she carefully scrutinized her suitor's character, a young woman could easily end up with a gambler, a speculator, a drinker, or a slacker whose non-industrious habits would eventually put the very home she essentially married for into the hands of tax or rent collectors.[12] Without an ability to earn a living on her own, that same young woman would be left destitute and forced to rely on the mercy of family or charity. At best, she would be deserted and left to her own devices; at worst, she would be locked into a continuing cycle of poverty and penury with a man for whom she had no respect and no real affection, which might otherwise make up for difficult external circumstance.

Many of the Real Womanhood writers' injunctions applied to a second false, but allied, reason for marriage: marriage for money or fortune. The advice writers and novelists strove mightily to stamp out the myth of the wealthy, indulgent husband who would supply his wife with a thousand expensive luxuries and who would leap to provide for her tiniest desires. The rich nobleman on the white horse who, seeing the beautiful but poor young maiden, rides up and whisks her away to an unnamed splendor, thereby changing her life into one of prominence and social status, might have been a decent fairy tale for children under the title of "Cinderella" or "The Goose Girl," but it was hardly a guide for wise young women. As these same Real Womanhood writers pointed out (both directly in injunctions and indirectly through negative portraits in novels), life did not operate that way. Even if the nobleman did come by, there was every chance that he would dally and seduce rather than court and marry. If he did marry, he would probably expect her to "adjust" to his way of life, which, as the primarily middle-class writers hinted, was characterized by high-flown friends who would despise her, high-living parties that pandered to alcoholism and sexual experimentation, or simply a life of well-upholstered but intense emotional neglect. Affection and love, according to these writers, arose naturally out of a full and continued knowledge of a good man's character and a basis in shared interests, not through a greedy contemplation of his fortune. The absence of true, mature love, then, indicated the suitor's lackluster character or the pair's incompatibility.

Such is the case of Graves's Elizabeth Harrington and Amelia Dorrington, who do not respect their husbands or share interests with them but marry entirely for money—and live to pay the consequences. The same is true for E. D. E. N. Southworth's heroine Nora Worth, who, through false ideas of love, marries a rich "knight on a white horse" who she thinks will bring her to "the big house" as his wife. She later dies in poverty as a result.[13]

Graves's Elizabeth Harrington acknowledges the core of the problem to her ubiquitous former school chum Graves early in the account; according to Elizabeth, her life at the point at which she renews acquaintance with Graves is "spent in harrassing anxiety and the wasting fatigue of fearsome labor" because she married for wealth and not for her husband's character or out of affectionate respect. Urged into a "loveless" marriage by ambitious parents, Elizabeth explains, she threw herself into the fashionable arms of one Mr. Horton, a wealthy older man and friend of her father. Not only does she not love Mr. Horton, but she finds him boring, characterless, and disgusting. Remembering her initial reaction to the choice her father made for her she notes: "I could scarcely command my gravity, when I recollected that this was the one whom my parents wished me to gain as a lover. His figure was ungainly, and he looked older than my father." Still, the lure of his fortune was very strong, and she became engaged, then later married him, despite her secret promise to a young man, Alfred Thorton, without fortune, whom she earlier had promised to "wait for" until he could make his name. Elizabeth is paid back for this moral outrage by both a poetic justice and a realistic universe. She soon discovers that, in addition to being older than she is, her husband is also a near invalid, and his fortune "for which I married him was much less than it was said to be." Indeed, she comes to detest poor Mr. Horton, who is "helpless as an infant," and hates having to nurse him. Wormwood is heaped on her head by two events: the return of Alfred Thorton and the bankruptcy of Mr. Horton. Alfred returns to claim Elizabeth not knowing that she has forsaken him and married another; ironically, he has made an enormous amount of money through his industry and has inherited a large fortune as well. Naturally (since this is a moral story), Alfred's fortune is considerably larger than Mr. Horton's, and all is gall to a cowardly Elizabeth, who cannot tell him she is already married and must watch as the man she used to love and who now is richer than her wildest dreams slips from her life. Upon finding out from others that she is already married, he promptly dies of a broken heart—just in time for Elizabeth's husband to go bankrupt and die also. Mr. Horton, it seemed, had loaned a worthless nephew large sums of money for a plantation venture in the West Indies. The nephew went bankrupt and thus bankrupted Mr. Horton, leaving Elizabeth to mourn that the nephew (or Horton, it is unclear which) "deprived me of the small competence which was to have been appropriated to my support and the education of my daughters. I was left penniless." Elizabeth, the girl who married for money, eventually returns home to live with equally impecunious and poverty-stricken parents and to struggle along running a boardinghouse that only just supports their needs, as Graves is quick to note.[14]

Although it is obvious, under the moral codes of mature love and devotion extant at the time, that Elizabeth has "sinned," it would be equally apparent to readers of Real Womanhood that she "sinned" pragmatically as well as morally in casting Alfred aside. A woman with such a lack of perception or foresight deserves (and will realistically get) the life she has at the end. Alfred Thorton, Graves tells us, is, after all, not a witless young drifter off in search of fortune and fame. Rather, he is a doctor—a professional man—who idolizes science and art, a young intellectual who is "singularly gifted with mental and personal attractions" and filled with an industrious compulsion to work.[15] It is this that Elizabeth turns down in favor of the supposedly large fortune of an invalided husband. Rather than choosing either man because of his fortune (or potential for making one), Elizabeth should have became trained to support herself (as she, ironically, is forced to do in the end) and then chosen Alfred because of his character. Were she properly trained, she would not be reduced to the bare subsistence of keeping a boardinghouse. Graves's point seems to be that, even if one were avariciously searching for a meal ticket, Alfred was a much better pragmatic choice in the long run than Mr. Horton: Alfred is young, a professional man, and ambitious, with brains and a desire to succeed. Mr. Horton is old, an invalid, dull, and inherited his money. Even on the grubby grounds of material self-interest—which of course one should not use—Elizabeth was a fool.

As if to make the same points from a slightly different perspective, Graves gives us the illustrative, sad story of Amelia Dorrington, subtitled "The Lost One." Extremely attractive, this former schoolmate of Graves merrily ignores all but the minimum scholarly or vocational requirements of the school and sets herself up as a flirt. Her parents, Graves points out solemnly, do not set her straight; rather, "their excessive and injudicious fondness" help them turn a blind eye to her lack of learning, her lack of preparation for life, and her wild association and "undue familiarity" with "many suitors." Like the mother in Arthur's "Married at Sixteen," Mr. and Mrs. Dorrington are fatuously proud of their daughter's social successes with large groups of (and seemingly unlimited numbers of) the opposite sex.[16]

Her mind undisciplined by intellectual training and experience because of inattention and laziness at school, Amelia impulsively chooses as a husband Charles Sefton, a young man who is as wealthy as he is eye-catching. Graves sounds the death knell for the relationship for the reader's benefit: Charles, she tells us, is a "spoiled child of fortune," a lazy young man "brought up in idleness," a "dissipated" gambler. Naturally, Amelia has thoughtlessly plighted herself and her considerable dowry to this man without so much as a simple check of his background, feeling herself secure both because of Charles's "fortune" and her own substantial inheritance. Not surprisingly, Charles eventually gambles away all his money—and Amelia's inheritance as well. During this time they live in a constant whirl of social excitement in the "fast set," and soon, in addition to gambling, Charles philanders. Amelia, as Graves tells us, in a simpleminded, ill-considered attempt at "revenge," begins flirting, then sleeping with, other men. Graves recounts her end in sepulchral tones: "This was her first, fatal step, and so rapid was her downfall, that even before the death of her husband, she was cast off by him and his relatives, as unworthy even to be the wife of one as degraded as he was. Her children were taken from her, and she was denied all access to their presence. After this she sank to the lowest state of vice and wretchedness, and her course is too revolting to repeat." Apparently, first for revenge, later by necessity, Amelia becomes initially a social, later a professional, prostitute. Her inheritance spent, her husband absent, her children denied her—and, of course, penniless despite her initial intention of marrying for money—Amelia dies of exposure and alcoholic delirium tremens in, appropriately, an almshouse.[17]

This gothic little story underlines again several key tenets held by the writers advocating Real Womanhood: a girl should spend her time during her schooling learning mental discipline and accurate assessment techniques and also provide herself with the ability to earn her *own* living by some means other than prostitution. She then need not try to secure her future by marrying for money or take no care for her future because of an inheritance she is due to receive. Both, as this story amply demonstrates, can evaporate overnight if a girl marries poorly. Second, using this careful mental training, a girl should employ some form of lengthy scrutiny to ascertain the character of her suitor before marrying him. Obviously, had Amelia done so, had she been intellectually able to do so, she would have known in advance about Charles's penchant for gambling and his expensive, idle habits. She then could have avoided her ultimate fate. Finally, this terrible tale points out the concrete and brutal reality of a social double standard that allowed Charles his women but denied Amelia her sexual revenge and, beyond that, cast her out to fend for herself when she was caught breaking that standard. Although Graves does not really approve of the harsh treatment of Amelia by Charles, his family, and society, she does recognize social realities and their consequences. Amelia is too thoughtless to do that— and not sufficiently equipped intellectually even to be a good businesswoman capitalizing on her immoral physical charms. This last is, of course, implicit rather than explicit, but it all adds up to the price paid for a poor education, lack of character, and wrong reasons for marrying.

Interestingly, Artemus Bowers Muzzey makes the connection that seems obvious in the case of Amelia Dorrington that marrying for money is a more socially acceptable form of prostitution but one with the same moral odor. Like Graves, he indicates that imprudent, thoughtless parents with an eye to getting their daughters "set up" by marrying well are initially responsible for such degradation; he castigates them roundly, asking angrily, "How many parents in this civilized and Christian land, thus sell their daughters. Give the transaction whatever smooth name you please, it is, after all, a bargain and a sale." He continues, relentlessly pointing out syntactically, if not specifically, the "road to ruin" Amelia Dorrington treads: "Marry for riches alone, and you will be a neglected unhappy wife, as sure as gold is not kindness. How many of your sex have sold their honor for paltry lucre. Our cities contain awful testimonies to this fact. Beware of that path, which leads to this fearful direction."[18]

Muzzey counsels that if a girl feels she must marry, she should marry only a "good man," one who is decent, intelligent, and industrious in his habits, and she should "act from principle and affection . . . in the formation of the marriage tie," not because she is selfishly chasing a chimera of the easy life. Indeed, even before trusting in her sense of principle and affection, he repeats, she should train and educate herself to earn a living. He offers to his young lady readers the following inspiration: "Prepare so completely to earn your own livelihood, that no one, friend or foe, dare say to you, 'She is obliged by her helplessness to marry someone.' There are honorable avocations, and not a few either, in which every young woman can support herself. Let all be acquainted with some of them, with one at least. Then may they listen to overtures of marriage, with the feeling, that, as for a home, that, they have already secured by the skill of their own mind and hands." Willard agrees strongly, exhorting girls to prepare to "become independent, useful, and happy, without marriage."[19] Other advice writers—Chapin, Weaver, Holmes, and Thornwell among them—agree to a greater or lesser degree.

How despicable it is to marry for money without affection and respect emerges especially in domestic novels of the period. Although Hentz's Linda may indeed end up well with her noble riverboat captain, she loves him when he is poor because of his sterling character and his "manly" attitude toward hard work and adversity. Linda's eventual good fortune is a reward for her lack of acquisitiveness, not a result of greedy foresight. Earlier, her evil stepmother, Mrs. Walton, attempts to talk Linda, then sixteen, into marrying wealthy Robert, Mrs. Walton's son from a previous marriage. This, Mrs. Walton explains with the bloodless enthusiasm of a Zurich banker, would amalgamate the two fortunes. Linda loathes and fears Robert (he has proven himself a lazy, idle, and sadistic suitor), and she finds Mrs. Walton's suggestion as contemptible as it is mercenary: " 'Fortune!' " repeated Linda, her eyes flashing scornfully through her tears. " 'Let him take my fortune, if that is what you want. I wish I were the poorest girl in the south-west, if I must be bought and sold like a negro slave. But I never will be. I never will enter into your mercenary scheme!' "[20]

Nor is Linda alone among domestic heroines in her instinctive distaste for mercenary marriage. Heroines in general despise it; conversely, their foils acquiesce to or seek it. In Holmes's *'Lena Rivers,* the limp-wristed, weak-willed cousin Anna Livingston (foil to the heroine 'Lena) agrees after some persuasion on the part of her mother to marry ancient Captain Atherton, a randy old gentleman living in the neighborhood, whose fortune is as large as his eye is roving. Anna is not a mercenary sort herself, but she is a weakling. Though her heart and spirit tell her that marriage without love, especially to an old man, should not, cannot, be borne, her protest is apathetic and muted. She demurs rather than demands and seems suspiciously soothed by the thought of sudden wealth.

Anna's brother, fiery John, Jr., urges her to denounce the betrothal and send the old man packing: "Be a woman," he advises her, "Tell him *no* in good, broad English, and if the old fellow insists, I'll blow his brains out!" Even armed with this generous offer, Anna finds herself incapable of refusing the marriage. Her answer to the horror to come is typical of those heroines much admired by the True Womanhood school: her delicate sensibilities overcharged, she faints, drifts into a "stupor," and then shows signs of approaching dementia. In other words, she is passive and self-destructive. It takes right-thinking 'Lena—a Real Woman—to "save" hapless Anna by arranging for the latter to elope with her real love, Malcolm Everett. Holmes notes coldly that 'Lena literally leads Anna (still in something of a stupor) to Everett and hands her over, "helpless as an infant."[21]

The portrait of Anna contrasts sharply with the pattern Nina Baym identifies in her discussion of the female domestic novel and its heroine, thus supporting the interpretation of Anna as foil and an example of behavior disapproved of by the novel's author and, by extension, its newly educated readers. Baym insists that the *real* heroine of the domestic novel (in this case, 'Lena), "has psychological strength, moral stamina, and intellectual ability—she is not at all like the weak, clinging, nonrational, and inferior creature of the era's [supposed] ideology. If the popular books do urge women to conform, they also celebrate female strength, ambition, and autonomy."[22]

One cannot place too much literary importance on the position of foils in these novels (both the Anna Livingston variety and the scheming fashionable women I will discuss later). Through these characters, authors suggest the alternative, but false, paths a woman may take and then paint, often in lurid detail, the natural consequences. Further, Anna, with her giggling, her fainting, her fashionable clothing, and her essential passivity, serves to undercut and indirectly invalidate those very qualities so prized by the competing Cult of True Womanhood, qualities which Real Womanhood writers feel are the spiritual and intellectual poison of the age for American women. True Womanhood's ideals, then, more and more clearly define, in the case of an Anna Livingston, woman's betrayal to the forces of societal materialism and her moral vacuity in the face of evil. How could an Anna ever have either the strength or the spiritual credibility with both men and women readers to preach, as Kelley would seem to label Real Womanhood's ideals in action, "the secular equivalent to the righteous reformist ethos of Protestantism"? If these novels functioned, as Baym suggests, even in the minds of their authors, not as "great Art" but as a force for moral reform through a kind of fictional "lay ministry," then use of such a foil was a splendid way to underscore the sermon's obvious message while simultaneously providing the audience with a titillating frisson arising from the horrors and degradations such True Womanhood ideology and actions based on it would bring in their wake, all of it safely remote in the pages of a good novel. The characterization of the foil representing True Womanhood inevitably follows certain conventions: she is usually "frail," often "sweet," always passive in the face of physical danger, moral judgment, or financial necessity, and uneducated in any true sense of the word. Frequently she has a pale, "ladylike" face and tiny feet, as well as delicate, doll-like features. She is, in fact, the victimized heroine of the old "literature of seduction," which enjoyed popularity up to the 1830s. As Baym points out, she is a heroine from past literature, left behind by a "major and significant change in the literary image of woman."[23] In the more realistic, healthy, and strident literature of the midcentury, such figures in domestic novels serve only as foolish or evil "arguments" to the heroine and her strong-minded and generous attempt to reform society and build her own character into that of a mature and responsible adult. Finally, one might call this passive foil the authors' attempt to reject an inferior and demeaning understanding of the nature of women and to protest continued attempts to force women into that mold by showing not only the disastrous results in the world they live in but their moral bankruptcy as well.

Mercenary marriage or acquiescence in the "slave auction" aspects of marriage is only one aspect of this moral bankruptcy; there are others, which are equally reflected in "false reasons" for marrying. Another false reason is the decision to marry to attain status, position, or prominence through the husband, using him as a surrogate. Although this reason often coexists with what girls call "love," as both advice writers explain and novels show, that love is generally initially suggested (or indeed advanced) because of the social prominence or status of the suitor. After all, as the loquacious Muzzey points out, a suitor with high social standing, a famous name, illustrious ancestors, or impressive rank is what "everyone" considers "a good match" and so is a competitive feather in the young lady's cap. She, not another, "caught" this one; by agreeing to marry such a man—a practice advocated directly and indirectly by the True Womanhood school as the acme of success—the girl proves herself to be of equal standing and social status as her suitor. This, Muzzey announces contemptuously, is a "royalist" or "European" way of looking at marriage—and it can lead very easily to disaster. As he points out, dazzled by a "good marriage" and an alliance with a family mansion or a coronet, the young lady can easily lose sight of the suitor's character: "The character, the principles, the disposition and heart of him, to whom a lady consigns her whole destiny are actually put out of view, for the sake of the family."[24]

This proves to be the problem in Graves's somber case history "Anna Percival," subtitled "The Maniac Mother." Here, however, the protagonist is the foil to Graves's other, more successful exampla heroines in her work. Dazzled by the blandishments of a Europeanized prominent American of "good family," Fredrick Elton, Anna marries him without any investigation or scrutiny. Her mother is too enchanted with the idea of a European honeymoon to counsel caution. Fredrick is an intimate of moneyed European spagoers, a friend of dukes, honorables, and viscounts. As Graves tells us disparagingly: "Fredrick Elton had spent a life of excitement" and was used to the "giddy whirl of brilliant attractions found in the theatre, the opera, the fashionable gaming clubs." His geographical preference is Italy, where he proposes to (and does) take Anna to live after they are married.[25]

Despite the excitement of an elaborate wedding and a splashy bon voyage celebration, Anna becomes unhappy almost as soon as the ring is on her finger. Though pleased to see Italy, Anna worries about leaving her widowed mother alone for such a long period and asks Fredrick if she might accompany them or at least join them soon. Fredrick's cold response is the first indication of his true nature; he says, with "a slight shade of displeasure," that Anna should remember her status as a wife: "Recollect, my Anna, your husband will be with you, and your Mother need not be alone, for I am sure that your friend [meaning Graves] will consent to remain with her until our return." This seems a moderate enough response initially (or perhaps a bit thoughtless because no one has consulted Graves), but it does show his notable lack of desire to please his new wife. His selfishness fully emerges soon afterward in Italy. He sneers at the devotional and quiet life of ordinary American couples and explains to Anna that he is used to a life of amusement, variety, and frequent sexual experimentation. He also explains that such is the way of the world in the sophisticated society of Europe and upbraids Anna for her "provinicial" morality. In addition to his other libertine habits, Fredrick drinks, and Anna usually sees him only early in the morning when he stumbles into the foyer inebriated.[26]

But things get worse, as Graves intones: "To neglect and desertion her husband added cruelty!" He denies her the right to see her mother; he refuses, even when they are back in the United States, to allow her to visit her old home or Graves; he will not allow Anna's mother to visit their home; and finally, even though Anna is pregnant, he forbids Mrs. Percival to come and aid her daughter. Says Graves with an almost noticeable shudder of horror, in Anna's moment of maternal anguish, "hired menials were her only attendants." It is not surprising that Anna comes out of the difficult birth with a clear case of postpartum psychosis. She falls into a "settled melancholy" and becomes a "maniac" when the baby is near her because, she says, it looks like her husband, whom she loathes. She feels that because her son looks like her husband, his character will be similar, and therefore the baby would be better off dead. In other moments, she accepts and croons over the baby. The "hired menials," however, are none too observant—nor, it turns out, are either Graves or Mrs. Percival, who have managed to gain entrance by devious means. Anna asks for her baby to hold, and they give it to her: "When gazing intently on it as its beautiful eyes were turned upwards to her face, she suddenly exclaimed, 'It is not my baby, it is the demon that haunts me, it tried to deceive me by coming in the form of a child, but it shall not cheat me thus!' Before we [Graves and Mrs. Percival] had time to reach her, she rushed to the open window, and threw out her child, exclaiming with a laugh of triumph, 'Now it will never haunt me again!' "[27]

Anna Percival, by Graves's account, has been turned into a maniacal child-killer because of a bad marriage; her husband's only kindly act during the entire marriage is an inadvertent one—he dies of delirium tremens "after a violent fit . . . a month or two previous to her restoration to reason."[28] Anna, though broken in health, is eventually restored to sanity and soothed with the tale that her baby was born dead. The wealth, position, and status she thought to achieve by marrying Fredrick have evaporated; nothing remains but delinquent bills, her husband's public name for drunken debauchery, and a hazy memory of her part in an "unspeakable act" that she may or may not have committed. By becoming an infanticide, Anna Percival has turned monster (however sympathetic); this seems a poetic, if unduly severe, punishment for the girl who desired to be "higher" than others.

Novels as well take up the warning cry so evident in Graves's exemplar stories: marriage for reasons primarily of "*name* and *pomp*," to quote Chapin, are doomed to failure, doubly so if the name and pomp are enhanced by yet another false reason for marriage, "sentimental love," by which the writers mean the notorious "love at first sight." It is important to understand that when either advice writers dealing with Real Womanhood or novelists of similar frame of mind write about marriages based on "love," they most definitely do *not* mean a sentimental, infatuated, or even romantic attachment. As Muzzey, Weaver, Chapin, Thornwell, Southworth, Hentz, Holmes, and even Sarah Josepha Hale agree, "real" love is based on respect and admiration for substantial personal attributes—industriousness, intelligence, piousness, kindliness, courtesy, well-roundedness—and grows slowly, ever so slowly out of a deepening and growing knowledge and awareness of these qualities in the suitor. Girls need time and scrutiny to come to understand these qualities fully (or even, Arthur suggests) to discern them initially. "Love at first sight" is a wicked delusion and a poor reason to decide to marry, the writers agree. Weaver scorns it as "a vision of the fancy, originating in a fevered or morbid state of mind," and Muzzey elucidates further that it is the result of "an unnatural predisposition and an inflamed and diseased imagination."[29] Abell, Burnap, and Chapin believe the condition is brought on by trashy novels and a poor education and feel that by delineating the nature of true love, they can eradicate the false reason for marriage of love at first sight.

At least one novelist, E. D. E. N. Southworth, seems to agree and, as usual, draws two female characters—one flighty, romantically minded, and doomed, the other hardworking, older, practical, and initially more assured of an emotional future. In this case they are sisters, and the younger one, Nora Worth, becomes the victim of her quest for pomp and name and her weak-minded capitulation to "love at first sight." Hannah and Nora Worth are "orphans, living alone together in the hut on the hill and supporting themselves by spinning and weaving," Southworth explains. They are obviously not part of the grand social order in Maryland, but industrious, honest mechanics who live marginally in the neighborhood. The Brudenell family, local wealthy landowners and American gentry, are comtemptuous of the county people. Unfortunately for Nora, they have a young and handsome heir, Herman Brudenell. Herman and Nora meet inadvertently at Herman's manorial coming-of-age party, when he invades the barn to show himself to the "lesser folk" who have been invited (in a mimicry of English tradition) to a feast in honor of the new heir. As the chapter title announces, it is "love at first sight" for both of them. Hannah Worth, the sensible older sister of the flighty Nora, cautions her against allowing herself to become emotionally attached to young Herman, answering Nora's sighing question, "I wonder who he'll marry?" with cold water: "Not you, my dear; so you had better not occupy your mind with him," Hannah replied, very gravely. In this, Hannah is in obvious agreement with the common observations and wisdom of the small community. Herman pays Nora marked attention during the course of the evening, smiles at her repeatedly, sits by her, tells her how beautiful she is, and, finally, dances almost exclusively with her for the rest of the night. Other women at the dance note the impropriety and danger of this situation: " 'No good will come of it,' said one. 'No good ever does come of a rich young man paying attention to a poor girl,' added another. 'He's making a perfect fool of *her*.' " Initially, since Southworth chooses women with whom Herman has neglected to dance as the spokespeople for this social dictum, we are unsure whether their remarks are wise or merely catty and envious. When Hannah's noble fiancé, Reuben Gray, objects and asks Hannah to be wary, however, we begin to doubt the efficacy of Nora's actions. Reuben Gray counsels Hannah that Herman Brudenell is of too high a rank to marry someone like Nora; his mother and "haughty" sisters will not allow it even if he should impetuously decide to. Reuben Gray has an even less sanguine view of Herman's character than this initially suggests, however, and Reuben traces the hypothetically chilling course such an affair of the heart will take. Even if Herman's sisters would accept Nora, Reuben explains, "his [Herman's]

Harper's Weekly, July 4, 1857

own pride wouldn't! And so he'd go away and try to forget her, and she'd stop home and break her heart!"[30]

Despite Hannah's and Reuben's sage advice, Nora continues to languish after Herman Brudenell, who stokes the flames higher by visiting her clandestinely at her cabin, meeting her out walking, and speaking of love to her. He declares his intention to make her his wife and straightforwardly approaches Hannah to ask permission. Hannah is loath to accept the match, but Nora is radiant with joy. This happy picture is suddenly darkened for both the reader and Hannah when Herman explains that, unfortunately, the marriage must not be made public because of his mother's certain disapproval for reasons of class difference: "I will not wrong Nora, and I will not grieve my mother. The only way to avoid doing either will be for me to marry my darling privately, and keep the affair a secret until a fitting opportunity offers to publish it."[31]

Herman, it seems, has convinced Nora that a public ceremony would cause a "rupture" between himself and his family; further, he convinces her that he needs time to "bring them around" and, once that is done, he will announce the marriage publicly after he has reconciled his sisters, and especially his mother, to it. Hannah's response to this sleazy arrangement is, understandably, negative. Hannah declares, "Secret marriages are terrible things!" but Nora's declaration that "I cannot live without him, Hannah! I cannot live without him!" makes her grudgingly agree to serve as a witness. Even though Hannah remarks that Herman's character is obviously weak and too pliable for true trustworthiness, Nora is adamant. Southworth announces apocalyptically, "Alas for weakness, willfulness and passion! They, and not wise counsels gained the day."[32]

Obviously, the advice writers advocating Real Womanhood would consider Herman a bad choice as a marriage partner. Rich, indolent, "open-faced," and therefore weakly pliable to the wishes of the strongest personality around, he is hardly a mature adult. Mother-dominated, vacillating, and impressionable, he is also rash and impulsive about an action that has the blessings of neither his nor Nora's family. His requirement of secrecy is one of the many red flags that domestic novelists (and even advice writers) during the period use as a warning. Anything that has to be done secretly, they declare, cannot stand the "light of day."[33]

This dislike of secrecy—secret courtship, secret marriage—is not limited, however, to Real Womanhood writers; as Welter points out, even the writers of the True Womanhood school dislike furtiveness. In fiction of the 1830s and early 1840s, seduction usually occurs as a direct result of a girl disobeying her parents, secretly reading love letters, and then leaving at night with the suitor.[34]

The difference between the two ideals in this regard, however, is important. The True Womanhood writers essentially view women as passive, emotional children, whose virtues are obedience and self-denial. Far from teaching young women what characteristics of the suitor and situations call for prudence and caution, as do writers for Real Womanhood, the True Womanhood writers assume that only a passive, unthinking, close adherence to parental dictates can protect the young woman from disgrace, dishonor, and an unfortunate demise. Despite their injunctions, however, the True Womanhood writers—both of fiction and of advice literature—make an icon of the foolish wanderer from parental advice, casting her as a "dying maiden," exalting her as a victim of intense sensitivity and loyalty to an unworthy cad.[35] They hardly bother to suggest defensive courses of action or useful guidelines or even careful habits which a young woman might cultivate to prevent her from becoming a victim of such practices; rather, these writers mourn the seemingly predestined loss of the pure young maiden and sing requiems to her intense sensitivity and unearthly power to forgive. As I have mentioned before, this is exactly the portrait and assessment of intellectually inferior and eternally victimized womanhood that domestic novelists struggled to oust from the popular audience's perception of a heroine.

The writers advocating Real Womanhood do not find such masochistic conduct in any way exemplary. Nora Worth, for example, may be a sweet and trusting girl, but she is also, as Southworth presents her, simpleminded both in her sentimental choice of a mate and in her subsequent romantic gesture of faith in him. To prove that she does not need to possess the means of "holding" Herman to his obligations, Nora explains that, if he deserts her, she would not care to live and makes a sentimental (and, as it turns out, tragic) gesture: " 'Why should I be armed with legal proofs against *you*, my Herman, my life, my soul, my self? I will not continue so!' And with generous abandonment, she drew from her bosom the marriage certificate, tore it to pieces, and scattered it abroad."[36] Generous Nora's gesture may be; as Southworth shows, however, it is also disastrously stupid. The marriage certificate is the only tangible, indisputable proof Nora possesses of her "secret marriage" and the only reliable claim her unborn son has to legitimacy or support.

The onus Southworth casts on secrecy does not devolve simply because the marriage is secret; Southworth deplores, as do other Real Womanhood writers, the reasons why such an event would have to be secret. As Arthur—and now Southworth—indicate, secrecy usually cloaks something irregular, even illegal. In the case of poor Nora Worth, the irregularity is Herman's inadvertent bigamy. Herman, rashly, impetuously, decides his first wife, the Countess of Hurstmonceaux, is dead, after seeing her name listed as one of the fatalities in a railway accident in a *single* newspaper. Without so much as a telegram to the house servants in England or an inquiry to the police, he rushes off with joy in his heart and marries Nora Worth, apparently getting her pregnant almost simultaneously. His horror is immense, five or six months later, when an equipage pulls up in front of Brudenell Hall and he comes face to face with his "resurrected" first wife. Herman, never a man to face things boldly, can only "cover his eyes with his hands and groan" and declare himself "a felon!" He berates the countess for not informing him she was alive (which she touchingly takes as proof of his concern for her). She explains gently that her right hand was crushed and she was unable to write; then she inadvertently spotlights Herman's characteristic rashness by adding: "I thought surely if you should have seen the announcement of my death in one paper, you would see it contradicted, as it was, in half a dozen others."[37] Herman, in his rush to marry Nora, did not bother to investigate thoroughly; since he did not allow his family to be cognizant of his plans, any information they might have discovered was not available to him either. The secret marriage—and Nora's destruction of the marriage certificate—leave Nora pregnant, unmarried, and subject to vile speculations and accusations, her good name lost.

Herman further exhibits his weak character by collapsing (we suppose) in his room, thus allowing the news of the arrival of Mr. Brudenell's wife to reach Nora before he does. Again, Southworth treats us to a picture of the passion and thoughtless frenzy characteristic of True Womanhood—and the "sensitive" and "emotional" heroines of seduction literature. Rather than formulating some plan, Nora rushes out into a snowstorm, hatless and cloakless, and walks several miles to Brudenell Hall to find out "the truth." She does—and faces the scathing accusations of Herman's mother, who assumes Nora is a discarded plaything of her son's, since it is obvious that Nora is well advanced in pregnancy. In attacking Nora, Herman's mother offers a certain pragmatic evaluation of the situation more than faintly reminiscent of the comments made by the other women earlier during the coming-of-age party; she asks Nora sharply what her relationship is with her son and Nora (noble, True Woman Nora) refuses to answer or to throw the marriage in the mother's face, afraid of "hurting" Herman. Her silence infuriates Herman's mother:

"You admit by your silence that Mr. Brudenell has been visiting you daily for months; and yet you imply that in doing so he means you no harm! *I* should think he means your utter ruin!"

"Mrs. Brudenell!!" exclaimed Nora in a surprise so sorrowful and indignant that it made her forget herself and her fears, "You are speaking of your own son, your only son; you are his mother, how *can* you accuse him of a base crime?"

"Recollect yourself, my girl! You surely forget the presence in which you stand! Baseness, crime, can never be connected with the name Brudenell.

But young gentlemen will be young gentlemen, and amuse themselves with just such credulous fools as you!" said the lady, haughtily.[38]

Though we know that Herman did not set out intentionally to toy with Nora's emotions or plan to ruin her, he obviously has; Mrs. Brudenell's comments, despite their inaccuracy concerning motive, are apt and sadly realistic in regard to the final result. Nora is dishonored, pregnant, and unmarried. She is, in fact, the perfect heroine, literally, of a seduction novel. Young gentlemen—especially rash, weak, and impulsive ones afraid of their mothers—will be young gentlemen, after all. Nora's sentimental gesture—destroying the marriage certificate that might have enabled her to make a case for a settlement for her child or save her good name (and her son's later), as well as her protective refusal to explain Herman's "mistake" in the face of cruel opprobrium and scorn—are only seemingly noble on paper. Nora Worth's nonmarriage and her subsequent (and to the reader, expected) death take up only 159 pages of a 718-page book; far from being the central tragic heroine of the story, she is merely the unfortunate mother of the true hero of the novel, the son, Ishmael, who overcomes the stain of illegitimacy brought on him not only by his father but by his mother's sentimentality (though it takes another novel as well to do so). Nora's gesture, then her silence, is the foolish, romantic, and destructive end to a foolish, romantic, and rash marriage choice, as Southworth's relatively brief treatment of it shows. Herman's whining and self-justifying explanation to Hannah over Nora's deathbed that his first wife, the countess, "trapped him" and he "pitied" her so he married her, his hair-tearings, ravings, and disappearance, leaving his son in Hannah's care, with a $5,000 check, indicate what a flawed idol Nora gave her life to protect and are especially bitter after an illiterate neighbor, when everyone is gone, uses the check to light a candle in the house.[39] Sentimentality—love at first sight in the moonlight, with a "prince" on a white horse—has a high and deadly price, not only for the woman but for her relations, who must pick up the pieces. Sentimentality loves the outward appearance, the flash of manners, the dazzling wealth and charm; love, real love, adores only after one has discovered the character. And Southworth shows strongly that Herman has no character worth mentioning. Even if he had, Nora would not have known it, having taken no time to discuss, as Real Womanhood writers suggest, "things"—feelings, thoughts, ideals, work habits, other marriages prior to the one proposed, other current wives.

Lest any of their readers not understand precisely what they mean, advice writers supporting Real Womanhood explain precisely and "scientifically" what constitutes the false and dangerous love at first sight and make distinctions between it and true love to serve as a rational guideline for their young women readers. Muzzey specifically states that to marry because of "beauty of person of suitor"—infatuation with a handsome face and elegant manners—is to marry for false reasons and to become a "victim to folly." With characteristic cynicism, Muzzey points out that good-looking men frequently are vain and pride themselves only on their appearance, becoming mere "shells of humanity" without any inward charms and, frequently, no strength or resilience when faced with life's vicissitudes. Brides of such men, hoping for a strong and helpful or caring companion with whom to face the trials of life, find out that they have "buil[t] their hopes on a foundation of straw." Chapin, too, deplores *sentimental love, that is as brief as youth, and as superficial as beauty,"* and Graves shows us just such a disastrous match in the previously mentioned case of Amelia Dorrington.[40]

Muzzey directly addresses a related issue that both Chapin and Graves skirt carefully—that of sheer sexual attraction and a desire to marry so as to have relations with a particular man. Muzzey lists this as "Number Eleven" of his "false reasons" to marry ("Marriage Because of Passion") and is very stern in his evaluation of it. A woman should marry only because she loves the character or the spirit of the suitor and feels the union will be spiritually "uplifting." To marry for reasons of sexual desire alone is to "lose integrity" as a woman and a human being because it capitulates entirely to "earthy" impulses.[41]

Though Muzzey and Chapin would seem to deny the sexual and emotional aspects of mature relationships for women, they in fact, reflect a common preoccupation with "transcending sexuality" shared by female domestic novelists. As Nina Baym points out, on one level both Christianity and Victorian society were "disinclined to acknowledge the body and physical sexuality as elements," especially as irresistible elements. Thoughtful people believed that "duty, discipline, self-control, and sacrifice (within limits)" were indices of moral development; to succumb to sexual attraction was to betray one's moral sense because it took no account of the suitor's morality or character.[42]

On another level, transcending sexuality also placed the novelists' ideal women in a position of greater spirituality through intellectual superiority. Men, those frequently uncontrolled and base creatures found skulking through hundreds of domestic novels, seem unable to see beyond a woman character's raven tresses and billowing hips. Domestic novel heroines, on the other hand, sturdily resist even the most Byronically handsome suitor if he is a cad, an atheist, or a "mere" creature of passion. Each heroine who resists the siren call of raw sexuality proves once again that women are capable of more than emotional response and value their intellects and lives beyond the artificial standards set by True Womanhood through its emphasis on woman as sexual victim. Despite the domestic novelists' predilection for presenting heroines as creatures of superior sincerity, sensibility, and emotional sensitivity, these heroines display fortitude and mental discipline in making decisions such as Evans's Edna Earl does despite strong physical attraction. Although no domestic author directly traces the course of a passionate and "earthy" union, several demonstrate the alarming results of courting and becoming engaged because of sexual attraction. Evans in *St. Elmo* does this through the character of that Byronic sensualist's previous victims and in the later novel, *Vashti*, through the obsession the coldly correct Ulpian Grey acquires for the mysterious "widow" in the neighboring mansion. Both obsessions—the girls' for St. Elmo and Gray's for the widow—end for the besotted ones in death scenes redolent of the macabre, as if to suggest as forcefully as possible that "carnal" and "charnal" are inextricably linked, since the former is an "earthy" passion subject to mortality.[43]

It would be hasty, however, to assume that all writers supporting Real Womanhood totally disavowed physical attraction or expected women to marry entirely for idealistic reasons. They spoke endlessly against "loveless" marriages and marriages of "convenience" in which no affection—or even amiable liking—existed. Graves's case of Elizabeth Harrington more than amply illustrates this point, as does the well-deserved fate of the selfish Lillie in Stowe's *Pink and White Tyranny*. Rather, Real Womanhood advice writers assumed that physical compatibility and conjugal enjoyment were the natural outgrowth of friendship, shared interests, affection, and respect and that to marry because of sexual attraction was to put the cart before the horse, dangerously and rashly hoping that the more important components of marriage—intellectual compatibility, friendship, and shared interests and values—would develop.

As their exempla and their short stories, their novels and their advice literature, show repeatedly, this last is a dangerous assumption with little basis in fact. The sensual man whom a woman marries for "passion" is often a man who also drinks, gambles, philanders, and, eventually, beats his wife; sensuality as a ruling force suggests the primacy of physical gratification in a man's life and a corresponding diminution or stunted growth in such areas of character as integrity, intellect, or industriousness. Better, the advice writers seem to suggest, that a marriage be characterized by strong friendship and only tepid or perfunctory sexual relations than the other way around.

One writer, however, granting the viability of such a mixed relationship, disagreed with some of the Real Womanhood writers' basic assumptions and proposed a pragmatic approach for dealing with the problem of sexual incompatibility. "Dr." E. B. Foote suggested that in marriages based only on strong friendship there was no guarantee of sexual compatibility and that a series of "medical" tests during the engagement period might determine whether the couple was capable of maintaining a "full" and satisfying relationship.[44] Although Foote, who includes chapters on electromagnetism, animal magnetism, phrenology, and birth control procedures, is perhaps not representative of the mainstream opinion either of True Womanhood or Real Womanhood, his philosophies intersect, at certain important points, with those of the writers advocating Real Womanhood, and his views on sexual compatibility illuminate an important consideration which these writers leave in the spaces between their words. Dr. Foote, for example, believes that people who were sexually incompatible should not be allowed to marry, claiming that present marriage laws are "haphazard" and that "ill-assorted matrimonial alliance[s]" are the direct result of "the prevailing ignorance of the laws of physical and mental adaptation." Foote describes three types of marriage that he believes are practiced in the United States: (1) the "mental marriage" in which "social, moral and intellectual adaptation has been secured, with little or no regard for physical adaptation"; (2) the "physical marriage," which is composed of "males and females well mated physically, with little or no mental adaptation"; and (3) "Lucifer matches," which are "contracted without regard to physical or mental adaptation." He rates the first "nearly happy," the second "tolerably happy," and the third "miserable." He also declares that miserable alliances are by far the majority.[45]

Certain tests of "electrical discharge," Foote claims, could discern the electrical and magnetic potential of fiancés and prevent either the acute hunger and misery of the Lucifer match or the tepid dissatisfaction of the mental marriage. Although he feels that a mental marriage (which bears a striking resemblance to those repeatedly suggested as a goal by Real Womanhood advice writers) is reasonably strong and agrees that a "powerful attachment," as well as a great deal of social harmony, exists between husbands and wives in such marriages, they still are not completely happy because they lack a full sexual dimension. Such marriages tend to be barren of children, he suggests, and are always vulnerable to the spouse being seduced and eloping with a partner who is more sexually compatible. He tends to agree with Real Womanhood writers, however, about the relative lack of viability of marriages based purely on sexual compatibility, though his projections for their future are less macabre and threatening. He points out that although physical marriages reap a harvest of fulfilling sexual benefits, they are barren of mutually experienced social enjoyments. In "physical" marriages, there is little talking or sharing, and the men tend to spend little time at home, thus opening themselves to the temptations that all-male events in the nineteenth century popularly were believed to carry: "In these marriages, husbands seldom find social attractions at home, but spend their evenings in business, in political caucuses, masculine gatherings of various kinds, or at the gaming table or club room." Indirectly, then, Foote's projection of husbandly behavior supports several of the tenets of courtship proposed by Real Womanhood writers, among them shared interests, intellectual proclivities, and recreational pursuits.[46]

Although the advice writers stress the accruing—and protective—benefits derived from a solid liberal education and its attendant gifts of self-discipline, intellectual acuity, and strengthened judgment, they feel that such an education does not fully prepare a girl to choose a marriage partner until she has had "life experience" during her late teens and early twenties. This need for life experience is one of many reasons why Real Womanhood writers insist on "late" marriage.

Realistically, as always, these writers point out that it is hard for a young woman to be judicious in choosing a mate if the only male companionship she experiences is that of her brothers and father. Life experience, the writers conclude, should include meeting a variety of men under relatively controlled social conditions. Junior partners in the father's firm; young men met at mixed social occasions such as balls, church socials, and hayrides; friends a brother brings home from college; carefully screened relatives of close friends all provide "types" to which a young woman can be exposed safely and come to know socially. Several years spent mixing socially and closely with all types of men will provide her with knowledge of what sort she does not want to marry, as well as helping her gradually come to understand what type she does. This experience will also dispel the aura of mystery surrounding men that may exist for the overly protected and isolated young woman.

According to Muzzey, such socializing carries an added benefit. Young women who have a great deal of social interaction with young men will be less subject to the twin temptations of flattery and proximity. Young women who are overly protected, he claims, are likely to mistake familiarity for love in the latter case and to substitute flirtation or fortune hunting for love in the former—none of which would happen if the young women had frequent social contact with men. Describing the problems of proximity, Muzzey notes that a girl who has been overly secluded from male company may be unprepared when she goes to visit a friend and suddenly finds herself face to flushed face with a brother home from college, a young unmarried uncle, or perhaps a handsome male boarder. A week's constant contact, sharing thoughts and pleasantries under somewhat intimate conditions, convinces the girl that she is "in love," when in fact she is simply becoming acquainted with a male who is not a relative. Muzzey does not exclude the brothers of friends as possible marriage partners for his young women readers, but he insists that if they choose such a man it is because of his "traits," the quality of his character, his intellectual and emotional sympathies, not "solely through the accidental Proximity of the parties." Weaver inserts provisos on this subject as well. Marriage, he claims, is too frequently regarded as a "lottery" in which one chooses blindly and haphazardly—a situation and state of mind made all too possible by the overseclusion and isolation of young women from young men.[47]

Muzzey and Southworth, when we consider the courtship of Nora Worth, warn against mistaking flattery for real love. Unsophisticated young women tend to be swept off their feet by a few cleverly turned phrases and a poetic line. According to Muzzey, such innocents turn a blind eye to faults in the male's character because the praise is so pleasant and seductive—especially if the recipient is either plain or only moderately interesting or accomplished. Such intense flattery—which, in fact, may be nothing more than a series of social minuet steps—reassures the moderately accomplished, somewhat plain girl that she is desirable and makes her commensurately less severe or analytical in her judgment of the flatterer.[48]

This certainly seems to describe poor Nora Worth, who in her cottage on the hill is a perfect example of social isolation from male companionship. The first time Herman Brudenell smiles at her "especially," she falls in love with him; his subsequent flatteries, lines of poetic nonsense, and hyperbolic compliments only ground her more solidly in her belief that it is "true love" for both of them. Nor is Nora alone in her susceptibility to flattery. Arthur's eighteen-year-old Miriam Darlington in the story "Taking Boarders" agrees to marry Mr. Burton only partly because he agrees to settle $2,000 a year on her mother; the other inducements come from his "slick" and sophisticated ways and his constant barrage of flattery and praise.[49]

Both the Reverend Burnap and Arthur suggest that, like the despicable Mr. Burton, many suitors have less innocuous motives for flattering young women than simply their desire to do the *au fait* thing socially. Burnap warns strongly against the slippery—and socially glittering—fortune hunter who will turn a girl's head with flattery so that he can marry her and possess her fortune. Such young men pay extravagant compliments and talk poetically, Burnap suggests, because that is the trademark of the professional fortune hunter: his tongue's ability to charm is the probable source of his eventual income. Fortune hunters have practiced and polished their lines in unsuccessful games of marital pursuit and thus have brought flattery to the level of a fine, seductive art. Their moral traits, needless to say, are either nonexistent or (more likely) vile; they are "without character, talent, or business, whose whole stock in trade is dandyism, dissipation and impudence." Women who fall into the hands of such "pirates" are sooner or later not only miserable and neglected but "stripped of all" their fortunes as well.[50]

Foreign observers such as the avuncular "M. Carlier," quoted acerbically in a *Nation* editorial of May 2, 1867, felt that many of America's marital woes could be traced directly to its courting practices, which allowed young ladies to mix too freely with young men. Native-born American advice writers supporting Real Womanhood, however, continued to stress the danger of "undue Reserve," as Muzzey called it, and isolation on young girls' ability to choose a future mate wisely. Muzzey, in what seems an oblique attack on the teachings of the competing True Womanhood ideal, with its stress on propriety and etiquette, sneers at a reserve that is more paranoid than prudent, more egocentric than modest: "Some young ladies are so trained as apparently to enshrine themselves from *all* approach, in the society of gentlemen. They are models of decorum, miracles of prudence, and drawn up, as if always anticipating a foe. They inwardly sneer at all sentiment, and deride those, who exhibit it, and pride themselves, above all things, in keeping every one completely at a distance." Shall we, Muzzey asks, "substitute an Anglo-American prudery" for "French freedom"? Shall even the smallest and most innocuous niceties and services which young men offer to young women always be met with aloofness, an icy hauteur, and censorious frowns? Muzzey and Weaver, as well as Arthur, Burnap, and others, feel that this coldness comes from being isolated from young men and perceiving them, thanks to etiquette books written chiefly (one supposes) by True Womanhood writers, either as slavering beasts or as princes on white horses for whom one "saves" oneself, rather than as human beings with weaknesses and strengths, interests and pet peeves. Dictates Muzzey, girls should learn to see men not just as lovers but as friends and social intellectual companions, which is possible only through regular socializing and repeated occasions during which they can engage in conversation aimed at more than the merely superficial.[51]

Ah, but what of the dangers of such mixing? What of the dapper but hypocritical and scheming young men of loose morals to whom the young woman might become irrationally attached? What of fortune hunters, libertines, and men of little accomplishment and decidedly unsavory proclivities? The answers to these obvious questions were, to Real Womanhood writers, equally obvious: the young woman should associate on an extended social basis only with the "right sort" of man. Then, after months of "getting to know the character" of a variety of these right sorts, she should commence to choose her initial candidates for suitors. After another intense period of "discovery" (as the advice writers call it), she should select the one she intends to encourage. Finally, she can allow herself "to fall in love!" As social historian Esther

B. Aresty points out, the steps outlined above were common, and the initiative for courtship in America, in accordance with what advice writers suggest, frequently came from the young woman; moreover, young American women usually made the final decision about who they would marry: "Dislike for masculine authority—or perhaps the urge to assert their own—stirred in American women. As girls, they did not think it necessary to 'ask Pa' when they chose a mate (more often they consulted 'Ma'), though some etiquette authorities held out at least a perfunctory request for parental approval."[52]

This, of course, was the freedom M. Carlier found so appalling, but it does substantiate an important point: advocates of Real Womanhood felt that young American women, *if they took the proper precautions*, were fully capable of choosing decent husbands especially if they were vigorous in their initial selection of the right sort with whom to socialize more than once.

The crux of the matter—and the largest problem—was what constituted the right sort. As Karen Halttunen, a modern critic, suggests—and novels, short stories, and editorials of the period bear out—the hypocrite and the omnipresent "confidence man" were the monsters to be avoided. Unfortunately, their very nature made them hard to detect because they cleverly took on the coloration of parlor etiquette and social rules: "These archetypal parlor hypocrites, the confidence man and the painted woman, were masters of the false art of etiquette: their artificial manners were assumed merely to dazzle and deceive an ingenuous audience. Sentimental critics of middle-class culture feared that etiquette, like fashion, was poisoning American society with hypocrisy."[53]

Obviously, then, applying *only* the standards of social etiquette was not sufficient as a pragmatic means of avoiding the wrong sort of man. As Graves, among others, shows in the case of poor Anna Percival, manners and courtesies exhibited during the courtship period could hide a multitude of sins of the blackest hue. The demonic Fredrick Elton, who ruins Anna Percival's life, is a master of etiquette; in addition to being extremely handsome, he is also "singularly refined and elegant" in his manners, exhibiting "delicate courtesy and deferential respect" to every woman he meets, as well as showing himself to be an excellent conversationalist, who is "fluent and graceful" on a range of subjects.[54] These talents, however, masked a sadistic and alcoholic nature, which expressed itself after marriage in philandering, inebriation, and wife-beating.

How, then, could one discern a man's true character? Weaver, Muzzey, Arthur, Graves, and Chapin all suggest that etiquette rules are of some use, but the ultimate designation must come from a personal judgment made by the young woman upon first meeting the young man. The dynamics of prudence are somewhat complicated here and need a bit more explanation so as not to appear contradictory. Although young women were encouraged to mix frequently with young men, this did not mean that they should socialize indiscriminately. Prudence dictated that the young woman should thoughtfully select favorable conditions under which to increase the chances of meeting the right sort of young men. Obviously, the wrong sort, masquerading as the right sort, could worm his way into select social gatherings or get himself introduced into decent company. The writers advocating Real Womanhood do not suggest that a young woman could avoid meeting all men of dubious character; they state categorically that she probably will meet some but that her powers of discrimination, backed up by enough time to probe, talk, and evaluate, should spare her from such men's evil enchantments. It was part of the young woman's duty to separate the moral sheep from the immoral goats by her own observations and intellectual evaluations.

All this being said, the advice writers did feel that there were guidelines, which, if the young woman followed them, would in all but the most hypocritical and subtle cases guarantee that she would meet men who were suitable and predominantly the right sort.

FOUR

Courtship and the Winnowing Process

[We see] the male beings that have no Employment. We have them about us—walking nuisances—pestilential gas-bags—fetid air-bubbles, who burst and are gone.

—Reverend George S. Weaver, *Aims and Aids for Girls and Young Women*

The process of meeting the right sort of man and scrutinizing his character and tastes in the hope of discovering intellectual and spiritual compatibility was rigorous. Young women, Real Womanhood advice writers noted, should be prepared to discover that no one met their standards, though they could expect to find some who did. The "winnowing" of suitors, then, could lead a young woman toward a decision for a single life as well as for an engagement. Far from suggesting that the unsatisfied young woman lower her sights, writers advocating Real Womanhood demanded that she be true to her values and either eschew marriage altogether or marry a man whose character, tastes, and intellect she found compatible. The trick, of course, was to discover someone who *truly* was moral, intelligent, hardworking, and compatible rather than one who merely *appeared* to be all these things. This was the rationale behind the advice books' and the novelists' lists of courtship procedures and those procedures make a modern FBI background check look positively haphazard.

In the initial phases of winnowing, etiquette rules played a useful role. Etiquette books clearly designated those men who were not the right sort and who, for reasons writers expounded bluntly, should not be dealt with socially even on a superficial basis. According to both etiquette books and advice books, young women should avoid the company of the "non-gentleman," the uneducated, the tasteless, gamblers, racy young men with well-known reputations for dissipation and "fast" living, non-Americans (especially Europeans with titles or claims to one), and those of obvious social, financial, or religious difference from the young woman (such as avowed atheists, acknowledged Catholics, or Jews).

The advice writers clearly stated the reasons for their objections to each of these types of men, and they smack much more of common sense than of arbitrary propriety. Drinkers, as Holmes in her novel *Mead-*

owbrook shows vividly through the character of "Herbert the Drunkard" (the heroine's brother-in-law), at best are improvident and throw their families into perpetual penury; as Graves, Hentz, Arthur, and Muzzey show, they are just as often brutal and vicious when drinking, beating both wives and children. Gamblers, for many of the same reasons, are an obviously bad choice as well—their vicious habits not only strip the family of income and reduce it to a shameful, pawnshop haunting poverty, but gambling is frequently allied with drinking and with associates in dissipation. Both dissipaters and gamblers, through their association with "low" people, can carry disease and spread it through the family— as poor Amelia Dorrington shows in Graves's book—or use the money meant for the family to support their mistresses. And as Muzzey and Arthur both point out, it is a tragic mistake for a woman to assume that she can "reform" such a suitor—though this is one of the True Womanhood myths. According to Muzzey, there are no "fifth act repentances" in real life: once a man is married, the superficial mask of reform slips off and the monstrous face of truth emerges. A woman who marries such a man runs terrible risks: she risks "her personal happiness, from his vicious conduct;" and, rather than her reforming him, he may, by example, by insistence, by habit, or by force, corrupt her. Her reputation—and that of her children, through her—may suffer and be lost. The risks in taking on an obviously dissipated man make Muzzey question the nonthinking and sentimental role-playing that lead the young woman to make such a decision. He asks, incredulously, "Will she calmly commit herself to the talons of the vulture, in hopes of taming his ferocity, and changing entirely his habits? The experiment is one which no woman of ordinary prudence will try." A young woman, he reminds us, is bound, as a Christian, "to love others as herself, if you please, even as much as herself; but not more."[1]

This startling rejection of the "save the sinner" tradition is more than supported by women's domestic fiction. Despite male critics' observations of the last fifty years, female critics like Baym point out that domestic fiction was hardly "sentimental," though it was "pious." The piety, however, was a matter more of internal values and general "elevated tone" on the part of the heroine than of external observance. As Baym states, and I will show with a review of selected novels, domestic fiction hardly excluded the Real Woman's experience with men who were coarse, brutal, and degraded. Furthermore, domestic authors refused to pretty up these qualities or present them in anything but the most censorious colors. Alcoholism, gambling, and philandering were certainly aspects of male behavior which domestic writers deplored, but they felt under no compulsion to sacrifice the heroine's life to "save" the ostensible antihero. Sentimental emotion for the drunken charmer; tearful forgiveness for the wife-beating husband now remorseful; loss of independence to bring a sinner back to the light: none of these, according to Baym, was admirable. Emotions of this sort placed a woman at the mercy of a worthless man and often proved to be a trap for her. The woman who immolated herself to save a man from himself was part of a different literary tradition—an English one, which many American women after 1820 despised, Richardsonian fiction with its pious, passive, and essentially victimized women. American women authors consciously rejected that genre of fiction and evolved their own national type in which the heroine's "trials and triumphs" were chronicled and her hardships described in loving detail. There was, however, an important difference. The American heroine, through her "intelligence, will, resourcefulness, and courage," overcame all obstacles and triumphed, becoming finally a full-grown adult of dignity, self-reliance, and affection, whom men respected and loved for herself, rather than for either her sacrifices or her body.[2]

As Esther B. Aresty noted much earlier, "Women were spun into their different molds on either side of the Atlantic." Aresty sees this process as dominated by males, but I would argue that it was, in fact, the product of determined efforts, primarily by American women themselves, especially by domestic novelists and female advice writers. American women writers rejected a model they found both unnatural and degrading and introduced one they felt was more nationally appropriate—one filled with traditional American virtues of self-reliance, common sense, control, individual dignity, and moral character. The American ideal woman did not allow Richardsonian arguments geared to play on her pity to dissuade her from her plans for self-support or to lure her into unworkable and disastrous alliances because a man threatened to kill himself or drink himself to death if she refused him. Despite Diana Reep's insistence that some of popular fiction's conventional plots required that the heroine rescue a male and bring him "to active Christianity, away from his evil ways," this scenario seldom appears in the most popular novels of the midcentury. At most, males who are reprobates go off somewhere far away (or the heroine goes off somewhere and leaves them) and "straighten themselves out" before appearing before the heroine again to try their suit. Such is the case of the demonic and nosebleeding Robert in Hentz's *Linda* and the swearing, atheistic St. Elmo in Evans's novel of the same name. Reep cites *St. Elmo* as an example of the female "rescue" by conversion but fails to note that Edna turns the villain down flatly and leaves him to do with his life what he will. That he eventually becomes a minister is entirely his own doing, not hers.[3]

Weaver takes a firm stand in his injunctions to young women to avoid obvious dissipaters, drinkers, and gamblers and, to some degree, blames them for the number of such men "in society." Young American women, he claims, "allow" men to display vicious conduct around them—or acknowledge that they have a reputation for it—and still see such men socially! Worse, claims Weaver, they allow these men to make advances. Weaver is appalled: "I am sorry to say it, but young women rebuke but very little the evil doings of their male associates. They chide not the waywardness of young men as they ought. They smile upon them in their villainy. They court the society of young men they have every reason to believe are corrupt." Not only should young women discourage the first hints of such incipient conduct in the otherwise good men with whom they associate, Weaver suggests, but they should "not know" (i.e., cut) confirmed dissipaters socially and cease inviting them to social gatherings if they have knowledge even of any "private" viciousness, however fastidious the men's outward manners may be. Furthermore, Weaver states, somewhat surprisingly given the date (1856), women should *"demand"* that "the same standard of morality and propriety" be used to judge and weigh men that men currently applied to women.[4]

Examples—both cautionary and uplifting—abound in fiction of the period in support of all contentions I made earlier. Holmes's Herbert the Drunkard reduces Rosa's sister to a miserable, poverty-stricken existence and, despite his "good heart," continues to drink, breaking repeated promises to his wife, Anna, that he will quit. Eventually Anna is so worn out with work and worry that she dies herself after Herbert's spectacular death in delerium tremens.[5]

Certain male writers also reject females' selfless sacrifice to save another, if only by painting appalling pictures of women who have. Arthur, in his story "Taking Boarders," focuses on the sin of gambling and points out the father of the family, Mr. Darlington, whom his wife has devoted her life to "saving." Though a successful lawyer with an inherited fortune, he ruins the family through speculation and common gambling. His fortunes (and his family) in peril, he falls prey to "inflammation and congestion of the brain" and dies, leaving behind his wife and five children, who, in abject poverty, must take in boarders.[6]

In the story "New Year's Gift" in the same collection, Arthur presents a formerly honest and hardworking farmer, Foster, reduced to working as an itinerant laborer because of drink; what money he makes, he drinks up. Nor can he be trusted to watch the children while his wife is out returning the huge bundles of sewing or laundry she has done to support the family. Left alone with the children, Foster goes to sleep in a drunken stupor and drops the baby: "The infant rolled upon the floor, striking its head first. It awoke and screamed for a minute or two, and then sank into a heavy slumber, and did not wake until the next morning. . . . In a week it died of brain fever, occasioned, the doctor said, by the fall."[7]

The drinker, the gambler, and the philanderer are easy targets for criticism and immediate exclusion. The next broad classification is somewhat harder both to identify and, once identified, to justify excluding, given the theoretical egalitarian and democratic ethos of the country. This group might be called simply the "inappropriate" and includes nongentlemen, those who are extremely different from the young woman in social status, family background, or wealth, and those who are unrefined, uneducated, and "tasteless." They should be excluded, Real Womanhood writers suggest, not for reasons of short-term propriety and snobbery so much as long-range practicality. "Nongentlemen" such as dock workers, migrant laborers, teamsters, saloon keepers, bartenders, and the like will not, Abell, Weaver, Muzzey, and other writers suggest, share the same values as the middle-class or well-educated young woman or hold the same things dear, find enjoyment in similar recreational or social pursuits, or agree about the way children should be reared. Social, aesthetic, and intellectual good sense militate against such unnatural alliances. One must assume that by now young women have a reasonably clear idea of what constitutes a "gentlemen"; class (i.e., middle class) is obviously one index, as I will show further on, but a variety of other criteria are applied to determine this classification. Class was not the sole criterion upon which men were judged as gentlemen or nongentlemen; moral values, education, or industriousness could either elevate a man into the category of gentleman or their lack demote him from this category even though his manners and social class initially placed him there.

Men who were uneducated, the advice writers advocating Real Womanhood explained, were incapable of sharing the interests and avocations of educated women—and such writers demanded that women be educated. Weaver insists that a marriage partner must be a "congenial spirit," one who will react, feel, and believe much as the young woman does in any given circumstances because he has the same "modes of thought and feeling." Weaver suggests that this congeniality in part rests on having similar opinions about controversial aspects of important subjects. The young man's opinions should be formed using the same information, a similar rational cast of mind, and a near-identical taste and sensibility as the young woman, not simply to be agreeable. Politics, archaeology, scriptural exegesis, literature, music, economics, and "science" are all subjects that can provide the basis for discussion. As Weaver points out, intellect is both our moral and rational guide, and its enjoyments "constitute a great portion of the real pleasure of life."[8] Therefore, to marry an uneducated man is not only to exist in a permanent state of emotional and intellectual isolation but to risk losing or obscuring the correct moral path of life as well. If ideally marriage is meant to provide the most profound companionship of mind and spirit as well as body, then marriage between people of dissimilar and unequal intellects perverts the purpose of the institution.

The reverse—an educated husband with an uneducated wife—is graphically illustrated in Harriet Beecher Stowe's *Pink and White Tyranny* and, interestingly, the less common version I have just mentioned, the uneducated husband in Holmes's *Rose Mather* in the case of Annie Graham. In the latter novel, Annie's husband, George, is a decent, spiritually upright individual, but his lack of education and his disinterest in music, literature, and art both distress Annie and reduce her life to an intellectual and aesthetic ghetto. Holmes dispatches good-hearted but uneducated George early in the novel by killing him in an early Civil War battle, thus leaving Annie free to marry her real love, educated, middle-class, and sensitive Jimmie Carleton. *Rose Mather*'s Annie is something of an anomaly among heroines of Real Womanhood writers; usually the heroines do not marry men who are their intellectual inferiors. Evans's Edna Earl pushes aside lawyer Gordon Leigh, who, even though he is "educated," cannot begin to compete with her in intellect and erudition; Holmes's Rose Lee in *Meadowbrook* and 'Lena in *'Lena Rivers* marry young men who match them in both refinement and intellect; Hentz's Linda Walton avoids Robert Graham initially and marries Roland Lee, who, though a riverboat pilot and not a planter, is as sensitive, intelligent, and industrious as she.

Sensitivity and tact as well as "gentle" personal habits are almost as important as education in determining whether a young man is appropriate. As Muzzey points out coldly, a man who is "coarse" and lacks "acute perception and deep sensitivity," a man who has no sense of a woman's feelings, becomes a constant irritant and a distress. He will soon become a "burden" because his every public appearance as her husband will be "nerve-wracking" as she scrambles to keep him from expressing stupid or vulgar opinions in conversation or watches with a baleful eye to prevent him from spitting tobacco juice on the floor, belching at the table, dribbling gravy on the tablecloth, or picking his teeth in the parlor. Obviously, a woman who marries a vulgarian spends a lifetime struggling to avoid—or, more likely, experiencing—abject social humiliation and private disgust.[9] The Real Womanhood writers' injunctions against admitting a suitor of markedly different social or financial background indicate that they feel the chances were high that such a man would spit on the floor or crack smutty jokes in mixed company.

Although the bulk of these writers' warnings seem to suggest that marriages between educated middle-class women and uneducated working-class men were the biggest dangers, they do not neglect the problems that accrue from educated middle-class women marrying "up." Rosa Lee in *Meadowbrook* faces snobbery and cruel remarks from Richard Delafield's sister because the former had been the latter's governess; Rosa overcomes these obstacles but only because Richard has intellectual sympathies and sensitivities that match her own. In the novel it is clear that Rosa is a superior, even an extraordinary, young woman; Rosa's happy ending is not as commonplace as the misery between Dell Thompson and Dr. Clayton. Another case, though an extreme one, is Southworth's Nora Worth and her secret marriage to Herman Brudenell. If a middle-class marriage "up" is uncomfortable, then one involving a working-class woman who aspires to be a "lady" of wealth and position is tragic. There is a discernible bias among advice writers advocating Real Womanhood in favor of the middle class. Frequently, in both novels and advice books, the "upper classes" of money and position are rotten with vice and morally weak; because they have money, the suitors tend to be idle and profligate, weak in character, and subject to dissipation and corruption because of boredom. Herbert the Drunkard in *Meadowbrook* is a splendid example; the mark of demonic inclination, in addition to his love of the bottle, is, according to Holmes, his Episcopalian heritage. The same is true of vicious (but sexually attractive) St. Elmo: with enough money to buy anything he wishes and the leisure to pursue every bestial desire known to man, Evans's antihero is another in a long line of violent, alcoholic, even satanic upper-class suitors in domestic novels. Edna Earl, stalwart intellectual, moral propagandist, and middle-class authoress, has no time for him until he chooses a "career" of philanthropy and good works, quits drinking, and finds God again, after having given the bulk of his money to charity. Southworth's Herman Brudenell, Holmes's Colonel Atherton (the old roué in *'Lena Rivers*), and Hentz's sadistic Robert Graham all represent both the false lure of wealth and the dangers of marrying "above" the middle class unless the young woman is absolutely sure of the intrinsically industrious, sensitive, educated, and refined character of her suitor.

The other category of unsuitable suitor is the non-American. As Esther B. Aresty notes, most etiquette authors were vociferously nationalistic in both their attitudes and their warnings: "For the most part they struck off in their own independent American direction and urged their countrymen to have the courage of their own manners."[10]

Muzzey, Weaver, and especially T. S. Arthur and Dio Lewis sneered at the European dandy with his ancient titles and his illustrious "house," suggesting that, like his upper-class counterpart in America, ancient lineage frequently meant a family tree consumed with moral dry rot. Muzzey attacks the "current" worship of the European suitor with a glittering coronet and the ability to make his American fiancée "Lady Somebody," finding the fad rank-conscious and out of keeping with American principles; it will also lead to tragedy because the dazzle of a noble name may blind both the girl and her parents to defects in the suitor's moral nature.[11]

Other authors join Muzzey in casting a suspicious eye on European or English men—titled or otherwise—and note that American men have a reputation the world over for their superior treatment of women. European men, such authors suggest, do not understand American women's desire for education, autonomy in decisions regarding housekeeping and family, or their degree of independence, preferring to treat them as brainless dolls or decorative ornaments. Warns Weaver sternly, women who marry such men advertise their own low opinion of themselves and therefore can expect a correspondingly low estimation at the hands of a non-American husband or an Anglophilic or Europhilic American one: "They [young women] must soon know that if in Girlhood they regard themselves as playthings and pets, in womanhood they will have to be drudges or the cast-off dolls of their boyish husbands, or the hangers-on to a society they would but cannot be a part of."[12]

In predominantly Protestant America, the European suitor (especially French, Italian, or East European) brought another possible problem: religious differences. A host of advice writers agree that major difference on points of doctrine and belief lead inexorably toward misery in marriage. Weaver, for example, points out sensibly that religion must be a subject upon which there is harmonious agreement, not only because specific beliefs frequently dictate both personal action and future family policy but because very few people are without strong feelings on the subject and will argue acrimoniously over differences. "Everybody of any worth has religious opinions and biases," he notes, suggesting that those who do not lack a moral basis. Indeed, characters like Evans's Edna Earl, Harland's Frank Berry in *Ruby's Husband,* and Ellen Montgomery in Warner's *Wide, Wide World* spend much time in the novels arguing about religious issues. Muzzey is specific about the extent of difference that may exist and still allow a marriage to survive as a companionable, as well as a spiritual, union. A young woman and her future husband may not be of the same Christian denomination, he suggests, but each should be able to respect and honor the other's "personal piety." This is possible only, he continues, if the two agree on "the main doctrines of religion." Again, whether such agreement is possible can be found out only by a "full and frank expression of opinion on points of faith and conscience, before marriage as well as after." Not to do so clearly and honestly before making a matrimonial commitment is to doom the marriage, Muzzey feels.[13]

Chapin, Abell, Burnap, and other writers inevitably stress the importance of religious agreement between partners, as well as the need for piety in a suitor. Clearly, religious differences are not to be taken lightly.

An obvious case of blatant religious differences—a Catholic, a Jewish, or an atheistic suitor—should, even on first meeting, warn the young woman away. Not only, these writers suggest, do religious differences lead to wrathful or distressing discussions, but they may well affect the way the children are reared and the practice of household and family routines such as compulsory sabbath school, infant (or adult) baptism, or the absence or presence of birth control.[14] Differences of opinion in any of these areas can be the source of bitter arguments and lifelong misery.

To the practical-minded Real Womanhood advice writers, gamblers, drinkers, dissipaters, nongentlemen, either very wealthy or poverty-stricken suitors, the uneducated and the tasteless, the non-Protestant and non-Christian, and the European would be less likely to be encountered if a young woman was selective about the activities she participated in or the social spas she frequented. A measure of control over circumstances of meeting brought prudent rewards. There were certain environments in which inappropriate men tended not to be present, though no social control was absolute nor were all situations foolproof, no matter how carefully chosen. Still, the odds were that appropriate men would grace certain occasions in specific locations. Church and church functions such as "sociables," picnics, choir practice, box socials, and community dances were generally considered by most advice writers to be safe from gamblers and dissipaters as well as non-Protestant Christians. Advice writers also seemed to suggest that those of markedly different financial status were attracted to different churches, the wealthy attending the larger and "tonier" cathedrals or churches and going to "socialite" activities, while the abject and poverty-stricken either worked on Sunday or went to the crude entertainments and cruder services of evangelical churches.

Again, domestic fiction supports this vision. In Susan Warner's *Wide, Wide World,* the pious heroine, Ellen Montgomery, must deal with her wealthy relatives in Scotland once she is sent there from America. Not only are they wealthy, Ellen (and the aghast reader) discovers, but they are severely lacking in religious fervor, undoubtedly because they attend the "social" Anglican church. It is a matter of some importance in the novel because the impious Keiths attempt, influenced by their faulty religious upbringing, to force Ellen into vicious irreligious practices. They try to keep her from going to church; they refuse to let her pray alone in the mornings; and finally, they literally force her to drink wine, as Warner notes in gothic tones: "The glass of wine looked to Ellen like an army marching to attack her. Because Alice and John [her American friends and pious mentors] did not drink it, she had always, at first without reason, done the same; and she was determined not to forsake their example now." Despite her demurs that she is unaccustomed to spirits, her uncle fiendishly insists: " 'It is of no consequence what you have been accustomed to,' said Mr. Lindsay, 'You are to drink it all, Ellen.' " Ellen obeys and then is sick—a literary device that demonstrates not only her delicate stomach but her outraged moral sensitivities as well. Fortunately for Ellen, the Lindsays have no suitor to foist on her at this point. Before an eligible Anglican wine-drinker can appear, John Humphreys arrives from America to rescue her. The point is clear that upper-class males who attend fashionable churches are often extraordinarily lax in both morality and proper behavior—and probably drink as well. Obviously the right men would also be detectable by their regular attendance at "normal" churches and their lack of participation in the racier activities regularly competing with those church socials.[15]

Fathers and brothers, like the church, could usually be relied upon to provide suitable men, either by asking a new clerk or a junior partner to dinner or by friends brought home from college. Under the careful eye of male relatives, dissipaters, idlers, drinkers, and gamblers hardly stood a chance. As Abell notes, the "mind, temper, habits, and principles" of the suitor were reasonably well known by such relatives, and the suitor's background was accessible to scrutiny. If a young man went to school with one's brother (and had a good reputation) or worked for one's father, there was every assurance that by social, intellectual, and financial measurements he was generally appropriate. There were, of course, cases when the father, blinded by the lure of wealth, attempted to arrange a match for his daughter with someone rich but inappropriate, such as a widowed senior partner or associate. Sometimes a "fast" brother brought home an even "faster" friend. In such cases, the young woman had her learning, her powers of reasoning, and her checklist of virtues to fall back on. The advice writers stressed that despite familial sponsorship of the fellow, the determination of suitability lay entirely with the young woman. Muzzey especially sternly orders young women to ignore parental pressure to marry for money and bluntly gives a name to such proceedings—prostitution.[16]

Muzzey would not have a young woman completely disregard parental advice (and he feels that ignoring parental advice is probably a bigger problem nationally than following it), but he does state categorically that the daughter should firmly resist parental pressure if the suitor is obviously inappropriate. He would, he claims, rather see an elopement than the young woman's capitulation to marriage with a man she neither respects nor likes with the inevitable misery such a marriage would entail for the rest of her life: "I would rather a young lady should be guilty of this impudence [elopement], if she sincerely love her companion, than that she marry one she does not love, nor can hope ever to love, for the sake of gratifying any individual in the world." Nor is he alone in his insistence on the young woman's intellectual determination as the final word on the appropriateness of a suitor. Weaver especially feels that the young woman's heightened judgment of a young man, based on intense scrutiny and conversation with him over a period of time, is her sole means of assuring herself of a decent life. As he curtly informs his female readers, courtship and marriage choice are *not* matters of chance or luck for a wise young woman; they are matters of sound judgment. He tells the young woman to "be sure you are right" and to be able to list the reasons for her decision: "There is to be no guess-work about it—no wish-work or hope-work about it. It is knowledge-work."[17]

Real Womanhood writers of fiction seem to highlight marriages which unscrupulous fathers or weak uncles have tried to force young women into (Anna Livingston in *'Lena Rivers* and Linda in *Linda* leap to mind). Nevertheless, there are also instances in fiction of young women meeting decent, upstanding, and lovable mates through the efforts of male relatives. Holmes's Rose Mather meets her husband, Will, because he is a friend of her brother Tom; Holmes's other heroine, 'Lena, has a fiancé, Durward Bellmont, who is a friend of her cousin John, Jr. In both cases the young men are sensitive, honest, intelligent, moral, and companionable; neither drinks, gambles, philanders, or curses; both value the heroines for their character as well as their beauty, though in the case of Rose Mather and Will, this character and beauty are discovered later.

In one of Graves's more uplifting exempla, the father's contacts and associates provide a suitable match. In "Sarah Sherman, or the Mechanic's Daughter," the election of Sarah's father to the state legislature provides a way for Sarah both to use her education from Mrs. Norville's

THE OLD STORY—"I sold myself to a loveless thing."

Harper's Weekly, December 1, 1866

school and to leave a home in which her mother insists that she do nothing but keep house. In the state capitol, Sarah serves as her father' official "hostess," and her "mild intellectual beauty" and "quiet dignity and refinement of her manners" make her an immediate favorite. While serving in this capacity, Sarah meets Charles Glentworth, a young law yer and associate of her father's; they come to know each other well and Sarah's father approves of Glentworth's character because he has a good reputation in the capitol; he is "universally spoken of as a young man of high promise and extensive acquirements." More to the point Sarah calls him her "dear friend," having discovered their mutual tastes intellectual interests, and shared opinions and enthusiasms.[18] Her deci sion to marry him is entirely her own, but her father's job and his initia scrutiny of Charles's background fulfill the advice writers' suggestec goals for male relatives: to produce eligible suitors, after eliminating those who are inappropriate because of a hidden reputation for viciou: habits or intemperate character.

Another environment in which the advice writers suggest a young woman could probably expect to meet suitable men like Charles Glent worth is through proper introductions at the homes of reputable friends As social historian Karen Halttunen explains, because of the pervasive fear of parlor hypocrites and confidence men, certain "laws of acquain tanceship" prevailed in middle-class society with an eye to avoiding in troductions to such men. Married hostesses had a special responsibility to scrutinize their guest lists, eliminating anyone of dubious or even slightly racy reputation.[19] Proper introduction of a young male guest to a young female guest implied that the host and hostess confirmed hi: suitability. The most dedicated hostess could not absolutely guarc against inviting someone of secret vices and a privately vicious char acter, however, and the young woman, again, was expected to use her good judgment to ascertain suitability. The hostess, however, was ex pected to winnow the crop to the best of her ability. The young woman then, was expected to examine the resultant grain with a careful eye choosing the best and eliminating any chaff that inadvertently go through. Obviously, this logic presupposes that the young woman': friends were appropriate themselves and that they had both the ability and the conscientiousness to prune a guest list of undesirables.

Neither assumption was always safe, as both domestic fiction anc some of the advice literature show us. Graves's book, for example, tell:

of Anna Percival, who meets the man who eventually drives her mad through mutual friends. Obviously having chosen Fredrick as a friend, these people were neither appropriate themselves nor were they conscientious. Graves, however, ignores their culpability and puts the blame for the fatal marriage on the shoulders of Anna and her mother; the mother should have provided wise counsel to offset Anna's romantic and unreflective infatuation when it first appeared, and Anna should have used better intellectual scrutiny and judgment. Such failures by friends to eliminate unworthy young men are perhaps behind Weaver's and Muzzey's strong recommendations that a young woman rely only initially on the "opinion of friends" or the "common report" of "fashionable acquaintances" in judging the character of suitors.[20] A young woman, then, should develop judgment, reasoning skills, and perception not only for ultimately choosing or eliminating suitors but for choosing her friends as well and, through them, proper men.

Having chosen a suitable environment in which to socialize and become acquainted with the right sort of men, the ideal young woman was ready to enter the second stage: determining suitability. The vast majority of men one met in the proper environment could be assumed to be suitable in general. Now it was the young woman's job to eliminate those who, for a variety of reasons given by Real Womanhood writers, would not "work out" for purely practical reasons. One of these reasons was a difference in age. Neither Muzzey nor Weaver (the two writers most explicit on the subject) suggests that the age difference is a problem only if the woman is older; rather, they suggest that any marked difference in age between husband and wife in either direction inevitably results in a chasm between the two emotionally and intellectually. Their ages, insists Muzzey, "should be somewhat near each other. How else can there be true sympathy between them?"[21] These writers' disquietude arises partly on purely practical grounds; how can there be common interests, tastes, and opinions if one partner is twenty-one and the other sixty-five? How can such a couple maintain common friends when one spouse wants to go to a concert, continue on to a theater party, and finish with a midnight supper, and the other spouse has to be in bed by ten o'clock or he becomes ill or cranky? Even assuming that, despite a major age disparity, both individuals have similar tastes and enjoy similar pursuits, will both be able to participate in parenthood with equal physical dedication? Will both enjoy good health? Will both be prepared for the inevitable secret sneers and eyebrow-raisings of those who assume the younger partner is a fortune hunter or an adventuress?

The domestic novels and the exempla in advice books are replete with negative examples of December–May unions, which bear every indication of being either bad or disastrous marriages of convenience or marriages made with an eye to financial gain. As we recall, Graves's cold-hearted Elizabeth Harrington ends her life running a boardinghouse, barely surviving, after marrying old Mr. Horton, a friend of her father's. Holmes's silly and passive Anna Livingston in 'Lena Rivers is prevented from marrying the ancient rip, Captain Atherton, only because 'Lena is strong enough and moral enough to save her from such a fate. Anna's motive—or rather her mother's because Anna is too passive even to have motives—is clearly fortune-hunting.[22] The evil Lillie in Stowe's *Pink and White Tyranny* marries middle-aged John to secure enough income to continue to buy fashionable clothes and French furniture and to have a carriage. She dies, denying her motherhood and, finally, admitting her guilt in marrying an older man for money.

In all these cases, the difference in age is extremely marked; in other cases, some difference in age is no barrier to true love. Frequently in Holmes's novels, for example, the man the heroine finally marries is as much as ten years older than his bride. Examples are Rose and Richard in *Meadowbrook*, 'Lena and Durward Bellmont in 'Lena Rivers, and the feckless Anna and her "true love" Malcolm Everette in the same novel. Holmes's other heroine, Rose Mather, is some ten years younger than her husband, Will, though Annie Graham is only five years younger than Rose's brother Jimmie in *Rose Mather*. Even Evans's indomitable Edna Earl in *St. Elmo* refuses the offers of marriage from publisher Douglas Manning, citing, among other reasons, the great age difference between them—and then marries St. Elmo, who is her senior by some twenty years.

Age differences brought other practical disadvantages to the minds of advice writers. There could be a great difference in the health and physical vitality of the pair. A young woman whose life became tied to that of a much older man might find herself functioning more as an unpaid nurse than as a cherished companion. Muzzey calls good health a concern "of no ordinary moment" and suggests that young women who are planning to marry invalids—either old or young—think twice. Even if the suitor is of an age with the young woman, even if he has a fine mind, a cultivated sensibility, a generous nature, and a spiritual outlook on life, if he is an invalid or suffering from an incurable disease, the marriage is doomed and ridiculous to contemplate for practical reasons. Notes Muzzey, "She can hardly be justified, who allies herself to one evidently incapable, for his physical debility, of sustaining a family. . . . There are other offices, besides that of the nurse, demanded of a wife, and the cases should be rare, in which all other considerations are merged in this." Such a man cannot be expected to support a family or do his conjugal duty with adequate energy. Muzzey's scorn is limitless for those romantically minded young women who insist on "sacrificing" themselves for invalided husbands, those who did not become invalids through an evil turn of fate but were invalids at the time of courtship. Both Muzzey and Weaver suggest that as young women are going through the initial process of determining suitability, they should find out, either through friends or relatives, whether apparently healthy men have family histories of hereditary disease, insanity, criminality, or senility. Not only should she avoid such "carriers" for her own sake, to avoid a life of drudgery or shame should these problems become manifest, but not to curse her future children with "bad blood." Indeed, men carrying hereditary taints, if they are true Christians, should not expect a young woman to marry them.[23]

Some men, however, are not as forthright as they should be. As Graves's mercenary Elizabeth Harrington explains bitterly, "I knew that Mr. Horton's health was enfeebled, but after my marriage, I found that he was the victim of a painful malady, which often prevented him from moving from one room to another without the assistance of a servant—and rendered him helpless as an infant. He became an object of detestation to me, which in my pride I concealed from others; but took little pains to hide from himself."[24] The picture of Elizabeth's situation is as graphic as it is realistic. She is tied to an enfeebled, dependent man, who before her horrified eyes turns "old and imbecile" and becomes a burden and a drain on her. Certainly, in the ways of exempla literature, it is a just punishment for the mercenariness and greed she exhibits in marrying him in the first place, but it is also a realistic picture of the long-term results of such an alliance.

With the exception of "hidden" diseases, such obvious criteria as age and health can be easily observed by young women. Other indications of suitability, however, are not so visible, and here a young woman must depend on male relatives, trusted friends, or the family lawyer or doctor. What is the suitor's reputation in the community for financial probity? Have his business dealings been above board and free of "sharp" practices that suggest a lack of moral principles? Is he deeply in debt? What is his habit of work? Most important, does he have a reputation for moral stalwartness or has he a mistress hidden away in another city or a path behind him of broken hearts and seduced girls? Finally, is the suitor truly "free" to "press his suit"? What are the possibilities that a fiancée—or worse, a wife—already exists?

It would be a mistake to regard such questions as merely salacious prying or morally intolerant. As Burnap, Weaver, Muzzey, Chapin, Hale, and others explain, if any of the questions listed above elicit disquieting answers, a young woman should avoid the suitor because involvement with him will lead to practical and emotional disaster. To understand both the practical reasons behind such scrutiny of a man's reputation and the awesome weight of reputation in the public mind, it is first necessary to acknowledge its very real usefulness.

According to Halttunen, the mid-Victorian period experienced a "crisis in social relations." Between 1820 and 1860, for example, America experienced a breathtakingly rapid rate of urban growth. The population of city dwellers rose by 797 percent as opposed to the national population increase of 226 percent.[25] The movement of people to cities, as well as an increasing rate of mobility, made the ability to check someone's background exponentially harder and harder. Suitors were more and more likely to be from somewhere else and to have obscure family and work backgrounds. The only real clue to their character was their reputation, especially in regard to work and among immediate acquaintances. Obviously, if fathers, brothers, and family lawyers could locate someone who knew the young man's family or had relatives in the town from which he came, such leads should be followed up. As this became impossible, immediate background must be the subject of investigation. The young man's acquaintances, his haunts and recreations, his work history, his employer's evaluation, and his record for probity among those who knew him even slightly had to suffice in initially evaluating him as a suitable future marriage partner.

The advice books stress and novels show in detail the need for young women to investigate the suitor's character themselves through serious conversation and observation, which must ultimately suffice as the basis for judgment. Advice books, short stories, and domestic novels draw grim pictures of the result of a young woman's failure to have inquiries made concerning reputation or ignoring family reports. Southworth's Nora Worth in *Ishmael* could have saved herself humiliation and heartbreak had her sister inquired about Herman Brudenell's marital status; conversely, Arthur's Miriam Darlington would have been ruined in a bigamous marriage with the amoral Mr. Burton had not her uncle thought to check around town and discovered that he already had a wife. Evans's intrepid heroine Edna Earl uses both her own powers of observation and the reports of those who have known St. Elmo to guide her away from a disastrous choice. Evans explains that the Murrays' black servant woman Hagar warns Edna about St. Elmo; Hagar's words would be more than disquieting to any woman with an ounce of sense: "If he finds you in his way, he will walk roughshod right over you— trample you. Nothing ever stops him one minute when he makes up his mind. He does not even wait to listen to his mother, and she is about the only person who dares to talk to him. He hates everybody and everything. . . . God knows I wish he had died when he was a baby instead of growing up the sinful, swearing, raging devil he is."[26] Edna's faith in Hagar's observations is only heightened when she sees St. Elmo beating his wolfhound until the dog's eye is almost put out and later learns of two of his previous girlfriends, one of whom bled to death on the church steps, jilted and waiting for him. Not surprisingly, Edna is not anxious to marry him. She accepts him years later only after she finds out through the common report of his sterling, charitable reputation and his new position as a minister—not because he tells her.

After all the foregoing precautions have been exercised and there is spread before the young woman a vista of several eligible young men, men neither too old nor too sick, men of upstanding local and social reputation, introduced by friends, given an imprimatur by family, and initially attractive to the young woman herself, she can begin the next crucial stage: courtship.

What the writers advocating Real Womanhood meant by "courting" was hardly what most modern readers have come to associate with that term. The latter vision, perhaps derived from 1890s valentines, of billing and cooing in the parlor, of extravagant flattery on one hand and coy archness on the other, of formal meetings in the presence of a watchful elder, does not match the seriousness or the texture of the assessment of each other that these writers suggest. This inaccurate pastoral portrait is, in fact, a facet of the True Womanhood ideal and one which the Real Womanhood writers despised. As Muzzey sneers, "All that is termed 'courting,' so far as that word implies assumption, pretense, and flattery,—and it too often means nothing more,—should be sacredly avoided." Weaver outlines the features of this unacceptable form of courting. He divides it into "stages" along the road to ultimate "conjugal infelicity . . . [the] earth's most firey [sic] hell." Stage one, the "meeting," he points out, occurs because both the young man and the young woman are attracted by the mere "plumes" of the bird. A tilt of the head, a handsome square chin, a blond lock of hair are the basis for the attraction, rather than an acute observation on current events, a well-played or well-sung piece of music, or intelligent conversation. The next event, Weaver suggests, is a meeting—or a series of meetings—in which "signs" and "tokens" of affection are exchanged so each can convince the other how enchanted and "captive" he or she is. Stage two, following hard on the heels of the exchange of tokens, is a period of fraudulence and artifice on both parts: "Every device is resorted to; smiles are profuse, deceits in standing, business, wealth, associates, character, dispositions, opinions, tastes, education, and almost everything else are now practiced; not with a view particularly to deceive, but to please." Stage three, says Weaver, is the moment of tragic *peripety* because after such a courtship "they know nothing of each other's *real* characters." After marriage, each learns things about the other's true nature that startles or disgusts him or her as "courtship character" fades away like the chimera it is. Revelation results in disappointment, sorrow, and regret and the knowledge that each must, for a very long lifetime, make the best of an unworkable situation "and *Bear it through*."[27]

A satirical wag, calling himself "The Doctor," referred in an article to this apocalyptic scene as a courtship made up of "three parts of the subcarbonate of cooing, dissolved in six parts of the oil of flattery." "The Doctor" goes on to give a tongue-in-cheek portrait of the false courtship which Weaver, Muzzey, Hale, and Arthur dislike so intensely. "The Doctor" refers to two classifications of the "sugar of courtship" and in his description gives a skewed but essentially accurate version of what the competing True Womanhood writers valued in a man's approach to the subject as evidence of "true devotion."[28]

The first category of courtship "The Doctor" classifies as "Poetical." To be an effective "poetical" lover, he cautions, one must wear a starched collar, roll one's eyes, and then in recipe fashion "hire thick volume of poems from the library, find verses on love, and commit to memory; curl hair, open eyes wide, and visit lady. Pull up collar, roll eye-balls, open mouth, and repeat verses; care should be taken to state that they are original; drop on right knee, seize hand, and inquire day. If lady says 'No,' faint vigorously, and repeat as before: if lady still obstinate, a pistol may be introduced with benefit: care should be taken that it is not loaded; bring down left knee and tear hair: if lady still declines, case desperate."[29]

Such ludicrous courtships occur regularly in domestic novels, though they are seldom effective and usually a cause for alarm in those written by Real Womanhood novelists. One remembers, for example, Hentz's heroine Linda and her horror at the disgusting Robert Graham, who, upon receiving for the third time Linda's point-blank refusal to marry him, immediately falls into a passion, has a spurting nosebleed, and threatens to shoot himself—and her. In Hentz's novel, this maniacal behavior confirms Linda's initial opinion that Robert Graham is totally unfit to be a suitor, much less a husband. Insanity, to a girl espousing Real Womanhood, is not an attractive proof of love. Edna Earl, though not faced with either a violent nosebleed or the threat of murder, is forced to endure St. Elmo's violent threat that he will go out and become a damned soul without her guidance, that he will steep himself in the stews of corruption and atheism even more than he already has. She, of course, rejects such specious arguments and points out that his soul is his own to look after and no concern of hers. The one heroine who does capitulate to hair-tearing and raving, Nora Worth in *Ishmael,* ends up a bigamous wife and a corpse over which her passionate "husband," Herman, continues to exhibit the same maniacal hair-tearing and sobbing that he used to lure her into marriage and that does her as much good as did his earlier protestations of "passionate" love. Obviously, this behavior does not exhibit the very important virtue of self-control, which advice writers of Real Womanhood unanimously consider absolutely necessary in a marriage. Emma Willard states that persons without self-control are *"infirm of purpose"* in the larger picture and unreliable. The spineless Herman Brudenell and the overly sanguine Robert Graham, who, despite threats to the contrary, never succeeds in "opening his veins," certainly fit this description.[30]

The satirical "Doctor" has another classification, if one does not choose to act like a lunatic, one that is more sensitive and less psycho-pathic: the "Sentimental Lover." This type, he explains, is "preferred by clerks and apprentices on the grounds of gentility: it is neat and power-ful." An aspirant to a sentimental courtship, "The Doctor" prescribes, should cut back on food, drink up to eighteen glasses of gin a day, and "persevere in this course of treatment until the patient [the suitor], if an adult, weighs seventy-two pounds; if under seventeen, sixty pounds; then chalk face and diet on green apples. If on third day no uneasiness in region of stomach, abandon apples and try cucumbers with skins on: continue till unwell; lay on wet grass till cough exhibits itself." "The Doctor" then suggests that the white-faced aspirant clean himself up and go courting, at which time he can talk about death and the moon and then can kneel before the lady, holding a handkerchief and coughing delicately as he switches to the "poetical" style.[31]

Following the strictures on the impracticality of allowing the ad-dresses of an invalid or one with hereditary disease, the young woman with Real Womanhood ideals would murmur a word of pity, put her own handkerchief over her nose, and exit immediately. Only in guide-books to True Womanhood do heroines delight in tending to suitors' physical infirmities or rushing to sacrifice themselves in an act of Night-ingalian "sutte" on the pyre of perpetual nursing. In both the poet-ical and the sentimental cases, "The Doctor's" satiric point is clearly in line with that of the Real Womanhood writers: such exhibitions are both fraudulent and manipulative at best; at worst they suggest a men-tal or physical imbalance which is undesirable in the *real* world in a future mate.

Part of the problem in establishing "true" courting may arise, suggests Muzzey, from a false idea of the degree of decorum one should main-tain. Far from accepting a rigid, conversation-restricting guidebook of "acceptable" and "unacceptable" public behaviors suggested by some etiquette authors, Muzzey feels that "where the heart is duly controlled, and the understanding cultivated, and fancy a servant, not a mistress of the soul, deportment will be spontaneously right, and commendable. Then all may be safely trusted to nature. The manners will be the ex-pression of gentleness, mingled with firmness."[32]

Obviously, a young woman surrounded by picket fences of rules about proper and improper subjects, proper and improper intimacies defined to a ridiculous degree, would find it very difficult to assess a suitor accurately. Rather than worrying about whether it is improper to accept a bouquet from a gentleman or borrow his book, Muzzey suggests the young lady abide by two very broad guidelines: she should avoid being either "forward" or "unduly reserved," and he defines both explicitly. Forwardness consists of making "advances of a character bold and obvious to a gentleman," of flirting in a "coquette" manner. Such behavior might include, according to advice writer Emily Thornwell, monopolizing the conversation or speaking in an excessively loud voice directly to a particular young man, as opposed to the company nearby. For Chapin, forwardness would include using "cant expressions" and "expletives," excessive "sarcasm," or expressing "prejudice" or "caricature." As he notes solemnly, tongues should not be "mere dissecting knives for cutting up of character." Another etiquette author, Florence Hartley, suggests that a young woman who indulges in deliberate double entendre or cuts into a conversation to attract a young man's attention will find her reputation endangered.[33]

The opposite behavior, which Muzzey suggests should be avoided, that of "undue reserve," seems once more a direct attack on the etiquette suggested for young women by the True Womanhood school. Thornwell especially castigates this "prudish reserve" and commands young women to avoid blushes, fluttering, and giggling, but rather to maintain a "dignified composure." She also suggests that maidenly decorum, which indulges in glancing modestly at the floor when addressed by a man, can be extremely counterproductive: "Always look people in the face when you speak, otherwise you will be thought conscious of some guilt; besides you lose the opportunity of reading their countenances, from which you will much better learn the impression which your discourse makes upon them."[34] She might have added that not being able to read their expressions also limited the young woman's ability to discover the intuitive and intellectual responses of her suitor— an important aspect of "true" courting.

The advice writers sternly prohibit fraudulent maidenly shyness and stiff decorum and portray it as unattractive. Dr. Dio Lewis, for example, paints a nauseating picture of a grown woman who, in the effort to appear modest and innocent, acts as though she were five years old and talks in baby talk, if she talks at all. Lewis warns that men of sense and sensibility shiver at and avoid such grotesques.[35]

Mary Jane Holmes has no time for such women in her novels.

Holmes's heroines tend to be "candid" and to look all conversational partners in the eye when speaking. The women in Holmes's books who practice false modesty tend either to be passive foils to the heroines or villainesses who use such wiles to lure weak and somewhat dense men into their matrimonial lairs. In *Meadowbrook,* for example, villainous Ada Montrose practices maidenly reserve and subtle clinging in her attempt to steal Herbert away from Anna. Ada, we know almost immediately, is a characterless vampire: she has "about her an air of languor, as if she had just arisen from a sick bed," and she lies about her age, telling everyone she is seventeen when actually she is twenty-two. As we know from the earlier chapter on physical fitness, the Real Womanhood girl was a healthy, hearty specimen with superb muscle tone and a brisk air about her; she was also someone who could conceive of no sensible reason for pretending to be seventeen. This evil portrait is further fleshed out when Holmes tells the reader that Ada is in the habit of "affecting a great deal of childish simplicity." Ada blushes, looks at the floor demurely, peeps at Herbert from under long lashes, and generally spins her web of intrigue. Unfortunately for Rosa's sister, Anna, even thick-witted Herbert "sees through" Ada Montrose finally and returns to his "true love," Anna, whom he proceeds to reduce to poverty and despair because of his alcoholism. Before sliding down the devil's road, however, Herbert denounces Ada Montrose, explaining, " 'As soon as I was engaged to Ada, she began to exact so much attention from me, acting so *silly,* and appearing so ridiculous that I got sick of it, and now my daily study is how to rid myself of her.' " He continues to state his intense dissatisfaction with one so "maidenly": " 'She hasn't soul enough,' he said, 'to really care for anyone, and even if she had, [I] would rather commit suicide at once, than be yoked to her for life; she was so silly, so fawning, so flat!' "[36]

Though it may not be obvious, Ada Montrose is yet another foil whose characteristics are meant to undercut the ideals of True Womanhood. Unlike Anna Livingston, whose passivity and simplemindedness clearly mimicked the naive and helpless maiden, Ada is a vision of what Real Womanhood writers saw bitterly as the true face of that spunsugar competing ideal—heartless manipulation, deceit, and fraudulence. Ada Montrose and similar villainesses employ the ostensible characteristics of the True Woman—her physical fragility, her deference to men, her helplessness, her ultrafeminine inability to solve problems, discuss money, or open jars—as bait to lure in unwary and chuckle-headed males who, we suspect, are already primed by a male culture that seemingly worships such frivolous folderol. In domestic novels, these idiotic men get what they deserve—after the fatal ceremony in which he places a ring on the True Woman's finger, the hero discovers what a gorgon he has married. Her selfishness, her indolence, her expensive tastes, and her complete lack of either a spiritual dimension or human compassion become glaringly evident.

Nowhere is this dilemma more horrifyingly evident than in Harland's *Ruby's Husband*. The oblivious (and fatuously uncritical) hero of the novel, Louis Suydam, becomes entangled in the web of the novel's chief villainess, Ruby Sloane. Batting her long eyelashes, reclining delicately in a chaise, pitifully explaining her poverty and her tiny-boned defense-lessness against the supposed evil plans of her brutish father, Nick, to marry her off to an elderly widower, Ruby plays on Louis's obviously conditioned response to the True Woman. Although she never explicitly asks him to "save" her, she swears with dramatic bravery to "get herself a job as a governess"—and then paints a pitiful picture of the drudgery that would involve and her total inadequacy to live in such a condition.[37] Obviously, Louis has grown up with the belief that truly feminine women do not, and cannot, work to support themselves and that it is cruel to suggest that they should do so. True Women such as Ruby are far too delicate and sensitive to toil in the mines of labor—even genteel forms such as governessing.

This touching scene takes place over an extraordinarily expensive lunch, which Louis, on a strict allowance from his wealthy and prominent family, can barely afford. As he watches Ruby's rosebud lips fasten around out-of-season strawberries—her second bowl—he vows to do something to prevent her from being sacrificed either to the elderly widower or to the disgrace of governessing. Harland makes it obvious through glaring clues throughout the meal (Ruby's greedy insistence on second helpings of everything, especially the most expensive dishes, the sudden edge to her voice, the not-quite-extinguished blaze of her eyes when Louis falters) that Ruby is a monster and Louis is being duped. Significantly, Ruby forces back her pique with Louis's snail-like pace in making decisions and repeatedly tosses her lovely hair while sweet-talking him, finally manifesting a single tear on each eyelash. This sad scene finally undermines his sense of caution and he proposes.[38] In sum,

Ruby acts the True Woman to perfection, and the result is a secret marriage. It has to be secret because Louis's family needs to be brought around to accept a girl from a dirt-poor, "clownish" family in the hinterlands, where Ruby's father functions as a guide to visiting hunters and stays drunk most of the time; her mother is a self-sacrificing drudge.

Ruby's evil nature reveals itself immediately after the marriage, especially during the seven months during which the couple waits for Louis's parents to return from Europe. Ruby's accelerating demands for jewels, furs, furniture, operas, plays, clothes, fine foods, and wines are completely out of keeping with Louis's austere lifestyle as a self-supporting doctor just starting a practice. Louis swiftly comes to hate Ruby, but with the poetic justice typical of domestic novels, he must continue the legal charade of marriage even though he has fallen in love with the novel's heroine, Real Woman Frank Berry. It is, however, too late for Louis, whose credulousness and vanity make him the perfect dupe for Harland's version of the arachnoid True Woman.

In 'Lena Rivers, Mary Jane Holmes portrays a young woman of true maidenly reserve, not an ersatz copy like Ada Montrose or Harland's Ruby; unfortunately, even the true-spirited variety, if excessive, has unhappy results. Mabel Rose loves 'Lena's cousin John, Jr.; her heart trembles at his approach; her cheeks blush; she feels faint. John, Jr., has a distant yet friendly regard for her, but he cannot love one so fragile and mute. He marries the brisk and healthily opinionated Nelly Douglass, and Mabel lapses into a fever and then dies.[39]

Conversely, in both periodical short stories and novels, the straightforward and dignified woman of opinion and sense, who neither faints nor is archly coy, attracts the right sort of man. In a brief story entitled "What Everybody Said," which appeared in Harper's Weekly, Mary Dashford verbally spars with and later falls in love with and marries George Newberne. Known for her witty remarks and penetrating observations, Mary is a bit too straightforward, verging on Muzzey's and Chapin's definition of forwardness. This behavior is soon corrected when George forces her to see her inadvertent heartlessness at mocking the scar on the face of a friend, Tom, by revealing that Tom received the injury when he was hit by an omnibus while pushing a little crossing sweep out of the way.[40] What is interesting here is that, despite Mary's need for mild correction, George obviously prefers a woman who is a tiny bit forward to one who is prim, overly demure, or kittenish—traits which, according to Barbara Welter, Madonna Kolbenschlag, and others, constitute the ideal demeanor of the True Woman.

As if writing an epitaph for the composite behavior of the True Womanhood ideal, Weaver tells his young female readers, "Multitudes of girls are as thoughtless and giddy as the lambs that sport on the lea. They seem scarcely to cast a prophetic glance before. They live as though life was a theater, good for nothing but its acting . . . I know they have been taught by the customs of society, by the follies of their elders, to regard themselves as the playthings of men, the ornaments of society, rather than the helpers of themselves and their race, and the solid substance of the social fabric." This behavior, he suggests, will result in tragedy in future life because they have created no adult expectations for their own treatment or status.[41] This foolishness, he and other advice writers suggest, can be avoided by participating in courting in the proper manner and for the proper reasons.

Courting, Weaver states, should not be an occasion for "wooing" so much as an opportunity for analysis. Weaver, Muzzey, Chapin, Hale, Hartley, Arthur, and other writers suggest that rather than participating in a contrived minuet of social responses and signals, the time be used to "get to know" the character of the suitor and discover whether the two are intellectually, emotionally, and spiritually compatible. Courting, then, is "a search for companionship" and not an "effort to please." Because it is such a serious procedure, courting should not be conducted, contends Weaver, "with excitement" or "in haste" but rather with "calmness and deliberation." After all, during this period—a time society deliberately sets aside for the couple—there should be a "court of inquiry . . . for the purpose of comparing their souls or their real characters; to see wherein and to what extent they are harmonious; to see how much they are alike and how much they are unalike; to see whether they are companions in heart or not."[42]

It may not always be possible to conduct this "court of inquiry" face to face because the exigencies of time and distance occasionally interfere. Advice writers agree, however, that much can be learned between personal meetings through an exchange of serious (as opposed to silly and mushy) correspondence, as long as certain rules are followed. Such letters should strive to elicit opinions and tastes on the same variety of important subjects upon which advice writers suggest women seek discussion face to face. While discussing those important subjects, young women should follow a few guidelines. According to Emily Thornwell, they should "avoid the introduction of too many quotations from other authors, particularly those in a foreign language." This Thornwell considers a "ridiculous affection" when an English phrase "would do just as well"; it also smacks of archness and an unfortunate attempt to deceive the other party by "shows" of pedantry and erudition.[43]

Muzzey expands somewhat on Thornwell's rules, returning once more to the true object of such extended correspondence—to acquire substantial knowledge of the suitor's views on important matters. As Muzzey explains, letters should discuss interests, tastes, and character so that "mutual Esteem and Respect" can develop. This is possible only if the correspondents are sincere, exchange confidences about true feelings, and talk "rationally." To this end, Muzzey stresses that, despite deep feelings of affection, letters should not "be crowded with nauseating compliments, with nonsense and vanity, but will contain good thoughts, no less than the expression of pure feelings, and generous sentiments."[44]

By contrast, Eliza Leslie—and others following the paranoid provisions of the True Womanhood ideal—see correspondence between couples as a fatal mistake. Leslie denies the propriety of any correspondence between young women and men unless the men are relatives, fiancés, or businessmen with whom the young woman is forced to deal. She sees in exchanges between unrelated couples as an ideal opportunity for the (inevitably) unscrupulous young men to puff their sexual reputations at the expense of their innocent but unwise female correspondents. The man, Leslie warns, will undoubtedly, even in the most high-minded, pleasant, or innocuous letter, "show the superscription, or the signature, or both, to his idle companions, and make insinuations much to her disadvantage, which his comrades will be sure to circulate and exaggerate."[45]

Few correspondents in fiction are so cautious, however. In Graves's "Emily Howard or The Gentle Wife," Emily's suitor, Mr. Harcourt, whom she meets while traveling with her father on a tour of New York, writes her both serious and delicately passionate letters over which she muses and which she answers in a similar fashion until he arrives for a visit.[46] Edna Earl corresponds regularly on matters replete with both business and intellectual concerns with Douglas Manning in *St. Elmo;* though she ultimately refuses to marry him on two occasions, there is enormous mutual respect between them. Roland Lee, the "young pilot" of the subtitle in *Linda* also writes to Linda with no evil result, as does Ishmael to his esteemed young woman in *Ishmael*, though with ambiguous ultimate results resolved only in a second novel.

Although correspondence did serve the purpose of getting to know someone whom distance and business concerns made absent, it was obviously much better to find out such vital information face to face if it could be managed, and that is the situation the Real Womanhood writers presuppose in the bulk of their advice. If this scrutiny of character was to be of any use, however, young women had to have a clear conception of what they sought. Weaver, Muzzey, Hale, Arthur, Graves, and others spend a great deal of time defining the healthy affection that should emerge from protracted conversation and the unhealthy attachment that might intrude and bring disaster. Muzzey especially is explicit about what love is not, and his statements crystallize the more general hints and provisos the others offer. Although Muzzey understands that affection and even desire might flare up initially for reasons of spontaneous "magnetism," he fully expects young women not to allow that to stand "without the revision of calm judgment." He unequivocally rejects the idea that love is the result of an irresistible impulse or a "disease" or a "weakness." This "fatalism," he concludes, as do Abell and Arthur, comes from reading trashy romances, and he mourns the result: "Who has not seen some young woman of talent and virtue sacrifice herself to this mistaken impression? The plume of the soldier, the gay air of the debauchee, the flippant beau, the half-insane tippler, could she not have seen her doom in being affianced to one of these poor pageants of humanity? Ah, but 'she loved; she could not help loving'; she gave herself a victim at the profane shrine, because she always thought she must love where and whom, her unbidden, irresponsible, feelings should direct her to love."[47]

Graves explains this infatuation even more clearly as she describes Emily Howard's initial reaction to Harcourt's absence. Needless to say, Emily later comes to love Harcourt for much more substantial reasons. At first, however, she idolizes him, as Graves explains analytically:

> The loved one then appears as he never will again, for we see him not as he is, but as imagination has fondly pictured him. We worship a creation of our own fancy, and forget the one we idolize is a being of earth and must share the frailties and errors of mortality. We vainly dream that every virtue and

gift of character and intellect are centered in him and regard him as the living prototype of every favorite hero of history or romance. And when a nearer view in the clear light of truth has awakened us to the reality, we too often suffer the blame to rest where it might not, upon him and not on ourselves. It is not he who has decieved [sic] us, it is our own self-delusion, and we should remember this when the disappointment comes.[48]

Graves's point is not to avoid feeling that "thrill through the heart" but to know it for what it is—an initial physical attraction—and to search conscientiously for esteem and love for the man based solidly on his real accomplishments, the true beauty of his character and spirit, actual sympathies of outlook and interest. Hence she advises a period of intense conversation, scrutiny, and discovery.

This period of scrutiny should, advice writers insist, follow certain lines. Subjects fruitful for revealing discussion should include favorite books read and why they are favorites; current events and controversial theological or scientific subjects; world politics and government; tastes in art, music, and architecture; great historical heroes and heroines; biblical scholarship; and favorite poetry. All of these, if discussed with an eye to learning each other's tastes rather than impressing each other, reveal the suitor's character, the topography of his mind, the state of his soul. One cannot be ignorant of Beethoven, the Renaissance, archaeological discoveries, chemistry, the classic revival, German biblical scholarship, the wars in Afghanistan, South Africa, and the American West, or the controversy over infant baptism and be either intelligent or cultured. As Emma Willard notes sternly, "Indolence of mind is a rock in the soil, to prevent the growth of that great root of Wisdom, the Knowledge of Truth." Lack of knowledge suggests mental sloth or dullness; lack of opinions suggests lack of character. Notes Weaver, "Opinions are among the best indices of character."[49] How much character could a man possibly have whose favorite book was *A Man and a Maid* or the Marquis de Sade's *Justine?* What sort of ignoramus would not reveal his true benightedness immediately by calling Stephen Foster the greatest composer who ever lived? What Europhile decadence might be hidden in a man whose heroes were figures like Frederick the Great and Napoleon and whose taste in architecture was entirely baroque? How spiritually aware could a suitor possibly be who had never considered the roots of the Reformation or questioned himself about his own belief in "revealed truth" or infant baptism or the nature of heaven? Indeed, what sensitivity or education, despite avowals to the contrary, could a man possibly have who preferred limericks to Longfellow or Tennyson? Conversation—intense, honest, and prolonged conversation—could reveal an enormous amount about the other person. As Weaver and others suggest, each young woman should seek a "congenial spirit," who under like circumstances would react, feel, and believe naturally much as the girl did because he had similar "modes of thought and feeling" drawn from a similar educational, cultural, and spiritual background. This was not to say the young woman should seek a clone or a toady; it was just as disastrous, Muzzey insisted, for a young man to be so malleable, so accommodating, that he would agree to every opinion the young woman expressed simply to be pleasant. Rather, as Weaver explains, one who shares similar opinions on important subjects, who dislikes, enjoys, approves, or condemns generally along the same lines as the young woman, should do so "not for the purpose of agreeing with us, but of his . . . own free will."[50]

Such a "congeniality of tastes," as Graves calls it, can sometimes mislead a young woman, however, if she is not cognizant of the nature of true love—she may be chasing a phantom of romantic infatuation and fail to acknowledge her own deep feelings for someone simply because her friendly feelings do not match the model offered by sentimental novels of True Womanhood. Emily Howard, for example, almost ignores Mr. Harcourt as a suitor in the early stages (before she becomes infatuated) because she *does* enjoy his company so much and feels so easy around him. Emily, Graves explains, "respected Mr. Harcourt, and was delighted with his intelligent and agreeable conversation, but she had no thought of him as a lover. It was true that his society gave her more pleasure than that of any gentleman she had known, but this she thought was owing to the congeniality of their tastes and to the intellectual graces of his own gifted mind."[51]

Thus it was all the more important for young girls, like Emily, to understand what they were seeking; those who are deluded on this point may very well have the perfect suitor under their noses and not realize it. They may continue to seek fruitlessly for the romantic cad (drawn in exciting strokes by the sentimental novelists) and waste a lifetime searching for him—or, worse yet, find him and marry him. Arthur's Alice Melville in a novel by the same name finds her dream in the shape of William Justin. A smooth reprobate with a thousand graceful ways and the heart of a calculating machine, Justin convinces Alice to run away with him against her parents' wishes. Delirious with the "romance" of the adventure, as well as the close approximation to romantic-novel reality, Alice does so. Her wealthy father disowns her, and of course William Justin is brutal, then deserts her, since he was actually a fortune hunter in the first place.[52]

Assuming, however, that the young woman does have a clear understanding of the true definition of love and has come to admire, respect, and enjoy the suitor before her, it is time to enter the next stage: personal assessment of feelings. As the advice writers explain coolly, the girl should decide at this early stage of courtship whether she has a strong attachment to the suitor and could consider marrying him. Does she find him a congenial companion? Can she respect him for his qualities of mind and spirit? Will he be a friend for a lifetime, a soul mate with whom she can share both triumphs and tragedies? If the answer to these questions is "no," then it is the girl's duty to end the courtship immediately, before she has given the luckless suitor "reason to hope" that the relationship will eventually terminate in marriage. If the answer to the questions is "yes," the young woman should openly encourage the suitor to make a proposal. Muzzey seems to feel that a young woman who is both sensitive and deft enough can usually prevent the suitor from making an unwanted—and embarrassing—proposal. In the event that the suitor springs the question unexpectedly, if the young woman is kind, she will answer as promptly as possible. Declares Muzzey, "It is ungenerous to trifle with the feelings of another" when it is within a young woman's power to end the suspense.[53]

At this juncture, the reader may wonder whether parents played any part in a girl's decision to marry a particular suitor. Weaver, Muzzey, Hale, Arthur, and the novelists do seem to believe that parents' advice can be useful, but it is not necessary to consult them. Aresty finds a significant pattern of independence from parental opinion among young women of this period. After all, the parents may, as we have seen, advise the young woman to marry for the wrong reasons—money, status, a lovely home. If they do, she must ignore their advice. Undoubtedly, though, her indecisiveness, which would lead her to seek parental advice, is evidence of a lack of sufficient feeling for marriage—and an indication of what her answer should be. Although advice writers of Real Womanhood urge their readers to be reasonable and calm in their assessment, they do not wish them to be completely cold-blooded—this is unnatural too. They feel that admiration, respect, and shared interests ordinarily result in affection. Indeed, if after vigorously scrutinizing a suitor's interests, values, intellectual gifts, and character, the young woman is still lukewarm, she should ask herself why; there may be a reason she has not yet acknowledged. Perhaps he lacks the level of intellectual ability she seeks; perhaps he is a touch too unrefined; perhaps she finds his opinions not so much congenial as colorless, and that is the reason no conflict has occurred.

Muzzey points out that there are ways of turning down a suitor that spare his feelings and reflect well on the young lady who handles the matter tactfully. First, he suggests, neither the proposal nor the refusal should be made in public; the shame, as well as the glory, should be private. He sternly admonishes young ladies not to laugh at or ridicule the suitor for his proposal, not to broadcast to all their friends the fact that he proposed and was rejected; nor should she show evidence of the proposal to anyone. The young lady should return all letters (and demand hers back) and give back any tokens of affection, which, if displayed, might exhibit the suitor's disappointment.[54]

But what happens if no suitor raises more than a lukewarm feeling in a young woman's breast, if no gentleman paying his addresses ever measures up to her standards? In that case, advice writers sternly admonish her to *choose* the single life. Despite Barbara Welter's statements to the contrary, all Americans did not regard spinsterhood as a fate worse than death. Muzzey states categorically, "It is not true that single ladies are usually despised, or subject to ridicule. Those who do suffer these things, have usually brought them upon themselves by a deportment, which might have been shunned."[55]

Muzzey, Weaver, Abell, Willard, and others feel it is wrong for women to assume they must marry. Muzzey finds this impression so "erroneous; and so disastrous [in] its consequences" that he suggests that parents, educators, and journalists should make a determined effort to root it out and remind women that God made all members of the sex to have character, "usefulness," and happiness but not all of them for marriage: "Woman was not made for marriage; but marriage for woman. If in any instance it shall appear that her improvement will probably be retarded by her entering the state, or her usefulness less extensive, or her happiness evidently sacrificed, then it is manifest that she belongs to the class of exceptions. It is her duty to continue unmarried." The young woman, he continues, should have the moral courage to wait for someone who matches her standards rather than throw herself away "on a dolt or a villain"; indeed, he concludes, "Better ten lives of singleness, than a few years of that wretchedness so often occasioned by marrying simply and solely for fear of being single."[56] One thinks almost immediately of the marriage hysteria of Arthur's Anna Wyman and her mother, with their obsession to have Anna be engaged at sixteen and the disastrous marriage to Thomas Elliott that follows, leaving Anna a brutalized, deserted wife with a baby in her arms. The novelists provided other examples—Carrie Livingston's loveless near marriage to Atherton in 'Lena Rivers or even Annie Graham's flawed relationship with George after her desertion by Jimmie Carleton in Rose Mather.

More common, however, according to Nina Baym in her survey of American women's fiction, the pattern that emerges is one of the heroine "facing up" to possible spinsterhood and electing it rather than making either a loveless or a mercenary marriage simply because women are "supposed" to get married. Even when heroines do marry, Baym points out, the plot shows that marriage is hardly the goal of the heroine's life; it is not regarded as either secure and permanent or unavoidable—it may be only "an episode in a woman's life" since many of the admirable secondary characters are either widows or single women. Certainly this is evident in novels like Whitney's A Summer in Leslie Goldthwaite's Life, which has absolutely nothing to do with courtship or marriage and features a thoroughly admirable spinster, Miss Craydocke, as a strong secondary character. Whitney's approving description of Miss Craydocke is particularly interesting because it ignores her physical appearance and lauds her character: "She had everything pretty about her, this old Miss Craydocke. How many people do, that have not a bit of outward prettiness themselves . . . [she sits and] grows silently [as] the century plant of the soul, absorbing to itself hourly that which feeds the beauty of the lily and the radiance of the leaf."[57]

In addition to being spiritually mature and intellectually beautiful, Miss Craydocke is a good sport, an active collector of flora and fauna, and a woman with a fine, appreciative sense of humor, who finds the young "Sin" Saxon's worries about possible spinsterhood and lost beauty in need of gentle correction. She warns the flighty Sin that beauty and youth inevitably fade and that inner strength, wisdom and a well-stocked mind should be the true objects of her energy. Yet despite this admonition, Miss Craydocke is neither envious nor censorious of the youth and beauty around her; the girls' comments amuse her, even Sin's wonder whether "I shall bear it, when it comes [spinsterhood and old age]." Whitney notes Miss Craydocke's reaction: "A droll twinkle played among the crow's-feet at the corners of her eyes. They could not hurt her, these merry girls, meaning nothing but the moment's fun, nor cheat her of her quiet share of the fun either."[58]

Miss Craydocke hardly seems to fit the model proposed by writers of the True Womanhood school, who suggest that all old maids have vinegary tempers, bitter mouths, and envious, censorious thoughts. Certainly such a description is not accurate for Evans's Edna Earl, who, until the last chapters of the novel, is not only a spinster but the bluest of bluestockings. She is also the champion at rejecting marriage proposals. Edna not only rejects St. Elmo repeatedly but Gordon Leigh as well, who offers a comfortable home and everything she "could want." Even as Leigh dangles this lure, Edna dashes his hopes coldly: "I am able to earn a home; I do not intend to marry for one." On her road to literary fame, Edna also rejects the advances of Sir Roger Percival because, though she likes him, she does not "esteem him intellectually" and therefore does not love him. As if dashing the hopes of Sir Roger, Gordon Leigh, and St. Elmo were not enough, Edna also twice rejects the literary notable and publisher, Douglass Manning; though she esteems his intellect and admires his work, he raises only a lukewarm affection in her.[59]

According to a long and thoughtful article about courtship in an 1868 issue of the *Nation*, Edna Earl's constant refusal to accept marriage proposals would be neither unknown nor to be deplored. In an article entitled "Why Is Single Life Becoming More General?" the author points out "the increasing infrequency of marriage at the present day" and speculates about the reasons for the phenomenon, eventually lauding such a decision as the product of "prudent hesitation more to be praised than the precipitancy with which thoughtless, ignorant, inexperienced, poverty-stricken children rush into the sacred responsibilities of parents." Far from being "unnatural," the decision for either late marriage or the single life was, the author felt, the result of a "process of civilization." Thanks to greater literacy, free time, and extensive middle-class culture, "men and women can less easily find any one whom they are

willing to take as a partner for life; their requirements are more exact-
ing; their standards of excellence higher; they are less able to find any
who can satisfy their own ideal and less able to satisfy anybody else's
ideal." The *Nation* author, however, does not see such a trend as one that
should "excite alarm and lamentation"; rather, the author explains that
such choosiness enhances the cultural level of the general population
since marriages are no longer being made because people are bored and
have no other outlet for imagination or amusement beyond courting. As
the article points out, "In cities they [amusements and resorts] are constant, abundant, and varied," providing endless sources of enlighten-
ment and entertainment, not only to city dwellers but to most of society,
thanks to the spread of entertaining culture via the railroads. Men and
women both now marry because of a sincere desire to obtain stimulating, intellectually fulfilling, and spiritually comforting companionship—
and they do so when they are able financially to have and maintain a
"decent" life. As the author explains, when thoughtful couples marry
now, they "have the *necessaries* and the *decencies* of life . . . furnace and
range, hot and cold water, marble mantlepieces [sic] and washbasins,
sofas and carpets, silver table service and pictures on the wall."[60]

Despite the overt materialism expressed in the above passage, it would
be a mistake to assume that the author speaks tongue-in-cheek; as he
explains later, material comforts are not to be sneered at because they
suggest a married life safely above an existence of grinding penury and
penny-pinching, which ultimately results in mutual accusation and
blame or the tension of trying to stay afloat financially while still maintaining a companionable marital relationship. It also avoids hordes of
ill-educated, neglected, unwanted children.[61] One remembers at this
point the injunctions of Weaver, Muzzey, and others against marrying
someone of financially disparate background and the advice writers'
dark warning that "romance" is not sufficient to make a stable marriage,
especially if it involves running off and living on bread crumbs and love
alone. Better, suggest the advice writers—and the *Nation* author as
well—to choose to remain single if the right choice does not materialize
than to commit oneself to a life of probable unhappiness and possible
poverty with a man one can never truly respect or enjoy, while trying to
rear a ragged army of demanding children as well. A pragmatic—as
opposed to sentimental—evaluation of the situation militates against
such a marriage, especially if a young woman is fully capable of sup-

porting herself, which of course she should be under the dictates of Real Womanhood.

Nevertheless, despite their approval of "blessed singleness," advice writers point out that most women eventually marry and that they need to understand the social and moral uses of the engagement period following their acceptance of a proposal if they are to contract satisfying and safe marriages.

FIVE

Engagement and Aftermath

[Marriage] brings into a relationship the most intimate possible two minds, that, if they do not harmonize, must act upon and react against each other with a disturbing force that necessarily precludes the soul's true development and perfection.

—T. S. Arthur,
Advice to Young Ladies

With their usual pragmatism, Real Womanhood writers did not view the engagement period as binding a young woman forever to the man in question. Though engagements should not be overly long, they provided an opportunity for a final investigation and intense searching, and the girl was expected to break the engagement if new evidence of the fiancé's unsuitability emerged. During this period, the young woman might discover enormities heretofore hidden by her suitor either deliberately or inadvertently—debauchery, a tendency to drink, brutality, family diseases, or a roving eye. During this interval, fathers, brothers, and family friends might expose something in the suitor's history that suggested that the relationship was unsuitable. Finally, the young woman or her suitor in their dutiful rush to reveal private sins of character—exposing their worst faults and lowest desires—might find that they could not live a lifetime with the truths so revealed. Any of these reasons constituted sufficient cause to break an engagement, and these writers urged young women to do just that. Engagement was the last chance to avoid disaster and secure a decent life. Divorce was unthinkable, though advice writers did suggest possible courses of action if, despite the young woman's best investigative efforts, the husband turned out to be brutal or impecunious to the detriment of herself or their children.

Given the extensive scrutiny young women had, ideally, practiced during the courting, advice writers suggested that engagements "should ordinarily be brief, at least, not needlessly protracted" because long engagements tended to have unfortunate results—the parties might outgrow each other or be molded in different and incompatible directions by extensive contact as single persons in the world. In marriage, conversely, the world affected them as a unit, and they grew together in the same direction under each other's beneficial influence.[1] An acceptable engagement lasted for four to eight months; this apparently was considered "brief."

This period, advice writers warned, should not be burdened with "extravagant Anticipations" in which daydreaming and imagination took the place of reality.[2] Rather, it should be a time of assessing the fiancé's position on more crucial matters than were covered during the courtship period—matters having a direct bearing on the manner and style of the future married life. It should also be a time to reveal oneself, including all one's deepest, most secret faults, to the suitor, who should do likewise, so that each could determine if he or she could live with the dark truth. Finally, engagement with its socially acceptable greater intimacy and contact, provided an opportunity for the young woman to discover the suitor's disposition, energy of character, amativeness, and equilibrium of temper.

Whereas during the courting phase, the young woman directed conversation to intellectual and artistic topics, during engagement she should seek to ascertain her fiancé's feelings about, among other subjects, the structure of "family governance" after marriage: the way he felt money should be handled; his feelings about child rearing and parental responsibilities (including specific obligations of the father); the nature and obligations of marriage in general, both financially and morally; the degree of opulence or "decency" the family should try to maintain in the eyes of the world; and finally, the intellectual opportunities the fiancé was prepared to make available to his wife so that she might continue studying or learning.[3] A lack of agreement about all such concerns, of course, could result in extremely unpleasant squabbles if there were no basis for compromise, as advice writers were quick to point out. In fact, to advice writers of Real Womanhood, marked disagreement on any one of these—disagreement with no chance of achieving a middle ground—led to a lifetime of unhappiness and was therefore a legitimate reason for breaking an engagement.

A brief examination of several of these concerns illustrates the very longheaded and pragmatic view of life advice writers advocated. In the question of family governance, for example, Weaver especially suggests discussing future lines of authority inside the family. Does the couple agree that the husband should have the final say on every decision involving the family, from relocating in another town to methods of disciplining children? Shall the wife have any area of responsibility that is hers alone, in regard either to housekeeping schedules, supplies, and management or to child rearing? Which partner will make decisions about the hiring and firing of servants—and who will do the deed? Who will decide what constitutes acceptable behavior in the home—and, again, who will enforce it? Is the couple committed to making such decisions together always or only some of the time? Such matters, suggest Weaver, Chapin, Hale, Abell, and others, need to be thoroughly thrashed out before a young woman finds herself surrounded by children and under the thumb of a suddenly despotic mate.[4]

Indeed, even if, theoretically, the young woman agrees to accept a less than equal role in family governance and decisions, the advice writers do not completely approve of such an arrangement. Both advice writers and domestic novelists portray a marriage of shared and equal responsibility in family matters as the ideal; never should the wife end up as an unpaid menial with no say in family decisions. As Hale notes tartly, "the idea that woman is only the shadow and attendant image of man[,] owing him a thoughtless and servile obedience," is not only "foolishly wrong" but immoral. What kind of partner would that be, she asks, and what help would she offer in the daily struggle of life? Writers advocating such a servile relationship seem to believe the husband "could be helped effectively by a shadow, or worthily by a slave!" Despite social historian Barbara Epstein's insistence that "woman's adoption of a subservient stance in relation to her husband" was advocated by all advice writers, as we have seen with the redoubtable Hale and as I will show with other writers, this was hardly the case universally. Weaver goes so far as to advise that both partners should "think, feel, and act in kindly independence" and says that they should encourage each other to be independent in all thought and action. Muzzey discusses the need for "a good Temper" in handling petty domestic matters and advises young women to seek mates whose tempers are reasonable and accommodating. Finally, Graves provides an especially uplifting picture both of a model "equitable" marriage as the goal to strive for and of the evil effects accruing from the dissolving of such an arrangement.[5]

Graves's illustrative story "Sarah Sherman" is interesting because it explores several important questions simultaneously, among them equality in marriage, the need for the wife to maintain intellectual engagement, and the unfortunate results of male dominance suddenly cropping up in an otherwise equal marriage. Sarah's marriage to Charles Glentworth seems model from the beginning. Charles respects the quality of Sarah's mind, considers her a "dear friend," and values her opinions. Moreover, true to the advice of the Real Womanhood writers,

Sarah has married a man who is both educated and rising in the professional world. Not only is Charles a lawyer, but his reputation for probity
and intelligence lands him a position as an assistant to a wealthy and
respected older lawyer, Mr. Melmoth, who possesses a huge law practice. On the basis of such solid prospects, Charles and Sarah get married,
and Sarah's parents rent and furnish a house for them. They are, obviously, well set up financially for a life of respectable middle-class comfort. As Charles's insistence on a library/study furnished expressly for
Sarah indicates, their marriage will be solidly egalitarian and intellectually stimulating. As Charles tells the delighted Sarah when she first
views the library/study, he does not want her to degenerate into "a
household slave"; rather, he expects her to attend to those domestic
duties not already attended to by servants, and then, "when your domestic duties are over, you can spend your leisure hours here free from
interruption, and when my engagements for the day are over, I will join
you, and we can read and study together." Sarah is, of course, overjoyed
with this suggestion and points out that it will allow her to continue to
be Charles's intellectual companion and equal, not a glorified housekeeper with nothing to contribute to discussions while he continues to
learn and think. Graves cannot resist underlining the excellence of the
arrangements, as well as their comparative rarity in the real world outside the covers of advice books: "Few married women are allowed to
pursue a system of mental culture, and even the little that is sometimes
gained by reading is momentarily seized on like a forbidden gratification, for few men ever consider it a duty to promote the intellectual
advancement of their wives. A well ordered house, a good dinner, and a
slavish attention to every capricious want, are by many rigorously
exacted."[6]

Graves's sense of the rarity of such male accommodation is more than
supported by Carl Degler's study of married women and the family. The
crux of the problem seems to be, not surprisingly, the much eulogized
state of motherhood. As Degler explains, supported by quotations from
journals and diaries of nineteenth-century women, motherhood often
left a woman no time for writing or serious reflection, no time even to
think because of the demands of family care, and certainly no time for
"self-improvement" or literary expression in journals or other media.
Indeed, the physical debility and mental depressions that often followed
pregnancy and childbirth were a large reason—even beyond the prob-

lem of finding time—why women felt they could no longer share their husbands' intellectual or recreational lives. A poignant letter from Mary Hallock Foote to Helena Gilder, written around 1877, illustrates this problem. Mrs. Foote mourns that she "could have cried," remembering how she and her husband had ridden over the hills, and of the "Sundays when I tramped with Arthur, following the steepest trails, without flagging a step. I thought to myself, I can never be *comrade* any more."[7]

Although Sarah is not yet a mother, Charles's willingness to supply her with the means of improving her mind and his vision of a companionable intellectual life together suggest a strong beginning to the marriage and a basic orientation that might do much to alleviate the mental distress suffered by many wives. Most men, Graves suggests, make no provisions for this kind of companionship at any stage in the marriage. Building such a relationship after the arrival of children becomes exponentially harder, given the lack of such suppositions in the first place.

Obviously, Charles Glentworth is no ordinary husband. Surrounding Sarah with books, maps, dictionaries, works of literature and science, globes, a study desk, and supplies, he seems all that a real young woman could want. And he is—until he gets infected with a competitive frenzy to outshine other lawyers. Here, Graves seems to suggest, was the weak spot in the courtship; during that golden period Sarah had not discussed such questions as the amount of money both could agree was necessary to "keep up appearances" or the weight her veto would carry in final decisions about expenditures. Alas for Sarah Sherman! At his employer's insistence, Charles begins cultivating business contacts by going to dinner at the fashionable homes of current and prospective clients. Once exposed to an atmosphere of silken luxury, Charles is stung by the contrast with his own "humble" abode and becomes increasingly dissatisfied. Spurred on by his dissatisfaction and Melmoth's sudden offer of a partnership and a higher salary (as well as that worthy gentleman's failing health), Charles insists on moving to a more expensive neighborhood and a new house, which Sarah points out they cannot afford. Charles refuses to listen to Sarah's cautionary reasoning that they should stay where they are and save the extra income from the higher salary for a possible financial emergency in the future. After a series of useless entreaties, Sarah reluctantly moves. Graves then soliloquizes on the evil habit of keeping up appearances and ends by discussing the burdens it places on the mate of a partner so obsessed: "Sarah deeply regretted the change, but with all the energy of her character she determined that her husband should not suffer from the effects of his imprudence, if they could be averted by her industry and management. She had always been an economist, but now she made it her constant study and exertion to strive to keep their increased expenses within the limits of their income."[8] It is obvious to the reader that disaster is looming on the horizon; it is equally obvious that, had Sarah an equal vote in family finances and governance, such disaster would not occur.

Sarah, however, does not have equal power in the relationship and must therefore scramble to keep the family's heads above water financially as Charles progresses deeper and deeper into expensive dinner parties, catered social evenings, and reciprocal entertainments. Charles demands, for example, that gourmet delicacies be served at his parties. Sarah responds by spending hours painstakingly preparing the foods herself. Charles insists that they hire a "fashionable" cook and a pair of waiters. Sarah oversees the cook and waiter personally to avoid pilfering, waste, or extravagance. She dismisses household servants and does all the heavy housework herself so that they can afford the cook and waiters. This bone-wearying regime affects both the quality and the amount of the much vaunted study time Charles earlier promised her. Graves notes caustically, "This unremitting vigilance and oversight left Sarah now no leisure hours she could claim as her own, and she was forced to give up everything like systematic mental culture."[9]

Although she feverishly concocts gourmet dishes, washes the silver, attends to the housekeeping duties, cuts and arranges flowers, writes endless invitations and responses, and supervises the specialized help, Sarah's efforts to maintain financial solvency are inadequate. Charles, it seems, has "various debts" (unknown to Sarah) "whose liquidation he was forced to defer from time to time." Though Graves does not state explicitly how he acquired this mountain of debts, she strongly implies that they are a result of his high-rolling associations with clients—possibly involving gambling.[10] Despite Sarah's unintentional reduction in rank from conversational intellectual partner to skivvy-in-residence, there is not enough money to pay the bills.

The final blow is yet to come, however. To smother Sarah's growing objections to his wild spending, Charles constantly holds out the expectation of taking over his senior partner's large and lucrative practice when that worthy gentleman dies. For two years Charles points out

Harper's Weekly, November 24, 1866

repeatedly that Melmoth's practice includes the richest clients in the city and that the large fees they pay will more than dissolve his debts and provide an income well above their operating expenses. Mr. Melmoth does die, but (since this is a moral tale by the relentless Mrs. Graves) Charles does not inherit his wealthy clients. They shift immediately to another law firm, one with lawyers of "more eminent reputation" than Charles. Facing bankruptcy and disgrace, Charles tells Sarah the awful news and, finally, hands over the financial reins to her. Sarah immediately moves them into humbler living quarters, liquidates the elegant house, its furnishings, and the expensive gewgaws Charles has acquired, and uses the money to pay off the majority of their debts.[11] The reader, of course, remembers vividly Sarah's earlier desire to save for a rainy day; in the midst of this veritable hurricane of disaster, Charles has the grace to remember it too and admits that he should have obeyed Sarah's wishes.

One expects that Charles, having learned the error of not consulting Sarah on important financial decisions and not weighing her advice seriously, has learned his lesson. He hasn't. Graves drives the point home with sledgehammer blows. The liquidation of their assets, it seems, did not clear all the bills. Through rigid economies, however, Sarah's unrelenting scrutiny of expenses, and her insistence that Charles pay strict attention to his practice, they manage to pay off the last of the debts. Charles then receives an unusually large fee from a grateful client and they are, once again, solvent. No sooner is this state of bliss achieved, however, than the "insanely ambitious" Charles immediately begins to neglect his practice (which barely supports them) to strive for high government preferment. Sarah manages to make him attend to business enough of the time that his reputation as a lawyer grows. Finally, because of his reputation—and his resentful but continuing acquiescence to Sarah's wishes rather than to his own political efforts—Charles is appointed "to a situation in an embassy to the court of St. James." Sarah, careful Sarah, remains in "republican simplicity," Graves tells us approvingly, in her dress and manners, continuing to keep a tight rein on the ebullient and potentially profligate Charles, picks up and continues her studies, and manages to make both of them the toast of the town and herself the much lauded "refined, intellectual Mrs. Glentworth," who is "frequently spoken of, as a beautiful model of what all American women should be."[12] The story ends on this cautiously happy note, though there remains the suspicion that Charles's contact with the elite always remains a potential tragedy in the making without Sarah's careful scrutiny.

Obviously, Charles would not have been ready to shoot himself over his financial disgrace if his wife had been granted a coequal and independent voice in family finances; just as clearly, there would have been no appointment to the court of St. James if Charles had not eventually granted that equality. Graves is hardly painting a picture of the ideal woman as "the passive submissive responder" to events that Welter and other historians of the Cult of True Womanhood suggest was monolithic.[13] If Sarah Sherman had "submitted her judgement" entirely to that of her husband, as Welter suggests was the accepted ideal behavior, she and Charles both would have ended their days disgraced and haunting pawnshops. Indeed, as we see, when Sarah allows her opinion to be overridden on one occasion, near disaster results.

With such books as Graves's *Girlhood and Womanhood* cluttering the literary landscape for over twenty years, girls were encouraged implicitly and explicitly to discuss financial planning, family governance, and decision making with their future husbands. Other advice writers encouraged them with equal strenuousness to use the period of engagement to ascertain the fiancé's temper and disposition because these would play a large part in the way the family was run and the quality of life for the wife. If Charles Glentworth had been of a vicious temper, Sarah could have suggested a change in financial priorities only from behind a barricade—and then only if she were willing to risk a beating for opening her mouth. Male advice writers in particular (strangely enough) employ bottles and bottles of ink urging that young women be careful to marry only men of good temper, equitable disposition, and kindly nature—and these writers do not mince words about the result if a young woman is foolish enough to ignore outbursts of "morose" temper or "feebleminded peevishness": they will be beaten after marriage over the slightest disagreement or the most trivial neglect of household duties. It is no less essential for the husband to have a good disposition than for the wife to have one, Muzzey claims. If during the engagement period, hints of a suitor's basically sour disposition peek through, despite how "artfully conducted" the courtship has been on his part, the young woman is "insane" if she continues the engagement. There are, Muzzey informs his young women readers, certain symptoms that denote later brutality. Does the fiancé become sullen and noncommunicative when crossed in an argument, when a change of plans is suggested, or when the young lady has an alternate suggestion? Does he become morose when she does not, for whatever sensible reason, approve of one of his plans or refuses to participate in an activity she considers either dangerous or immoral? Is he selfish about material possessions, food, or her attention to others? Finally, is he unkind in his treatment of her—snapping at her, brusque, or hateful verbally? All these denote a poor disposition. If this poor disposition is matched by an inability to control his temper or his passions, the young woman should dismiss him immediately. Muzzey points out that if such evidence appears during the courtship or engagement period, it does not bode well for later married life: "When the restraints of unfamiliar acquaintance are at length thrown off, what can you anticipate, but captiousness and peevishness, if not actual violence?"[14]

Muzzey, Weaver, and Abell all point out that "playful" slaps or shoves or physical restraint at this stage—especially against the young woman's protests—suggest later brutality, especially if such "playful" occurrences happen with any regularity in connection with disagreements between the engaged pair. Muzzey cautions the young woman in strong terms that "better had she been bound to the dead" than to such a man and advises her to seek a man of good temper, excellent self-restraint, and even disposition: "Spare no efforts in ascertaining how near the individual who addresses you approaches this ideal. An utter failure, should present, in your view, an insuperable obstacle to a connection with him for life."[15]

Abell adds a cautionary note on the subject of disposition. She advises young women not to allow a fiancé's behavior toward pets or other animals to outweigh the other symptoms Muzzey and Weaver suggest are indicative of an evil and potentially cruel disposition. Rather, Abell suggests that young women observe a much more homey proof of the young man's disposition; his temper, she asserts, "is seen and made apparent in the treatment of mothers and sisters, far more than in animals and pets. I have known men so devoted to a dog, or a horse, or a bird that a wife was a secondary consideration."[16]

Domestic novels are replete with examples of nasty behavior toward mothers and other female relatives, which underline a suitor's potential explosiveness in the marriage. St. Elmo's barely controlled anger toward his mother, Robert Graham's intemperance toward his, and Herbert the Drunkard's vicious denunciation of his mother all are accurate premonitions of their character in marriage. Only John, Jr., in Holmes's *'Lena Rivers* seems to have grown into a decent, temperate manhood despite his fourteen-year-old physical cruelty to 'Lena; this achievement of decent adulthood, however, may have been more the result of nine-year-old 'Lena's response to his behavior (she slapped him soundly, knocking a cigar out of his mouth) than to any inborn correction on his part.

Advice writers do make a distinction between a man with a temper and a man who has a bad temper but can control it. As Muzzey points out, George Washington had a sudden, violent temper, but he also was able to exercise control over it. Many people with strong convictions possess tempers; the suitors to avoid are those who make no attempt to contain its manifestations.

Again, Graves offers an enlightening example to illustrate how a man with a temper (but possessed of self-control) might react in a marriage, in her story "Emily Howard or The Gentle Wife." Graves, never one to let didactic opportunity slip by without wringing several messages from it, also points out the problems that accrue in marriage when a young woman is not educated enough in domestic pursuits as well as intellectual ones. Emily Howard, a young southern girl, is touring the northern states with her father after a stint at a "fashionable" boarding school. The tour group the Howards have joined travels by boat up the Hudson, spending several days at Saratoga, where Mr. Harcourt (Emily's future husband) first meets them. After due consultation with Emily's father and a request from him that Harcourt "join them in their excursion to the lakes," Harcourt changes his travel plans and does so. Courting commences under the benevolent eye of Emily's father. Emily's contact on an extended basis with Mr. Harcourt reveals him to be "a man of taste, intellect, and varied information." They talk at great length, and Emily is enchanted with Mr. Harcourt's mind, though, in sensible Real Womanhood fashion, she has not yet allowed her emotions to become engaged. Their tour to the lakes over, Harcourt reluctantly takes leave of Emily, promising (after having obtained Mr. Howard's permission) to write to her and to visit in the fall. And write he does—long, affectionate, intellectually stimulating letters. Here Graves shows us some of the drawbacks of the lack of personal observation over an extended period of time; Emily soon decides, despite ignorance of all but the most superficial behavioral traits Harcourt has shown in public after an extended correspondence, that she does indeed consider him a lover. Unfortunately for Emily, she has had little time to observe his behavior on an extended basis, nor has she learned any more about his home life than that he is the only son in a family made up of sisters and a widowed mother and that he has a wealthy, reputable background. When Harcourt comes wooing in the fall, Emily agrees to marry him (again with her father's permission), and they become engaged and then married.[17]

Emily is not the only one who discovers surprises after the marriage; so too does Mr. Harcourt. Emily is graceful, intelligent, and sweet, but Harcourt discovers to his dismay that she is utterly lacking in "household virtues and skills." Raised in the South, she has been accustomed to the instant obedience of "numerous and faithfully attached attendants in her youthful home," as Graves delicately alludes to the presence of slaves, and has had no experience running a household and dealing with "the impertinence and inefficiency of hired menials." The household is in chaos—food ill-prepared, burned, or not prepared; supplies absent or running out; wash piled up and not done; housekeeping accounts in a tangle and unsystematic; bills due. Harcourt is appalled and criticizes Emily, especially after these disasters occur three and four times. Emily cries and is emotionally crushed at Harcourt's censoriousness; he is put out of patience and in a temper by her inefficiency. Had Emily had more personal contact with him before marriage, she might have discerned his punctiliousness about small household matters; had they discussed the duties each thought the other ought to perform in marriage, neither would have been so shocked. A few more inquiries on Emily's part might have revealed that Harcourt's position as the only son in a family of women had made him, as Graves notes, "accustomed to have every thing arranged for him according to his own fastidious tastes, without even having the necessity of expressing his wishes; and he naturally expected the same from his wife, forgetting the manner in which she had been reared by her fond but too indulgent father."[18]

Harcourt's temper, however, manifests itself in sarcasm, not in blows, and he remains accessible to reason, controlling his desire to throw things and slam doors in favor of discussing the situation. After one half-raw roast too many, Emily and Harcourt sit down and talk of their problem openly. Harcourt, good man that he is, understands the educational disability Emily is laboring under and promises to teach her what she needs to know. He reaffirms his love for her and—a significant point to Graves—promises to be less irritable and critical of her efforts while she is learning. He also vows to have a hand in raising their new daughter to be better prepared in domestic skills than Emily was, and Emily agrees wholeheartedly. Both agree that the "New England" model of house-wifery is the *ne plus ultra* for womanhood. Emily forgives Harcourt for his hypercriticalness and sarcasm because, after all, he is basically a good man with a fine mind and the right instincts.[19]

Weaver instructs young ladies that displays of temper (minor, not ma-jor) once shown should be "mourned" but "readily forgiven" unless they continue to occur on a regular basis or become physically dan-gerous. In *Hopes and Helps for the Young of Both Sexes,* Weaver advises a sort of "Eugenics of Temper" to follow if one wants to produce children with moderate dispositions. According to Weaver, young men or young women who have "extreme" temperaments (that is, a tendency to ex-plosive bad temper) should choose partners who are moderate—never ones of the same temperament. He adds helpfully that a young woman or man with red or light hair should probably marry a partner who is dark-haired; those with blue eyes should marry brown eyes; one with an olive or dusky complexion should seek out and marry a fair one. These genetic considerations will, he feels, go far toward ameliorating the effects of negative temperamental characteristics in the next genera-tion and thus produce happier and better-balanced children. Weaver hastens to add, however, that he does not mean that a young man or woman should seek out and marry a suitor of the opposite character (that is, nonindustrious for industrious, dull-witted for intelligent, shifty for honest, atheistic for devout). The complementarity should involve only physical appearance and temperament—nothing else. As for choosing one's "opposite" in important matters such as those listed, Weaver announces, "No greater error was ever inculcated!"[20] In this last injunction, he again supports Real Womanhood's vision of a couple sharing similar interests, character, background, and beliefs.

As we have seen in Graves's story of Emily Howard, one last stage in the engagement period was both useful and necessary to a successful final adjustment: the confession stage. Advice writers agree wholeheart-edly that before the marriage, toward the end of the engagement, the young woman and the young man should confess their worst faults of temper, disposition, character, and activity to each other, laying them out in grim detail, not attempting to shade the facts to put them in a better light. According to the redoubtable Muzzey, it is better to risk losing a partner by telling the ugly truth initially than to marry and try to maintain a facade that eventually will crack under the day-to-day strain of living together and reveal the ugly truths. A frank discussion during the engagement period of one's habits of messiness, or a tendency to temper at being contradicted, or oversensitivity about small things, or stubbornness or selfishness or overcriticalness all should be set out for the fiancé to peruse and discuss. Any marriage contracted without this vital step was in danger of floundering when these traits came out; any marriage that took place after such full-hearted confession could not be shaken by surprise, and, in fact, the partners would have acknowledged their willingness to live together despite these unfortunate traits.

Muzzey stresses that women especially are subject to being idealized in the minds of men, who later express shock and an angered sense of having been swindled when the angel they married sets her jaw and retreats into icy silence or throws crockery during domestic arguments. Says Muzzey, "Sunday exterior and manner" are a trap; a woman can only fall in her husband's estimation when the facade fails, and mutual disappointment and misery are the inevitable result.[21]

Finally, if the emotional cards of both partners have been placed on the table and both still want to marry, they should do so in an appropriately brief period of time; the date should be set and the wedding planned. There are, however, still several acceptable reasons why, even at a late date, young women may break the engagement. Advice writers and novelists both set the standards of "just cause," and in most cases, they seem sensible even to modern readers.

The first reason was, of course, if during the entire courtship and engagement period the suitor had intentionally deceived the young woman and had held back information "which he knew would have prevented her from consenting to an engagement, had [it] been disclosed."[22] Information that would fall into this category included secret vices such as drinking and fornication; hereditary diseases; family feeblemindedness or insanity; prior engagements (and marriages!) to other women; illegitimate children; lies about employment, position, or financial status; atheism; felonies or periods spent in jail; gambling debts; impotence; venereal disease; and "abnormal propensities." Such information may emerge, Muzzey points out, after the young woman's male relatives have completed an exhaustive scrutiny of her suitor's background; if he is from another part of the country, this information might not emerge until very late in the engagement period. If it does, the young woman is expected to confront the suitor and present him with the proof. If no satisfactory explanation is forthcoming, she should dismiss him immediately—not only because of the nature of the information that was withheld but primarily because he thought so little of her that he intentionally deceived her.

In the Real Womanhood courtship model, a man capable of such atrocities would have been—should have been—detected earlier in his malfeasance through certain telltale signs. The drinker and the fornicator's local reputation and lack of steadiness of hand should have alerted the careful young woman; a significant reticence about immediate family and the suitor's discouraging the girl from meeting or writing to them should have provided a clue about their mental state or physical problems; a suspicious amount of free time, especially during the morning, should have made the young woman reconsider what the suitor had told her about his employment.[23] If there were a problem with his health, surely the observant young woman would have noticed a suspicious paleness, an unhealthy languor, a queer lack of enthusiasm for strenuous physical recreations such as horseback riding, rowing, walking, or dancing, a tendency to tire easily after ordinary exertion, a cough, or blood on a handkerchief.

Hidden sexual dysfunctions, however, have no apparent outward manifestations that any large number of advice writers allude to. Other than vague remarks about "affectionate natures" and "warmth" there are few measures or symptoms by which the young woman can judge her suitor without actually doing the unthinkable—having intercourse before marriage. Several marriage manuals state that they are intended to be read not only by couples already married but also by engaged couples, but even in them, suggestions of how a young woman should determine a future husband's conjugal suitability are indistinct. The subtitle to Dr. Frederick Hollick's *Marriage Guide* reads *A Private Instructor for Married Persons and Those about to Marry, Both Male and Female,* but there are no concrete suggestions on this topic. Given the highly specific nature of the book, its many finely detailed drawings of sexual organs both stimulated and unaroused, and its chapters on both male and female sexual dysfunction, perhaps the good doctor assumed that the young woman—or the young man who was her suitor—would discover the truth and apply it as a diagnostic tool. Hollick's somewhat evangelical tone and his obvious belief in the necessity of both young men and young women understanding the various stages, problems, and physiological reactions of sexuality would seem to indicate that this was his hope. As he notes in his preface, "A very large portion of the *disease* and *unhappiness* which many married persons suffer arises directly from their forced ignorance." He adds that he hopes that his book will provide the needed information both before and after marriage that can prevent conjugal misery and that it will serve as a handy reference throughout life.[24] His explicit chapters concerning female orgasm and its dysfunction, frigidity, as well as a chapter on male impotence containing a description of symptoms, perhaps provided sufficient information to enable the young woman to deduce whether her suitor had displayed "normal" interest in her or had exhibited suspicious reserve. Since Hollick's book was in constant publication for thirty years, running to five hundred "editions," perhaps such deductions were reasonable.[25] The enthusiastic Dr. Foote would have been more to the point; impotence or "abnormality" would have been blatantly exposed by his premarital "electrical magnetism" testing, which he felt should be a mandatory part of the marriage licensing procedure. And it needed to be exposed! As Carl Degler indicates in an article on women's sexuality in the nineteenth century, wives expected male "amativeness" to result in female sexual satisfaction. Without such satisfaction, it was thought that the wife could suffer mental and physical illness. Hence "normal" sexuality in a potential partner was very important.[26]

There were other just causes for breaking engagements, which did not involve horrendous disclosure of a "terrible secret" so fondly mentioned by gothic novelists and were more often met in everyday life. Two of these were a sudden, marked, public erosion of character with a change "decidedly for the worst" and a tendency to flirt obsessively with other women. On the degeneration of character Muzzey cites among other things the suitor suddenly turning violently and openly atheistic or sneeringly "scientific"; he also mentions a sudden turn to profligacy. One assumes that by this last he refers to a suitor unexpectedly inheriting a large sum of money and spending it wildly—something he had shown no sign of before because he never had enough liquid capital to do so. Under this injunction we can see that Graves's Sarah Sherman, with her competitive and luxury-loving lawyer husband, would have had just cause to break the engagement had Charles shown any sign of these traits before the marriage. In another fictional case, Holmes's Rosa Lee, though initially rejected by Dr. Clayton, lives to see how fortunate she was that the engagement was broken because Dr. Clayton lands himself in a financial mess by spending wildly above his income on the strength of his fiancée's (and later wife's) supposed inheritance. In addition to all of his other unworthy traits, Southworth's Herman Brudenell, the bigamist in *Ishmael,* reveals a fine and cavalier profligacy which even Hannah notices and comments on critically. Even had he been free to marry, Southworth indicates, he was a bad risk for any number of reasons, not the least of which was his uncontrolled spending habits.

In the case of a fiancé flirting or showing undue attention to another woman, the advice writers are equally stern: if no sufficient explanation and immediate cessation of the behavior is forthcoming, the young woman should send the suitor packing and cancel the wedding. Muzzey, Abell, and Weaver all indicate that such actions during an engagement do not bode well for future fidelity. Chapin indicates that life with a neglectful or roving-eyed husband is a private hell, which young women should make every effort to avoid. Chapin instructs young women not to expect their husbands to pay "a perpetual service of affection" to them, but he has no regard for neglectful husbands either and urges the young woman to take a critical view of a fiancé who engages in neglectful behavior. He calls such a fiancé—and later husband—a "traitor" and warns the young woman that such a man will "[use] the vows of marriage as a mere form, or as mock-words. Who [will toss] aside the heart he has won, like a toy."[27] The advice writers suggest, however, that young women at least give their suitors a chance to explain their behavior and show their sincerity by desisting from further displays. As Muzzey and others suggest, the other woman to whom the fiancé seems to be paying undue attention may turn out to be a cousin, an old acquaintance, or a friend of the family, in which case the insult is unintended and the violation only apparent. The young woman should present her fiancé with her objections immediately and in no uncertain terms to give him a chance either to explain or to stop or both.

Emily Thornwell, in her etiquette book, *The Lady's Guide to Perfect Gentility,* provides a sample letter which the young lady may use as a guide. Thornwell feels that a suitor's apparent flirting with someone else demands the formality of the written word, rather than a tearful, face-to-face confrontation, because the former is more in keeping with the honest, forthright, dignified tone the young woman should take on such a personally painful occasion. She suggests that in response to the young man's flirtation with another, the young woman should write, "Need I remind you that our vows of constancy have long been pledged, and often reiterated—more times than I can number." She should then demand an explanation of his behavior and a pledge of more appropriate behavior in the future. Never one to leave loose ends when giving advice, Thornwell has two other sample letters in the event that the fiancé apologizes or that he "intimates his wish to discontinue acquaintance." In the first case, Thornwell again suggests a somewhat aggressive approach to discourage the fiancé from further violations of the code; in accepting his apology the young lady should say, "That you have offended me, I have not attempted to disguise from you," thereby registering on paper a second time her absolute rejection of his behavior. In the infinitely more complex second case, when the fiancé indicates after the young woman's questions that his affections have moved to another, Thornwell demands a strong-minded and courageous reprisal: the young woman should tell such a cur stoutly that she will "banish you from my affections, as readily and completely as you have banished me," and she should follow this statement with a stern demand for the immediate return of any letters she sent him and the assurance that his will be sent back posthaste.[28] Obviously, if Thornwell felt that sample letters were useful on such occasions, it was not inconceivable or inappropriate to end an engagement or demand explanation of inappropriate behavior. ʼ

Finally, assuming that no just cause emerges and that each knows and accepts the other's faults, the marriage should take place. On its eve, advice writers have one last piece of advice. Young women who are about to become wives should realize that the road ahead of them is one that, even under the best and most cautious of circumstances, is fraught with rough spots and brambles. As Chapin notes solemnly, the young woman must be prepared to work in partnership daily against the problems that inevitably arise, the "occasions of trial" that will occur. As Muzzey reminds the young woman, there is joy in marriage, but it often comes from "an unlooked-for-source," frequently from traits she initially undervalued or had not seen fully manifested. A young woman should not be obsessed with the fulfillment of satisfaction in particular areas which she projected while she was engaged, but rather be prepared to enjoy other, less obvious, satisfactions that develop. The key, according to both Muzzey and Chapin, is a realistic adjustment and the wholehearted desire to make the best marriage possible under whatever circumstances present themselves, unless those circumstances are extraordinary such as physical brutality, gross lasciviousness, alcoholism, or gambling. If these problems arise, the general consensus among both writers of advice books and novelists of the same mind is that the woman should remove herself and her children somewhere else (often returning to live with her parents) and live autonomously, depending in whole or in part on herself for financial support. If she has followed the Real Womanhood ideal, the young woman, however heart-bruised by this turn of events, will have both the training and the fortitude to carry on alone. Despite arguments to the contrary by Henry James, divorce was not really an option, especially in a society worried about how children would be supported after a divorce. The editor of the *Nation* sternly told his readers to be aware of its risks before entering matrimony; indeed, speaking as the voice of society, he says that "marriages are not perfect; that in a vast number of cases the woman marries the wrong man, and *vice versa*, I admit, my dear friends, with sorrow. But they make the choice themselves, and I have as yet hit no substitute for their freedom. Nor do I see any likelihood that, if I let them divorce as often as they pleased, matters would be any better, for they would be just as likely to err in the second alliance as in the first."[29]

Despite the seemingly obvious rejection of separation on the grounds that children would need to be supported, the *Nation's* editor notes that if divorce were easy a man could conceivably scatter the landscape with cast-off children for whom he was financially responsible legally but whom he would be unable or unwilling to support in light of each new marriage and family. One marriage significantly reduced the number of children he was legally responsible to aid and which the state could reasonably and practically force him to support.[30] The *Nation's* editor also objected to divorce because he felt it cheapened the meaning and the obligations of the marriage ceremony and encouraged the lightminded to approach marriage casually and without seriously considering its responsibilities, thereby inadvertently hastening divorce for reasons of marital incompatibility and unhappiness. Easy divorce encouraged such persons to dismiss the commitment and seek newer and more interesting casual sexual unions without any consideration of duty, thus promoting "changefulness," selfishness, and irresponsibility nationwide. The editor's worry over an attitude of national selfishness is best understood as a concern over the growing tendency to regard marriage—and worse, its products (children)—lightly. The editor's chilling words—that the choice was freely made—underline the extreme caution the Real Womanhood advice writers advocated for the entire process of selecting a future mate. Though they may have concurred that occasionally, even with the most stringent preparations, mistakes in judgment occurred and that in extraordinary cases of physical violence and injury, the responsible woman should escape with her children and live apart from her husband, they still felt marriage was a lifetime commitment and the selection of a partner should be treated as such. Making the marriage work should be considered a "duty" for both partners—one from which neither their own moral consciences nor society would willingly free them. Caution in choice and adequate criteria for judgment were, then, the only real safety.

SIX

Employment and the Real Woman

The want of Employment, and the dependence of many women, have ruined their characters, and made them little else than nuisances to their fellow-men. Thousands of women have no Employment and live through life in a state of abject dependence. What are they, what can they be, under such circumstances?

—Reverend George S. Weaver,
*Aims and Aids for Girls
and Young Women*

To those of us reared to believe that decent American middle-class women plied only their needles and not a trade in the nineteenth century, the Reverend Weaver's words come as a bit of a shock. If, as Barbara Ehrenreich and Deirdre English suggest, society expected good women to exist as the "antithesis of economic man" and, as Madonna Kolbenschlag claims, they were theoretically excluded from "worldly achievements, assertive behavior, initiative, and autonomy,"[1] Weaver's and many other nineteenth-century writers' injunctions to women to pursue salaried and benevolent employment require explanation. Once again, that explanation lies in the competition and disagreement between the Ideal of Real Womanhood and the Cult of True Womanhood about the requirements of being a "good" woman. Both ideals had their spokespeople, male and female, and each defined not only employment but the need for it differently. This chapter outlines Real Womanhood's understanding of the term "employment," as well as the various categories of it to which those advice writers refer; explains the conditions under which women were expected to seek employment; lists the benefits (moral, physical, spiritual, economic, and patriotic) women could expect to derive from employment; and provides a partial list of the forms of salaried employment advice writers suggested and domestic novelists and short-story writers demonstrated as the "proper" work of the decent, self-reliant, middle-class woman of the American Northeast during this time. Further, I will explain how this employment fit with other aspects of Real Womanhood such as academic and domestic training, the woman's maintenance of her health, her ideals concerning the man she would (or would not) marry, and her expectations about the economic security of marriage. Real Womanhood, though diametrically opposed to the passive economic dependence and victimization inherent in the True Womanhood ideal, is hardly a strong ally of early feminism either; on the matter of salaried employment, the Ideal of Real

Womanhood plays for the first time that ragged old tune modern working women frequently hum today—"I'd rather stay home with the children, but I *have* to work for financial reasons."

With an ideal as tightly integrated as Real Womanhood was, there is bound to be some repetition from one topic to another. I stress the interrelation of marriage choice and employment as they relate to employment, but it is important to understand that employment—or the desire to be employed and the ability to be employed for a salary—is central to the question of marriage. In the advice works outlining the characteristics of the Real Woman, employment is less frequently discussed than marriage or even education, but advice writers presuppose the woman's ability to be employed when they tender advice to women about their health, their courtship practices, and their educations.

Initially, however, it is vital to understand what these advice writers meant by "employment." A dictionary used in common schools in the mid-1860s defines employment as "n. business; service; occupation; agency"[2]; it does not suggest that salary is necessary to the definition, though, as in the case of "business" or "occupation," it may be. Any productive labor was "employment." Indeed, with this definition in mind when one reads the literature, many formerly obscure connections become clear. There were three broad categories of employment which advice writers and novelists urged, and only one of them involves employment for a salary. All of these, according to writers, conferred the inestimable moral benefits of work on the woman; all provided for her physical well-being; all were an avenue for her to prove herself a good Christian and a good American.

The three—charitable or philanthropic employment, domestic employment, and salaried employment—either directly or indirectly taught the woman self-reliance and weaned her away from various forms of dependency. Changing circumstances (economic, social, or marital) apparently demanded that the woman engage in different categories of employment; no circumstances—even riches and a secure home—allowed for idleness. Work in its own right was both a virtue and a necessity for the character; good women, advice writers cautioned, should always be "employed" if they expected to remain morally upright. With this expanded understanding of the definition of employment comes also a wider understanding of Real Womanhood's vision of woman's sphere as one in which work played a central role and without which no woman could consider herself a good mother, wife, daughter, sister, friend, or member of society. As the unrelenting Reverend Weaver explains coldly, "A lady and a woman are two very different things. One is made at the hands of fashion; the other is the handiwork of God through the instrumentality of useful Employment. A lady is a parlor ornament, a walking show-gallery, a mistress of tongue-tied etiquette. A woman is a consecrated intelligence—a love baptized—a hand employed in the work of good." Nor is Weaver alone in his insistence on the virtue of employment; Dr. Dio Lewis states that there are physical and mental, as well as moral, dimensions to working, noting that "without a regular occupation, no person, male or female, can preserve a sound mind in a sound body."[3]

Domestic novelists tend to agree in their portraits of heroines and their foils. Although the heroine's aunt, Fortune Emerson, in Warner's *Wide, Wide World,* is hardly a pleasant or aesthetic model, she is a strong, Yankee-blunt, "employed" alternative to Ellen Montgomery's weak and passive mother, who eventually dies leaving the child to the tender mercies of unknown relatives. Says Aunt Fortune, the farm owner, sneeringly to Ellen, "I'll give you something to do; and something to learn too, that you want enough more than all those crinkumcrankums; I wonder what good they'd ever do you! That's the way your mother was brought up, I suppose. If she had been trained to use her hands and do something useful instead of thinking herself above it, maybe she wouldn't have to go to sea for her health."[4] Much of the rest of the novel revolves around little Ellen Montgomery's initiation into the world of self-reliance and work and away from a life devoted only to books and dreams. Although Real Womanhood encouraged higher education, it was never to be at the expense of employment in some form. Ellen's mother not only read too much, but she refused to engage in domestic employment; her poor health at the beginning of the novel and her relatively early death paint a vivid fictional portrait of the woman who does no work and what happens to any children she leaves behind her. It is a thought-provoking picture.

Two forms of employment that play large parts in a "good" woman's life are charitable employment and domestic employment. These distinguish Real Womanhood from early feminism because they suggest the value of "at home" or benevolent work for no salary. They provide as well a clear context for understanding the transitory nature of salaried employment among Real Women—a context in which one form of work is as morally beneficial as another, and each form comes at the dictates not of ideology but of circumstance.

A labor historian's statistics on actual jobs held by mid-nineteenth-century women is not at issue here, but rather the jobs and work that advice writers and novelists suggested they should hold ideally. This is an important distinction. Whether women actually did hand out leaflets to factory workers or do their husbands' bookkeeping at night or worked loading cartridges at the firearms factory is immaterial; advice writers urged—and expected—them to do such things. Though occasionally, for purposes of illustration and contrast, I mention what women really did, the focus of this discussion is on the ideals espoused, not on actual working conditions.

Perhaps the least clearly understood aspect of employment under the Ideal of Real Womanhood involves the concept of charitable or philanthropic endeavors because the vision of this work is one of apparently syrupy "do-gooderism." Many critics fail to realize that such benevolent works were only of importance secondarily to benefit the poor; their main function was to provide enormous benefits for the character and health of the young misses as they busily went about their merciful rounds. Rich young women without homes to care for, husbands, or families of their own, writers suggest, are especially vulnerable to character defects; idleness, fashion, and enough money to provide for all their whims provide perfect breeding grounds for boredom, selfishness, callousness, and sloth, unless parents take stern measures. One way out of the dilemma was for parents to urge their "more fortunate" children to spend their time helping or "improving" the lot and the character of the "less fortunate." As Dr. Dio Lewis explains, "I have advised idle young ladies, who were longing for something to do, to look up poor unhappy families, and minister to their hungry bodies and hungry hearts." Each of these young ladies could become, Lewis feels, "a devoted friend of the sick and the suffering"; this benevolence, in turn, would cure them of the evils brought on by "[being] a slave to a round of fashionable dissipations." These dissipations seem to consist, in Lewis's book, of eating chocolates, reading trashy novels, pouting and whining for presents, failing to exercise, and wearing rib-crushing corsets.[5]

Domestic novels are replete with heroines doing philanthropic or charitable work while their vicious and selfish foils lounge on sofas, complain, have headaches, dress in frilly clothes and kid slippers, and try to entice or entrap the heroine's boyfriend. Susan Warner's model woman for heroine Ellen Montgomery to emulate, Miss Alice Humphreys, is an example of a well-off philanthropic character, set in contrast to Ellen's "fashionable" aunt and grandmother in Scotland. These two, Mrs. Keith and Mrs. Lindsay, are not only rich and antiphilanthropic, they are neither truly Christian (they drink wine and go to the Anglican church) nor imbued with what advice writers would consider American values. Both women resent Ellen's desire to "do good"; they even call in a doctor to examine her when she begs leave to pray by herself for an hour early each morning and attempt to make her "forget" the words of wisdom offered her by Miss Alice and her brother, Mr. John Humphreys. Since this is a pious American novel, little Ellen succeeds in reuniting herself with the godly Humphreys and manages to throw off the suffocating mantle of wealth and stultifying privilege the Lindsays and Mrs. Keith would thrust on her. Ellen ultimately refuses a life of well-upholstered inactivity and seeks a path for herself marked by learning, writing, and doing good.

Her model, Miss Alice, is exemplary of such a life. Miss Alice is the motherless daughter of the local minister, and she makes it her duty to "tend" to the sick, the impoverished, and the distressed in her neighborhood. It is not merely because she is a minister's daughter that she feels it is incumbent upon her to do these good deeds; rather, as a "good" woman, a Christian, and one of the "fortunate" in America, she feels it is her duty to be actively employed, as she explains to little Ellen, who becomes one of Miss Alice's more successful "projects." She takes Ellen with her on benevolent rounds, leading her up the mountain to visit Mrs. Vawse, an elderly Swiss-born grandmother who is poor but honest and in need of comfort. Miss Alice counsels Ellen to be kind to Mrs. Vawse's impish, sometimes malevolent granddaughter, Nancy, pointing out that the girl is wild and ignorant, not "bad." Nancy becomes one of Ellen's first successful "projects" in the arena of benevolence, for under her tutelage Nancy learns to read, swears less, and develops (through Ellen's kindly persuasion and shining example) "gentle ways."

Busily delivering soup to the hungry and Christian tracts to the neglected, organizing food and clothing drives for the impoverished, and reading the Bible to shut-ins, Miss Alice and Ellen are busy most of the day, taking time out only for lessons in English, Latin, biology, history, French, and horseback riding or practice in cooking and housework. Little Ellen, formerly a skinny, pasty-faced child, blooms under this regimen, profiting not only from the healthy effects of do-gooding but also from the long tramps up and down the mountain, the good food, and the sunshine. Miss Alice is not so fortunate; delicate already, she overtaxes herself by searching in a snowstorm for Ellen and winds up with pneumonia, which kills her. Although this would seem an indirect indictment of benevolence as a way of life, closer examination of the novel reveals a fictional imperative to get rid of the character so that a grown-up Ellen can take her place, both benevolently and actually in the Humphreys household. Indeed, when imprisoned in Scotland, little Ellen, denied the right to serve the community benevolently, forced into a life of idle, fashionable routine, herself soon sickens. Despite Miss Alice's demise, it is obvious through the example of Ellen's illness under inactivity that a life of employment—even if it is unnecessary to do so for a salary—is important to maintain mental and physical health.

Susan Warner is not alone in portraying the benefits of such a life. Other novelists and (through extended exempla) advice writers preach the same gospel. Marion Harland's antiheroine Ruby Sloane in the 1868 novel *Ruby's Husband* not only provides a black-gilt frame for the novel's true heroine, benevolently employed Frances "Frank" Berry, but ends up, as a direct result of her selfishness, an imbecile and a cripple.

The heroine, on the other hand, spends her life caring for the sick. Word of Frank's goodness and charity precedes her appearance in the novel; she has nursed the Suydams' eldest son in Florence as he lay dying. Though she is no relation, Frank is a friend of the Suydam family and feels compelled by compassion to try to ease the eldest son's pain, fear of death, and loneliness. Not only does she play the piano for him, wipe his fevered brow, and read him the newspaper, she also brings him to Jesus before he dies.

Exemplary Frank Berry also carries the burden of a rattled, cancer-riddled, coquettish mother, who, well beyond the years of flirtation, covers up her fear of death by acting the belle in public and being nursed by Frank in private. For the majority of the novel, Frank is the only person Mrs. Berry allows to know about her cancer; Frank is forced to read medical books, deal with her mother's growing addiction to narcotics, and bear the strain of nursing and the worry alone. Despite the physical and emotional strain of nursing such a woman—as well as the effort she exerted earlier in Florence—Frank still is strong and vital enough to help out old Katrine, the Suydams' retired nanny, and to take over their second son, Louis. Through Frank, Louis learns to face up to his responsibilities, acknowledge his guilt, and, eventually, clear his name. Benevolence and the busyness of such employment obviously agree with Frank; she is rarely sick, walks miles, and is generally strong and active, as well as rosy-cheeked and beautiful.

Needless to say, the novel's arch-villainess, Ruby, is a woman who has never been employed in her life, not even in taking care of herself. Although she comes from a poor family, Ruby depends on her mother to take care of her, and her mother has made herself a slave to the beautiful girl, granted her every whim, and stayed up nights until her eyes were bloodshot making clothes for Ruby out of her own old dresses. Ruby's monstrous selfishness, indolence, and languor are representative of the character flaws people—especially beautiful women—develop, according to advice writers and domestic novelists, if they are allowed to spend their lives in idleness and self-satisfying frivolity. Frank Berry is the attractive alternative. Naturally, Louis Suydam falls deeply and passionately in love with Frank Berry, drawn by her erudition, her common sense, and most of all, her generosity and goodness, in contrast to the poisonous, demanding selfishness of his "secret wife," Ruby. Beauty and an attractive character are two of the side benefits, authors suggest, that accrue from a life of employment.

Frank and Ruby, as opposites, further illustrate several dicta of the famed advice writer Dr. William Alcott (cousin to Louisa May). According to Alcott's manual on health, benevolent activity provides enormous benefits to both the constitution and the mind by taking a person "out of herself"; it gives a young woman something to think about besides her own troubles, and therefore she ceases brooding. Moreover, going about her business, she is able to contemplate green things (apparently Alcott assumes that outdoor benevolence occurs only during spring and summer), and beautiful foliage soothes both the spirit and the mind. Such employment, notes Alcott, gives purpose to one's walk—and this helps with respiration. It also tires out the young woman so that she passes no lonely nights brooding over her lot but sleeps soundly so as to be fully prepared to do her benevolent work the next day.[6] Alcott's description fits both the constitution and the ordinary activities of Frank Berry before her mother's last weeks; the neglect of such a regimen results in the brooding, the pallor, and the spiteful spirits of Ruby.

Benevolent or charitable work, however, is only one form of employment that the wealthy should practice, and help for the poor or compassion for the unfortunate is only a secondary reason why the rich should seek such employment. There are less philanthropic reasons to be employed for no pay; apprenticeship and vocational training, for example, are excellent hedges against a sudden loss of fortune in the family. As with philanthropic employment, entering an apprenticeship has primary beneficial effects on the character, which can prove useful even if the young lady's father never loses his fortune. Charity work can be done in and for the family, as well as outside it. Girls learning how to clerk in a father's store learn the value of a dollar and the habits of industry and application; moreover, they help out the family, as well as gaining experience in a skill that will make them fit to earn their own living in the event of a disaster.

Advice writer T. S. Arthur tells a moral tale of just such a familial charitable situation in his best-selling book *Advice to Young Ladies*. In this illustrative story, a merchant friend of Arthur's complains about his two eldest daughters, Jane and Edith, who employ themselves in nothing more strenuous than reclining on sofas and trying on new clothes. Warned by the meddlesome Arthur of the bad effects on their character, Jane and Edith's father insists that they cease their lives of idleness and apprentice themselves to, respectively, a dressmaker and a milliner. With many tears and much grumbling, the girls do so, spending five years as apprentices but yearly growing more healthy, more cheerful, and more mature. They finish their apprenticeships just in time for their father to be ruined financially. His business lost, he proceeds in typically American male fashion, according to both novels and advice literature, to have a stroke that paralyzes him. Jane and Edith come home to take care of him. Fueled by financial necessity (and trained in habits of perseverance, hard work, and honesty), the girls design circulars advertising their skills (dressmaking and millinery) and distribute them. Soon their industry, good taste, and honest toil have won them a small but steady clientele; eventually, they have enough trade that they are forced to hire, Arthur assures us, twenty assistants. Ultimately, the girls become wealthy, provide nursing home care for their father, and educate their younger siblings.[7]

The "shopkeeper and his lazy daughters" seems to be a favorite moral tale in advice books. Dio Lewis, too, has a moral tale to tell, involving not two but three idle daughters, thereby adding a more overt fairy-tale quality to the story than it already has. As Lewis explains it, a friend confides to him that his dry goods store is edging toward ruin. Lewis's friend is forced to call his idle, selfish daughters back from an expensive vacation in New Hampshire (a vacation they harried their father into providing for them—on credit). He tells them of the impending family disaster and asks them to clerk in his store to save on salaries. They whine, object, and cry that such employment will "ruin" them socially, but they eventually agree and pitch in, just as Lewis predicted they would. It seems that in the past Lewis had warned the shopkeeper about the bad character traits his daughters were developing without a "regular occupation," but the father had not listened. After several weeks of working in their father's store, however, the girls show their "true" characters. Their father tells Lewis, "It is just as you told me,—that their life of indolence and selfish indulgence had brought every mean trait to the surface; but that when the depths were stirred I should find that they were true women. Yes, thank God, they are true women, as brave girls as ever lived."[8] The girls save their father from bankruptcy, become happy and "chipper" in the process, and learn a trade./ Employment not only prepares them for the possible hard times to come but improves their mental health./

The Reverend Weaver seems to make the conclusive statement on the matter of employment for rich young women, and in so doing he strikes a curiously egalitarian note: "No matter if they are rich. They need Employment just as much. A rich young man is not excused from business—from acting nobly his part in life, and doing something worthy of a man. And if he excuses himself he will only be despised by the community in which he lives. . . . Why should it not be so with a young woman?" He paints a dreary picture of the stultification endured by rich, fashionable women, treated like small children by a society determined to limit their lives to an endless diet of monotony, triviality, and boredom: "They are attended by servants wherever they go, who do what they ought to do, and often think what they ought to think. The woman who always asks her servant to do what she may do herself, soon becomes dependent upon, and loses a good portion of herself in her servant."[9] The terror Weaver displays at dependence on servants is

Left: *Harper's Weekly,* February 24, 1866. Right: *Harper's Weekly,*
December 1, 1860

crucial for understanding the impetus behind domestic employment. In
short, domestic employment involves two separate but related activities,
both of which may help save money. The first, doing domestic tasks or
other work that would otherwise have to be hired out, obviously saves
the cost of the salary to employ someone else to do the job. A good
woman, therefore, is prepared to do such work herself to save on either
her own or her family's expenses, both immediate and extended. The
second activity involves being able to do all the tasks generally assigned
to domestic servants so well that those servants, as Weaver implies, are
not in a position of power because of the woman's dependence on them.
They are not, therefore, able to "blackmail" the mistress into granting
higher wages or being lax in discipline because the woman is afraid they
will quit if their demands are not met. This bogey haunts several short
stories of the period and works its way into novels.

One striking example occurs in Mrs. H. C. Gardner's uplifting two-
part story "Labor; or Striking for Higher Wages." The mistress, Mary,
finds her untrustworthy Irish cook, Nelly, threatening to walk out only
hours before a big dinner party if Mary refuses to raise her salary sub-
stantially. Sly but not shrewd (like so many stereotypical Irish servant
characters), Nelly outlines her crafty plan to the servant next door, un-
aware that Mary is at the window within earshot. Mary is piqued but

not distressed; she is more hurt by Nelly's treachery than by the possibility of her quitting. Mary, Gardner has explained earlier, always thought she should do the cooking herself because she had grown up without servants and accepted Nelly only at her new husband's fervent request. Swiftly, Mary makes her plans, enlisting the marginal help of her maid, and plans dinner around Nelly's supposedly "surprise" departure. She does not turn a hair when Nelly announces that she is leaving after Mary has coolly turned down her request for higher wages. Shocked but backed into a corner by her own lies, Nelly departs in a storm of tears, having lost both her ploy for more money and her job.[10]

The second part of the story opens with Mary preparing for the dinner party alone. Her objective (with the help of her maid to serve it) is to maintain the fiction that Nelly is in the kitchen working so that her husband will "never know" that she has had to cook the meal herself. As Gardner draws him, the husband must be kept in the dark so that he will not be embarrassed in front of his friends by his wife doing a "domestic's work." As we see later, when Mary reveals all to him after the party, part of the purpose of Mary's heroism is to "educate" her husband so that he will understand the value of domestic employment for wives—even the wives of comfortably fixed, "important" men. In this effort, of course, she succeeds.

She convinces him in part because of the brilliant success of the dinner and the party. Presiding genteelly at the head of the table, she excuses herself three times to "check on the meal"; in truth, she rushes back to make the final preparations on the next course, dish up a complicated dish, and finish the dessert. She returns each time to the table and waits coolly for her maid to bring out the dishes, which only short hours before she had prepared in a frenzied effort. No one—especially her husband—is any the wiser, even when the guests wish to compliment Nelly on the meal; Mary explains that Nelly is shy and would be embarrassed to come out and face "company." Given the comic vagaries of Irish servants in fiction, this ploy works and the guests have a merry laugh at Nelly's quaint ways.

After the guests have left, Mary's husband insists that she fetch Nelly so that he can tip the cook for the meal on which she "outdid" herself. Mary is then forced to confess that Nelly has quit and that she herself prepared the dinner. Her husband is astounded—and he soon agrees that every woman should be as well equipped domestically as his Mary is. Nelly, incidentally, comes whining to Mary, begging her for her job back; Mary hires her at her old wages out of charity and continues herself to help prepare the meals, happily keeping employed to attain mental as well as physical health.[11]

Novels of the period also feature upright, domestically employed heroines who scotch the open revolt of servants or make them unnecessary. Though the obstreperous servants are slaves, the case of the dinner and party in Holmes's 'Lena Rivers not only further underlines the virtues of the woman able to perform her own household duties but provides negative examples of women who cannot. The heroine, 'Lena, has come, for financial reasons, to live with her uncle and aunt in Kentucky, where she is treated wretchedly and constantly sneered at by her fashionable aunt, Mrs. Livingston, and by her hateful cousin Carrie, both of whom are living embodiments of "fashionable" idle women. Maple Grove, the large mansion where the Livingstons reside, has a full complement of house slaves as well as a cook; Mrs. Livingston is not only idle, she is cruel to her slaves as well. Only hours before the prominent Graham family is expected for dinner and a party, along with scores of other notables, most of the household slaves, including the cook, come down sick—or so they claim. Faced with a mansion that needs to be cleaned and a dinner to prepare, Mrs. Livingston becomes hysterical. Rushing into the kitchen, she attempts to start the dinner and ruins everything she touches. Gently, the despised 'Lena (a Massachusetts girl of faultless New England training) sends her aunt upstairs to get ready and then cleans the entire house, including all the guest rooms: " 'Lena, confining her long curls to the top of her head and donning the wide check-apron which her aunt had thrown aside, set herself at work with a right good will."[12]

Not only does the fifteen-year-old 'Lena clean the entire house, she also has dinner ready, thanks to the help of her other cousin and one loyal slave, and greets the arriving guests while Mrs. Livingston and Carrie are busy primping upstairs.[13] The dinner, needless to say, is a success—and so is cool, self-possessed 'Lena, especially with the eminently eligible Durward Bellmont, Mr. Graham's stepson and one of the most accomplished and upstanding young men in the region. Carrie, who had intended to impress Durward, finds herself cast into the shadows by 'Lena's domestic abilities and her healthy vigor and common-sense attitudes. As the novel progresses, Carrie continues to lounge round the house, slapping servants and twitting 'Lena, who can turn er hand to any domestic concern that needs doing. Carrie is also portrayed as selfish, whining, and frequently sickly; 'Lena is in splendid ealth and, of course, ends up marrying Durward Bellmont, while Carie finds herself betrothed to an ancient roué who has lied about his ortune. Domestic employment, like benevolent employment, not only ids in encouraging attractive character development and a healthy outook, but it also dramatically separates Real Women from, as Weaver lassifies them, "ladies," in the eyes of prospective suitors.

Blackmail—or obstreperousness—on the part of servants implies either having to hire more servants or saving the expense by doing it oneself. Salaries are no small item in a household budget, as any number of authors show when they have their model young women ave their fathers or their husbands the salaries of bookkeepers, cooks, caterers, or clerks. A clear picture of the value of domestic employment emerges when we consider the role it plays in economy within a narriage.

Graves's redoubtable Sarah Sherman ("The Mechanic's Daughter") is n outstanding example of the use of employment in the domestic phere to save money. Trained by her book-hating mother in domestic rts of housewifery such as putting up preserves and making teas, Sarah s an expert when she marries Charles Harcourt. This is indeed fortunate ecause Charles spends them into enormous debt. Sarah manages to keep them afloat by doing all the cooking and the catering for his clients herself and by keeping his books from the law office. Without her fforts, Charles would owe salaries to servants and clerks; indeed, it is ecause of the enormous potential outlay for servants' wages that Sarah s able to convince Charles to get rid of the servants and let her do the work.[14]

Novels abound with well-trained domestically employed young women who save money by doing for themselves or their families. Whitney's heroine Leslie Goldthwaite, for example, is a thrifty little person who makes her own exquisite underwear. Holmes's Rose Mather is despised by the other women because initially she has no idea how to sew or cook or knit; she earns their respect later (and saves money while waiting for her husband to return) by making socks and shirts to send her husband while he is at the front during the Civil War. The lawless Ellen Montgomery, in Warner's *Wide, Wide World*, helps run her aunt's farm when her aunt is sick and keeps up the house as well because Aunt Fortune cannot afford hired help in the house. Even in a book as out of the mainstream as Fanny Fern's *Rose Clark,* the heroine learns the millinery trade in her aunt's shop and clerks there to save her aunt an extra salary; in this progressive novel, marked by a bohemian female artist as a secondary role model, domestic employment is portrayed as being valuable.[15]

Although the benefits, both financial and moral, of domestic employment are obvious, they pale in comparison to the greater benefits advice writers suggested that young women could accrue from salaried employment. Like both domestic and benevolent employment, work for money kept the woman busy in useful, productive labor; additionally, it fostered independence of spirit and pocketbook and provided a strong safety net for an immediate or extended family. Finally, it provided a way to escape a bad or brutal marriage and an alternative to marriage.

Despite all of these inestimable benefits, however, it would be a mistake to see in the novelists' or advice writers' exhortations to salaried employment any quasi-modern idea of personal fulfillment or careerism. Always such writers as Weaver, Lewis, and Arthur see such occupations in the larger context of an extended woman's sphere in which Christian benevolence, responsibility for one's own or extended family, and usefulness to the community are the outlines of a female lifelong duty to God and country.

Its transitory, crisis-oriented nature perhaps best explains one of the most difficult concepts to understand about salaried employment as it was *ideally* represented. Working for money was the correct female response to financial hardship when the good of one's family or the support of oneself was at stake. Being economically self-reliant built character, but so did benevolent employment or occupying oneself fully at home. The strength of character salaried employment added was merely a side benefit. Money to buy shoes, pay the doctor, keep the landlord from the door, or prop up a husband's failing business was the primary benefit—along with freedom from fear or from the degradation of accepting charity. Salaried employment made it possible to hold up one's head and live with a bad marriage without having to run to a father or mother (or worse, a benevolent institution) for money on which to live. It also meant that when a husband drank, or gambled, or speculated with the rent money (as many novelists and advice writers suggest was a better than average possibility) a woman could still support her family—or leave and take the children with her. It meant that the death of a spouse or a father did not require that a family be broken up and farmed out to various relatives or that the widow had to remarry immediately to provide the income to keep the family together.

Nor were alcoholism, compulsive gambling, and speculation the only honorable reasons for a woman to engage in salaried employment. Sometimes—both in real life and in novels—husbands, however kind and thoughtful, were hapless about getting or holding a job.

One excellent example is the life of advice writer and sometime novelist Lydia Maria Child. A successful editor and the author of twenty-one books of both fiction and advice, Child supported both herself and her husband, though, fortunately, no children. Gerda Lerner offers an interesting perspective on Child's marriage, noting that she was "married to a gentle and ineffectual man who seldom made a living, but who offered her moral support."[16] Apparently, this was a satisfactory trade for Child, who valued her work and her independence.

Child's routine activities provide an excellent example of the integration of domestic, philanthropic, and salaried employment expected of Real Women in America. In her "List of Activities" for the year 1864, Child includes the following, among others: writing six articles for the newspaper, correcting proofs for a forthcoming book, making twenty-five needle books for freed women, gathering and making a peck of pickles for the hospital, knitting socks and making suspenders for her husband, cutting down and reconstructing three gowns for herself, writing forty-seven "autograph articles," making five visits to "aged women," cooking 360 dinners, mending seventy pairs of stockings, and making a silk dress.[17]

Although advice writers like Weaver strike what seems an early feminist note, we must remember that it is a severely qualified one; their discussion of self-reliance is understood to mean in case of a crisis, not as a way of life for a married woman. Despite the assertions of Ehrenreich and English that writers urged mid-nineteenth-century American women to be intuitive, emotional, tender, submissive, nonrational, noncompetitive, and "even masochistic,"[18] another body of advice writers disagreed violently and deplored the fact that women were not prepared with job skills to meet the emergencies that would undoubtedly beset them. They argued against training women to be ornamental dolls, without skills or purpose, lest these dolls shatter under the weight of adversity; they denounced different vocational expectations for boys and girls because they believed both would face economic difficulties, the girls more than the boys because they would have children. Thunders Weaver:

> I would not make the boys self-reliant and vigorous by generous Employ-
> ment, and the girls weak, puny, and dependent by idleness and folly. I
> would not give the boys opportunities to develop their powers and become
> noble men, and deprive the girls of all these glorious privileges. I would not
> open a thousand avenues to distinction, wealth, and worth to the boys and
> comparatively none to the girls. I would not send the boys out into the field
> of life bravely to earn their own living, and grow strong in doing it, and the
> girls out to beg their living of the boys, and grow weak and worthless in
> their dependent beggary. I like the girls too well to have them thus mis-
> treated.[19]

Despite such exhortations from advice writers, a curious anomaly crops up in the domestic novels and short fiction of the period. Advice writers counsel women to learn specific job skills, laud them for gaining higher education, and urge them to become doctors and lawyers on occasion. Heroines in the fiction, however, rarely exhibit such a range of skills. Susan Warner's Ellen Montgomery is a scholar and a benevolent helper, but she is hardly a doctor or even a milliner; Holmes's Rosa Lee in *Meadowbrook* is both a teacher and a governess but not a lawyer or a university professor; Olive West in the *Harper's* story is a poet and a doll dresser but not a photographer's assistant, a telegraph operator, or a smallwares businesswoman. All of these alternatives are skills, trades, or professions which advice writers suggest are eminently suitable for women.

Women, it seems, were being told in genteel advice books to choose such trades, but they were shown in fiction doing more dramatic or glamorous jobs or more transitory ones. Certainly these heroines are never idle—like Child they are frequently employed not only in benevolent or domestic pursuits but also in salaried ones. Just as surely the novelists openly despise women who are idle, frivolous, or weak.

What could be the reason for such a disparity? Perhaps the answer is obvious: domestic novels and short stories, however didactic in intention, are not works of expository prose; they are works of fiction—and fiction demands drama, glamour, extremes, and excitement. Reality—even in so-called realistic novels (though most critics consider domestic novels sentimental, not realistic)—is always subordinated to the needs of the tone and the plot. For Holmes to cast heroine Rose Lee as a telegraph operator or smallwares seller would hardly allow her the opportunity or scope to show her colors as the brilliant, brave girl who at thirteen first supports the family by teaching rough sixteen-year-old boys in a one-room schoolhouse, then later meets the hero, Richard Delafield, a rich plantation owner, while working as a governess. Conversely, sorting pins in a pin factory or working as a weaver in a mill hardly suggests the hopeless depths of degradation and poverty that taking in wash and sewing shirt collars does for Arthur's heroine Mrs. Foster in the "New Year's Gift." Sorting pins or working as a mill weaver was reputed to pay too well for the degradation to be believable.

The domestic fiction tradition expected its readers to experience strong emotion; heroines, therefore, must be either degraded, noble, or exalted. As a result, married women (or heroines supporting their siblings and parents) are too busy making ends meet to pursue a medical or legal education. Rather, they work at noble occupations such as teaching or governessing, or work their way up from lowly positions such as doll dresser or seamstress, meanwhile secretly writing poetry or short stories or articles, which they later sell and which earn them, ultimately, fame and success, like *Harper's* heroine Olive West and Edna Earl in *St. Elmo.*

All of the heroines in the domestic novels and short fiction I have mentioned throughout this work are not limited to schoolteaching or seamstressing, however; some have glamorous professions. These heroines form a separate category, however, because they are dedicatedly single, with no intention of marrying. Augusta Evans's Salome Owen in *Vashti* is a miller's daughter who eventually becomes famous in Europe and America as an opera singer. Salome is problematically drawn, in contrast to Miss Jane Grey, who is a rich character practicing assiduous benevolent employment by taking in orphans like Salome and giving them a good home. Other characters denounce Salome's ambition, her brains, and her drive as "selfishness" and "coldness"; one in particular, Miss Jane's brother, Dr. Ulpian Grey, particularly attempts to "reform" Salome, who carries a torch for him. His cold, correct Christianity, however, is hardly attractive, as Evans paints him, and indeed, the author rewards his righteous cruelty to Salome by having the faultlessly correct doctor fall in love with a married woman, whose corpse he inadvertently kisses, becoming the victim of a grim practical joke on the part of his author-creator. From the outset Salome refuses to consider settling down and becoming some man's good little wife, and she fights for the right to an artistic career and an independent single life. Her character shows on her face: as the novel opens, Evans tells her readers that Salome has "thin lips, whose outlines sharply index more of decision than amiability of character."[20] This heroine is obviously not going to settle down to an ordinary, pious, but humdrum life. Her choice to remain single with a glamorous career is depicted with both severely qualified admiration and a hint of censure. Salome's flamboyantly aggressive desire to live for herself pushes the definition of self-reliant Real Womanhood dangerously to the limits.

Evans's other heroine, Edna Earl in *St. Elmo*, also repeatedly refuses offers of marriage but finally succumbs in the last chapters of the novel. An orphan, Edna becomes a scholar and, eventually, a world-famous authority on comparative religion and mythology. She publishes books and articles in New York City, pushes away the romantic importunings of editors and lawyers, and makes a name for herself. Since Edna has no family dependent on her, Evans makes it clear that she can accomplish success; she has both the time and the energy to sit for hours perusing ancient "Chaldee" texts and Aramaic inscriptions. She also has the moral freedom to do so; unlike Salome, who has brothers and sisters, Edna has no emaciated children pulling at her skirts begging for something to eat, nor, like *Meadowbrook*'s Anna, has she a swinish husband roaring for his supper.

Another curiously glamorous figure in a novel is not a heroine but a secondary character—Miss Craydocke in Whitney's *A Summer in Leslie Goldthwaite's Life*. Free to come and go as she pleases, Whitney's cheerful spinster collects flora, fauna, and rocks; she is a trained "naturalist," who seems to enjoy life much more than the bored mamas and dispirited daughters with whom she shares hotel space in the mountains. Up at dawn, climbing over rough terrain, sample case in hand, Miss Craydocke serves as a model of a woman with a fulfilled and busy single life. Perhaps the bored mamas would be cheerfully accompanying Miss Craydocke over hill and down dale if they did not have the dispirited daughters heavy on their consciences and pocketbooks; certainly this implication exists in the novel, especially when heroine Leslie muses about Miss Craydocke's interesting life.[21]

These portraits of glamorous single women, unencumbered even by extended family, illustrate the other influence at work in the fictional treatment of women in domestic literature—crisis orientation. If Real Women saw their role as one of constant, albeit varied, employment, moving fluidly between domestic, benevolent, and salaried work according to the needs of the moment, then professions that could not be picked up at a moment's notice, or trades that demanded steady application to avoid a loss of skill, or occupations that required years of sustained, intensive preparation would hardly be recommended. Only single women, unencumbered by families (and not intending to have families), could risk preparing themselves for an occupation such as opera star or doctor, which, were they married, they would have to "lay out" of and stay home from after the babies came, until a crisis drove them back to work. Such professions could not be picked up after a ten-year lag, nor could a woman with the rent due the next day simply go out and start working at them. Occupations and professions like teaching, with its seasonal schedule and its dependence on a solid education and current reading, or writing for magazines, which allowed one to work at home, or doll dressing and seamstressing, which extended a domestic skill already in place, all suited the perceived nature of salaried employment as a means of revenue to tide over a family, not as an end in itself.

This same bias toward pick-up employment may well explain why, despite exhortations to the contrary and pages of admonitions to learn vocational skills, only a few advice books in the popular mainstream list specific jobs women might hold. Virginia Penny's various editions of *Employments of Women: A Cyclopaedia of Woman's Work* and less popular specialty works such as the Reverend James Porter's *Operative's Friend, and Defence* are alone in the field in discussing such bread-and-butter issues as how to obtain a job and how to go about the application process; they alone delve into wages, hours, working conditions, safety, and advancement possibilities or requisite training to land a job and hold it. Occasional articles discuss these aspects of employment such as the *Harper's New Monthly* survey "Working-Women in New York," or the *Nation's* "Working Woman's Statement," but most discussion of salaried employment is in the most high-toned, idealistic, and general terms.

Many of the advice writers favor acquisition of vocational skills and salaried employment, but they refuse to discuss the particulars or to suggest attributes a job might have. Since such employment ideally is occasional and in response to grim financial necessity rather than a way of life, perhaps they see no reason to delve into the grubby details. It is enough simply to suggest a handful of useful employments (book-keeper, teacher, writer, copyist, governess, milliner, dressmaker) for which a young woman might need to do an apprenticeship before marriage or to insist that she receive a solid academic education so that she can eventually teach, write, or edit.

The popularity over fourteen years of Penny's detailed work, which dealt with those grubby particulars, suggests that, even though other advice writers ignored these subjects, a need did exist which she was fulfilling; indeed, some of the more conscientious (but more lofty) advice writers refer their readers to Penny's work. The ambivalence of most of the advice writers about salaried employment seems representative of a cultural embarrassment concerning the subject. Such works as Penny's were not needed in large number, the argument would insist uneasily, because they were for the rare single woman or the few "unfortunate" married women faced with a crisis at home. That these same advice writers extensively discuss the pitfalls of unwise marriage, the scrutiny one should afford prospective suitors, and the necessity of a full education and vocational training illustrates that they acknowledged, if indirectly, that married women could—and did—become in need of salaried employment more frequently than anybody would like to admit. Writers such as Graves can speak feelingly of the hard plight of women forced by necessity to work, can wring the heart with stories of women who see their hard-earned wages taken by intemperate husbands, but these writers find the solution in "enlightening public opinion" about a woman's right to her own wages or teaching her how to avoid such a husband by being more careful during courtship.[22] Rarely do the writers discuss savings banks in which to put wages out of the reach of husbands, nor do they suggest, as Porter's book does, putting money out at interest or into investments. Such approaches seem to smack too much of the rare choice of a single life or the economic-mindedness of male financiers, rather than simply extending the definition of most women's "natural" sphere.

Despite this general lack of concrete advice about salaried employment among either most advice writers or domestic novelists, a book such as Penny's (or similar articles) is valuable because they give an indication of what popular opinion, when it chose to consider the matter, understood as the economic realities of female salaried employment during the period, when that employment proved necessary. To test their reliability, Penny's projections of conditions and salaries can be checked against women's actual historical experience and these can be correlated with the references to specific jobs that pop up in fiction and some of the more general advice works. What, for example, might a schoolteacher have earned in Michigan in 1862? If Holmes shows Rosa Lee bravely teaching school, what might Penny have taught young women considering teaching as a profession to expect in wages and training required? If Augusta Evans tells her readers that, as a girl of eleven, Edna Earl is working in a factory to earn money for schooling, how much money would a mid-nineteenth-century reader have expected her to make, and would factory work have seemed a practical way to make money? Would women's experience as box makers or hands at a shoe factory in 1850 validate this picture?

Penny was not alone, however, in insisting that apprenticeship or vocational training was extremely important—if only because the work available to the unskilled was not only dangerous and tiring but paid wretchedly. Those with education or vocational training or who had served apprenticeships could swell the numbers of the skilled trades and make a living wage as well. Woe to the woman who suddenly had to face the world of labor armed only with a knowledge of watercoloring and ornamental French, warned advice writers. She was destined to fill the bottom strata of society, melting into the army of ghosts dragging themselves from garret sewing room to slop work superintendent's shop and back, sewing collars for pennies apiece and working by the light of a candle, weakened by skipped lunches and breakfasts, freezing for lack of heat.

Neither Penny nor more general advice writers, such as Graves, were under any illusions about the nature of regular working life for women—even under decent conditions. Sexually discriminatory inequalities in pay, the roughhouse resentments of men in the workplace, the fierce competition for jobs, and poor working conditions even in some decent jobs were well known, though they were accepted as "the way things were." These problems were raised by a power of five if the woman faced such a jungle without marketable vocational skills. Graves gives a vivid picture of unskilled American women at work: "Unjust laws, prejudiced opinions, and tyrannical usages entail upon her, even here, a fearful amount of suffering. Let any one consider the numerous disabilities to which she is subject; the impositions to which she is obliged to submit; or her ill-required labor, where she is compelled to work for her own support or for that of her helpless off-spring: let him listen to her tale of misery, of oppression, and of wrong, and it will be seen that even civilized communities are sadly wanting in justice to women."[23]

Nor had the picture improved some forty years later, as the exhaustive survey in an article entitled "Working-Women in New York" attests. The author describes the army of unskilled female labor in the city: "There are many . . . thousands in the city with no special ability and no special value, who toil, and blind themselves, and wear themselves to death, for an unimaginable pittance, who plod along for the sake of mere existence, enduring more than will be believed, filling every waking hour with labor, sacrificing themselves in every way, and willing to suffer so much to prolong it that the simple possession of life, though it is imbittered [sic] to the extreme, seems to be sufficient compensation for a martyrdom."[24]

Vocational training for women before entering the work force was one way to avoid such a fate, but it was not the only vital preparation advice authors suggested. Virginia Penny, T. S. Arthur, and even the Reverend Porter insisted that women should be trained to manage money, understand contracts, and be wary of the frequent scams practiced on the naive newly employed—especially the unskilled ones.

Being taken in on an apprenticeship fraud was one of the hazards of entering the work force unprepared. Though many apprenticeships (especially those in factory work) were legitimate paid work, others were neither. Penny outlines the way an apprenticeship scam is accomplished and warns those expecting to pick up vocational training on the job that they should carefully consider the arrangement being offered them. In the artificial flower business, for example, unskilled young women were taken on with the understanding that they would spend six months in an unpaid apprenticeship learning the trade and then receive "fair wages" for their work. On the surface, it seems a hard but fair proposition; in six months the girl could learn a skilled trade and then earn a decent wage. Callous exploitation and fraud lurked just below the surface, however, as Penny explains. Artificial flower making in its elementary form could be learned in seven to ten days, so the six-month apprenticeship gave the manufacturer five months and two weeks of free labor. The final cruelty then occurred: after the six months were up, the apprentices were fired, explains the indignant Penny, "on the plea that there is no work to give them, and new apprentices are taken." The vicious cycle started again, staffed by naive apprentices supervised by a smattering of old hands in key positions. Even these old hands earned only $4 a week, according to Penny.[25]

Other slimy practices that the unskilled should regard with caution involved selling items on commission or working as an "agent." According to Penny, the world of selling was frequently, though not always, a jungle, filled with unscrupulous companies attempting to rob the agent of her wages. Often the agent was expected to purchase a stock of what was to be sold. As Penny explains, "It being on a cash basis, they have few lady agents," especially if the item to be sold was large, like a sewing or a washing machine. In the latter case, the company would deduct 20 percent from the price to the agent; if the agent bought six or more machines and sold them, she would receive 30 percent off the item's price and a commission. Obviously, neither an indigent widow nor a mother desperately seeking a job to support a hungry family would consider selling as a job, despite the lavish claims companies made in advertisements for agents. An advertisement in the *Nation* in 1867, for example, asked for "male *and* female agents" to sell sewing machines for Secomb and Co., based in Cleveland, Ohio. Agents could make "between $75–$200 a month salary" or "commissions." According to Penny, an average salary between $30 and $80 a month was more realistic—and the woman would receive that only after proving herself on commission for thirty days.[26]

Still other forms of "unscrupulousness" awaited the unskilled woman in the job force, as the author of "Working-Women in New York" explains with horrifying clarity. Sewing machines again figure prominently in the story. Those unable to use a machine, who knew only hand sewing learned at home, were generally reduced to occasional piecework farmed out by a jobber. Fifty cents a dozen was the standard wage in 1880 for making twelve men's shirts—and out of that wage had to come thread, candles, and needles. Even on these paltry wages, unscrupulous employers frequently practiced cruel, petty chiseling; the woman unused to sharp business practices was warned that "there are employers who are never able to make the exact amount of change on pay-day and who deduct a few cents from week to week until the total loss to the unfortunate employees is many dollars." Others demanded deposits, supposedly as security for the shirt pieces they were farming out, but never gave back the deposits; still others "further impover-ish[ed] the fagged-out woman [and] deduct[ed] something on the ground that their work [was] not so good as the sample, or that it [was] delayed in delivery."[27]

Women who decided, sensibly, that they could not support them-selves sewing by hand often ran afoul of another scam, according to advice writers—buying a "new" sewing machine from the jobber to learn on and use, with a deduction from the wages of daily work as a form of time payment. As the "Working-Women in New York" article explains—and Penny agrees—the weekly payment (usually between $1 and $3) was frequently for a very old machine that had been refurbished to appear new. The cost of such an ancient machine, eked out of wages over months, even years, at best was two or three times its real value and, indeed, often twice the price of a new machine. In many cases, the machine was new, and the jobber told the desperate seamstress that it would be "all right" if she let a payment or two slide, she could "settle up" after she got ahead financially. This settling up was usually brutal: after the seamstress had provided free (or nearly free) labor sewing shirts or collars to buy her machine, the jobber, using the justification of a missed payment, swooped down on the unfortunate seamstress and repossessed the machine, claiming that she had violated the agreement. That machine was then refurbished and sold again as new to another unfortunate.[28]

Fiction provides some interesting examples of just such unfortunate unskilled women, though usually they are not the heroine; the heroine, by contrast, is trained or educated so that she is skilled when the need comes to use it. Arthur's miserable little story "The New Year's Gift" features a woman who must sew piecework and take in washing to support her family. As that story shows, such unskilled labor is not lu-crative enough to provide for her family; her children have to risk injury in a factory to earn enough to make up the difference.

Graves's moral stories in *Girlhood and Womanhood* also provide exam-ples of the fate of the unskilled. Amelia Dorrington, for example, learned no skill, and when her marriage fell apart and her husband deserted her, she turned to prostitution, sinking "to the lowest state of vice and wretchedness" before dying of delerium tremens. Another unfortunate victim of Graves's didactic pen, Elizabeth Harrington, who married for money and failed to finish her schooling, ends up running a boardinghouse after her husband loses all their money in a West Indian plantation speculation. Taking boarders, Elizabeth sadly tells Graves, was "the most eligible means of support and the only one for which [I was] fitted."[29]

For women who owned a building that had to be maintained and who had no marketable skills or apparent income, taking in paid boarders was a possible way of getting by. As we have seen in Graves's story—and in Arthur's "Taking Boarders"—it was a desperate and degrading option as far as makers of popular opinion were concerned. Despite historian Susan Strasser's assessment that operating a boardinghouse offered "a source of income to women with small children and household duties who could not or would not go out to work," according to fiction and advice writers, it also placed one's family in close proximity to a nefarious population. Boarders were, by nature, a transient group. Although, as Strasser suggests, boarding in the United States was a common way for many single and married people to meet the housing shortage between 1840 and 1880, there was still a healthy proportion of "single gentlemen" such as the salesmen or other drifters who collected there as well.[30] As in Arthur's story, such persons, if not carefully watched, could lure daughters into disgrace and false marriage. Even if boarders avoided the daughters, Arthur, Lewis, and others indicate, they frequently pocketed the silverware, clipped knickknacks, and tried to skip out on the rent.

Even if one screened the applicants (as writers suggested), running a boardinghouse was a hard, toilsome job—the entire family, however much they tried to hide it, became a staff of domestics, cooking, cleaning, washing, and fetching for others day in and day out and receiving, as Penny notes carefully, between $1 and $3 a week for each guest (the latter price includes "washing") for the privilege of doing so.[31]

Operating a boardinghouse was marginally respectable because the woman owned the house and was, in fact, running a business. It did slide perilously close to domestic work, however—the bottom rung of employment to most middle-class women readers, since domestic service, even more than factory work, was regarded as degrading and totally unsuitable for anyone except foreigners and immigrants like the Irish. Even the most skilled servants—ladies' maids and cooks—were paid very little, though fancy cooks could earn as much as $12 to $16 a month in the 1860s, and the best private cooks in the Northeast received no more than $20 a month, according to Penny. To keep this figure in perspective, we should remember that a decent job in a factory at the same time often paid between $3 and $6 *a week*. Generally, a maid or nursemaid received board, lodging, and about $5 a month in wages—and was "on call" twenty-four hours a day, except for half a day off on Sundays. Native-born American women (as opposed to immigrant women) supposedly could not stand the live-in slavery implied by domestic service. As Penny notes caustically, "Girls, especially American girls, prefer to work in factories to being servants, as they think it more honorable, and it secures them more time—in short, they are more their own mistresses."[32]

There is another factor at work that Penny only implies but modern historian Susan Strasser spells out: domestic work was the work of foreigners; to do it was to be little better than the "Celts" swarming off the boat. As Strasser points out, between 1825 and 1890 over 90 percent of domestic servants were non-native-born, and most were Irish. Not only were they forced to live in cramped attic rooms, eat leavings in place of "board," and be on call perpetually at the mistress' slightest whim, but they had a bad reputation as well. In her story "Labor; or Striking for Higher Wages," Gardner's depiction of her Irish cook is fully in the mainstream tradition, according to Strasser: "According to the literature, most servants put on airs, stole from their employers, left their positions without notice, and performed their duties without skill or care. Bad servants came and went."[33] Quasi-racist as it is, the reputation the Irish servant gave to domestic service eliminated it as a viable option for advice writers to suggest to young women without vocational training or higher education. Running a boardinghouse was as far down as one should go.

Despite the extensive discussion of the plight of the unskilled, middle class advice books only warned against such a fate; they did not presuppose it as normal. The books primarily suggest means to avoid it, such as academic and vocational preparation and a careful courtship process to weed out men who would likely force a woman to seek employment

The middle-class ideal was firmly skilled or professional. As Burton J. Bledstein points out, the middle-class American usually "owns an acquired skill or cultivated talent" and, historically, the American middle class "has defined itself in terms of three characteristics: acquired ability, social prestige, and a life-style approaching an individual's aspirations."[34] These characteristics presume skilled or professional employment, not the drudgery of slop work or cooking, and advice literature indicates that women to some degree were expected to share these assumptions with men.

The advice books did suggest trades and skills that might prove to be appropriate sources of income for "nice" women. Again, I stress here the popular perception of such work, not the historical views of labor statisticians. Penny's various books list over five hundred occupations requiring some degree of skill. Lewis, Weaver, and Arthur also suggest specific salaried employments, and the "Working-Women in New York" article lists a sampling of women's skilled or semiskilled work which is "so long that a mere enumeration is impossible." Some of those semiskilled and skilled trades (those requiring either specialized on-the-job training or formal apprenticeship) in which New York City women, according to the article, were actively employed in 1880 and are actively urged to attempt include staining and enameling glass; painting china; making glass signs; cutting ivory, pearl, and tortoiseshell; working in gutta-percha; cutting hair; making willowware and cane chairs; feeding printing presses; setting type; making and packing candles; molding tablets of watercolor paints; making clocks; enameling clock dials and jewelry; painting clock and jewelry cases; making and dressing dolls and toys; weaving twine into netting; painting broom handles; making paper collars; burnishing jewelry; making buttons; gilding with gold leaf; silver plating; bookbinding; weaving braid; making and bleaching straw hats and bands; and making artificial flowers.[35]

These skilled and semiskilled trades are not unique to the 1880s; Penny suggests that women choose most of the same occupations in the 1860s, and a handful are mentioned in Arthur's advice book in the 1840s. Writer Caroline Dall, in 1845, claims that women worked in large numbers in mills, especially textile mills, and as bookbinders, printers, bonnet dealers, bootmakers, confectioners, fur sewers, and corset makers.[36] Penny adds a few not listed in the "Working-Women in New

York" article such as hairdresser, florist, photographer's assistant, colorist, copyist, and photographic tinter, as well as lace maker, engraver, etcher, telegraph operator, and baker.

There was, according to popular advice literature, no shortage of decent jobs for well-prepared women who wanted or needed to draw a salary. Dall agrees about the variety, if not the quality, of the jobs, stating that 6,412 females were employed in shoemaking alone in 1850.[37] Despite wage discrimination and long hours, advice writers judged the pay to be adequate and the conditions usually clean; a woman could, therefore, both profit and keep her dignity—or so the advice books claimed.

Perhaps the most startling aspect of this subject is the stance taken by both advice writers and the occasional novelist on factory work for women of the middle class. Despite its repudiation by the middle class in England and Europe, factory work was suggested by American advice writers such as Penny, Dall, and the more obscure Porter as a better than average means of making a decent wage. Several provisos apply, however. Penny especially keeps track of the ominous number of "foreigners" employed in any factory. If the proportion of foreigners is well below that of Americans (native-born), Penny feels the factory is a good place to work. If there are too many foreigners, the mill or factory ceases to be viable for a "decent" woman. One reason seems to be that immigrants were willing to work for lower wages; another factor, Penny explains, is that foreigners tend to work longer hours with a higher production rate, set a grueling pace, and thereby raise the minimum number of finished items required for a worker to receive the day's salary. Penny especially mentions the "Germans" employed in Rhode Island in jewelry making who drove out the real Americans by their high production standards and long hours.[38]

Nevertheless, Penny, Lewis, and various articles point out that young women going to work in a factory and possessed of a "good common school education," general intelligence, and steady industry can often start in a legitimate paid apprenticeship program, and as their skills increase, they can expect to work their way up to top-paying jobs. In a pin factory, according to Penny, an apprentice could earn $3.25 a week while learning the skills, then earn up to $4 a week as a regular, finally swelling that salary to a phenomenal $21 a week through a combination of salary and piecework. Another example Penny offers is that of work in a dyeing and bleaching factory, in which she projects a steady climb in both salary and skill. Women can start as apprentices at $2 a week and work their way up to finisher ($3 to $5 a week), then yarn dyer and washer ($5 a week) or pattern printer ($6 to $12 a week). She cautions that women are kept from the truly lucrative work in the dyeing vat room, which allows only men, but she concludes that "the prospect[s] for females are good—eventually they will supercede the men in one branch of the business."[39]

Penny and the article in *Harper's* also consider the following factory work acceptable: hook-and-eye factory, Sharps Rifle Company (loading cartridges and inspecting primers for $1 per day because of the hazardous nature of the work and the skill required), lantern factories, boot factories, and buggy whip factories.

Advice writers saw major differences between work in American factories and work in European or British ones, which they announced proudly in their books. Notes Penny, "The factory operatives of this country are more favorably situated than those of most countries" because they have more wholesome food; they live in clean, reasonably comfortable boardinghouses; and they are not "confined in factories from early childhood . . . consequently, they are not stunted and deformed, and prematurely old."[40] Nor is Penny alone in her opinion. According to an insightful article by historian Judith McGaw, mills were often regarded as a "good place to work," as a woman from Sheffield, Massachusetts, Amy Fuller, declared in 1848.

That some middle-class advice writers urged their readership to consider the rewards and advantages of factory or mill work would hardly surprise McGaw. She believes that such work was an occupational choice in America, not something into which women merely drifted. McGaw points out: "Occupation choice by women workers such as Fuller has not merely been neglected by scholars, it has been presumed not to exist. With the exception of certain transitory and aberrant cases such as Lowell, scholars have pictured women moving passively into their jobs." As she indicates—and as writers such as Penny, Porter, Weaver, and others prove—the Lowell experiment was not an isolated historical phenomenon. Young women apparently chose such work over domestic service, sempstressing, laundressing, and even, on occasion, schoolteaching. If conditions had been abominable, wages miserably low, and the physical work intolerable, such choices would hardly have been made in the numbers they were. Dall, in fact, claims that

75,710 women (and only 55,828 men) were employed in the textile mills in 1845.[41]

Both Penny and, more recently, McGaw provide clues about what the mills and factories offered the northeastern woman during the midcentury beyond mere wages—the same advantages advice writers stress to their readers. Both Penny and McGaw mention that factories offered greater freedom, family time, flexibility in wages, and steadiness of employment than other fields. As McGaw explains in her study of mills in Berkshire County, Massachusetts, women chose among a variety of mills: woolen, textile, paper, cotton, and mixed textile. There may have been a variety of reasons for a preference. In paper mills, for example, women could work under a "mixed" system: "They were guaranteed a day's wage for accomplishing a minimum of work, but earned 'over work' pay if they performed additional work," notes McGaw. Penny's discussion of this possibility in several factories (including a pin factory) reveals a similar interest among women in obtaining "good" jobs in which they might earn higher wages if they exerted greater effort. Factories, unlike sempstressing, in women's perceptions, also allowed for increasingly remunerative employment. Unlike schoolteaching, factory work apparently required little scrutiny of the woman's "outside" life. Unlike domestic service, when a woman went off shift, she was truly off—her time was her own. As McGaw points out, women paper mill workers could expect to work three hundred days a year, as compared to less steady employments such as school teaching, which was seasonal. Cotton mill work in the 1860s, explains Penny, meant steady employment all year, time off for holidays, meals, evenings, and Sundays to be with family, and, in the case of some mills in progressive Massachusetts, New York, and Rhode Island, mandatory free schooling for three months for mill workers' children who were under age fifteen.[42]

Advice writers such as Penny and novelists like Augusta Evans additionally suggest that single women were able to make and save enough money (in part because of subsidized boarding) to pay for higher education for themselves or to start businesses. This is indeed the alternative that Augusta Evans has her orphan Edna Earl choose after her grandfather dies—to go to a factory and make enough money for schooling. It is hardly any wonder, then, that advice writers suggest strenuously that girls get "good, solid schooling" and learn habits of application and industry, since these are the repeatedly stated requirements for mill or factory work of this period. It is also hardly surprising that they regarded mill or factory work as less degrading than domestic service or taking in wash. Even in Arthur's "New Year's Gift," the mill pays well enough that a child's wages keep the family from ruin. In addition, despite accidents from machinery, most mill work was not regarded as significantly more dangerous to health by advice writers than was sewing for ten to twelve hours by candlelight in a freezing garret, taking in washing, or making artificial flowers by hand. Indeed, in the latter case, the dyes used often produced respiration problems and skin sores, according to Penny.[43]

Despite the perceived benefits of factory work, however, both novelists and advice writers more frequently mention skilled trades such as dressmaking and millinery when they urge young women to consider future employment. Millinery is an especial favorite, extending a domestic skill and benefiting from an apprenticeship program. The Reverend Wise, Weaver, Lewis, and hosts of other writers also suggest millinery as an excellent skilled trade to follow. A woman with good taste, a winning personality and deft hands could, these writers suggest, build a large enough clientele to start her own small shop. Dressmaking (often suggested in combination with millinery), if, as Penny notes, it was "custom" work, rather than slop or piecework, could pay well, especially if the dressmaker owned a sewing machine. One of the main problems clothiers faced, however, Penny informed those considering the prospect, was seasonal lags and a possible lack of employment. Spring and summer were the busiest seasons.[44]

Other skilled trades that employed women, according to both Penny in 1862 and the *Harper's* article "Working-Women in New York" in 1880, included those requiring artistic skill such as jewelry making (working in media such as gold, silver, jet, ivory, and hair), cameo cutting, enameling, engraving, plate coloring, and toymaking or doll dressing. Olive West, in the *Harper's* story got a job because of her taste and design ability, as well as her workmanship. She is an excellent fictional example of a woman possessing the skills to which Penny alludes, and she also had an imbecilic father at home and could make use of the side benefits of such employment. As Penny elaborates, "Doll dressing requires taste, experience, ingenuity, and economy in cutting the materials." One of the side benefits is that during the busy season (Olive and her father arrive in town before Christmas), the woman is allowed to take the dolls home and dress them at her own pace in the evening.

Although the work, done by hand, is not munificently remunerative, it does keep Olive and her father in lodging and food. According to Penny, doll dressers earned at least $4 a week at the time of the "Olive West" story.[45] Skill could provide enough income to keep a family going, if only barely.

Another artistic skill which Penny emphasizes is engraving or coloring plates for magazines. According to Penny, magazines such as *Frank Leslie's Illustrated News* and *Harper's Weekly* paid well for women either to make the engravings or to color them for the magazines once they were printed. Women earn, she notes approvingly, the same wages as men for the job, between $3 and $7 a week, with the possibility of much more once they get established and their work is known—as much as $500 for an engraving. This skill required many of the same talents as did the even more remunerative work of coloring and retouching photographs. According to Penny, the latter, after three months of paid apprenticeship, could net a woman as much as $30 a week in large cities if she worked for a photographer with an established reputation. Even receptionists in the studios earned between $3 and $8 a week.[46]

One other skill is mentioned in a novel as well as in Penny's book— that of florist and florist's assistant. According to Penny, women could work at a florist shop making bouquets and wreaths for hair ornaments to sell to women going to concerts and dinner parties; such work earned them approximately $5 a week. Working as a florist required a solid knowledge of botany, a good aesthetic sense, and nimble fingers. Florists did more than make bouquets; they made arrangements for public buildings and weddings as well as funeral displays. To become a florist required a long apprenticeship (3 to 4 years), but bouquet making could be learned in as little as 3 to 4 months. Once employed, the young woman could learn the business in its entirety over a period of years.[47]

In Harland's *Ruby's Husband* the Suydams' old nursemaid Katrine eventually takes her savings and, with her ailing husband, opens both a greenhouse and an informal florist shop. She makes a living supplying arrangements and bouquets to the ladies in the neighborhood. Heroine Frank Berry visits her daily, not only to render the older woman benevolent service but to "learn the trade," as she puts it. Frank is, in fact, becoming an informal apprentice.[48]

Yet another skill, rather less popular because it smacked of exalted domestic service, was hairdressing. According to Penny, both men and women in the United States dressed women's hair, and they charged artisan prices for doing so. Many women, she explained, had their own establishments, though they occasionally visited a patron's home on request. One such hairdresser, responding to Penny's survey questionnaire, explained that she charged $.50 for styling, $.75 for shampooing and dressing, and tacked on an extra dollar if she had to go to the house rather than have the woman come to her hairdressing establishment. This same woman had a lucrative sideline giving lessons and training apprentices at $1 per lesson; four lessons were needed to master basic skills. A hairdresser could earn approximately $5 a week dressing hair in the shop and more if she went to patrons' homes. Hairdressers who were unable to afford shops of their own could start by living with the employer and receiving board plus $10 a month and more for being on call when needed. Penny does not suggest this as the optimal situation because it too closely resembles a live-in servant and has many of the same drawbacks; it was, however, a way to get started.[49]

One last skilled trade Penny lists is interesting because it suggests that it was becoming increasingly possible for women to gain jobs through the growth of technology. Penny discusses the position of female telegraph operator at some length. According to her survey information, a woman could learn both sending and receiving in Morse code in only six weeks. She also needed a "solid knowledge" of orthography, arithmetic, and geography, as well as "ordinary mechanical ability." Once established as an operator, Penny claims, a woman could earn as much as $25 a month, the same wages as male telegraph operators, and she was required to work only ten hours a day. Best of all, the work was skilled, steady, out of the weather, and involved no hazardous working conditions.[50] With board and room running approximately $6 to $8 a month, a telegraph operator had more than enough left from her salary to buy clothes and necessities; for a woman with a family, it was, ideally, enough above rent to provide for children as well.

No discussion of women's employment would be complete without mention of women's work as literary agents or independent commissioned book and magazine subscription sellers. Selling on commission was not the most reputable trade one could enter; it often required the woman to buy the stock of goods and then sell it. Frequently, because of the nature of the work, especially with book sales, it was necessary to travel, which made it an unfit occupation for married women with families. Apparently, popular opinion did not rule out such employment because ads for "lady agents" abounded in respectable popular magazines of the period. One such ad in the *Illustrated Christian Weekly* in 1876, for example, asks for "A Lady Agent" for "every city and Town in the United States" to sell a brand new (and salacious) exposé on the Mormons supposedly written by Brigham Young's "Wife Number Nineteen," Ann Eliza Young. Lady agents selling this book, the ad states, can expect to make $75 per month from the publisher, H. S. Brubank in Philadelphia. An advertisement for the firm of Fowler and Wells in *Harper's Weekly* in 1860 seeks "young men—and women also" to be agents and "to engage in a local or traveling agency for our Books." The ad states neither the money supposedly to be made nor what, if any particular book the agents would hawk—but the ad appears in all the 1860 numbers of the magazine.[51]

Penny explains that such work is at least semiskilled because it requires an "educated lady" to do it, that is, one with a wide range of acquaintances and an eye to the favorable literary features of the work. She adds that decent publishers may not require the lady to buy a stock of the book but will let her work directly on commission, making $.50 on the dollar for each book sold. She cites the case of a lady of education and refinement in New York who "wished to earn a livelihood and, not seeing any other way open, she became a book agent. She got a horse and buggy and rode through the country and was very successful." Penny points out that the job involves a great deal of traveling, however and is therefore better suited to a single woman or widow without children than to a married woman. Such jobs as book agent and magazine subscription seller, Penny notes, can eventually lead to setting up one's own "news depot" (apparently a newsstand) or small subscription circulating library. The latter two occupations had the advantage of better working conditions, no traveling, and higher social status.[52]

Despite impressions given by critics to the contrary, advice writers encourage and novelists show women in business for themselves. This, too, was a way for women to support themselves and their families in times of crisis, though working for a business as a clerk was the more commonly mentioned employment. Several novels feature women, usually widows, running their own businesses.

Unfortunately, almost none of these fictional characters are totally admirable; all tend to be decent but "hard," as if the nature of business and trade dried up their natural juices of compassion and sensitivity. The storekeeper in Warner's *Wide, Wide World*, who takes pity on poor little Ellen Montgomery, is an exception, but in the same novel she is overshadowed by Ellen's Aunt Fortune, who owns and runs her own farm, selling the produce in town. Aunt Fortune is as hard as nails and curt to the point of rudeness. She does do her duty by Ellen, however grudgingly, and is admirable for her self-reliance and hard work. Aunt Fortune also apparently sells fowl and rabbits to establishments in town—a business Penny applauds, pointing out that it can be "built" from the humble beginning of selling "extra" eggs laid by farm hens. Penny suggests that a woman so inclined could also try selling chickens, plucked and ready, to hotels, steamboats, and restaurants and, as her reputation grows, branch out to raising and selling turkeys, rabbits, and pigeons as well, becoming eventually the sole supplier for her customers. The price per pound that these animals bring varied, but Penny insists that chickens can be sold for as much as ten cents a pound, turkeys for twelve cents, and rabbits and pigeons for even more.[53]

Mrs. Sloane, the overworked, besotted mother in Harland's *Ruby's Husband*, practices a variation of this business. She not only sells her extra eggs and milk in town and occasionally to the railroad, but she caters meals and provides lodging for a fee when her husband brings rich young men out for a day of hunting, he himself serving as a combination guide and gunboy.[54] Agnes Sloane is firmly in the tradition of women forced to work to help support their families. She provides not only the necessities but tiny luxuries for her only child; her husband is marked not only by sloth but by "ignorance and clownishness" as well.

Other women who have their own businesses in novels include Aunt Dolly, who owns her own millinery shop, in the poorly received novel *Rose Clark* by popular writer Fanny Fern, and Mrs. Vawse, who not only nurses neighbors but peddles wool, thread, and other smallwares in Susan Warner's *Wide, Wide World*. Aunt Dolly is remarkable for her mean spirit, "sharp" practices, and cruelty to her niece, Rose, and her second apprentice, Daffodil. Unlike the other women mentioned earlier who own their own businesses in more widely read and popular novels, Fern's Aunt Dolly is an extreme example of the supposed effects of the worst of the competitive business practices of the time—she cheats customers and employees alike, producing inferior goods which she sells at exorbitant prices after having stealthily skimped on the material to keep a length back for herself.[55] Perhaps Fern's bitter portraits of so many unattractive people in the novel is one reason for its limited success, certainly her portrayal of the self-employed independent business-woman is extreme in its censure and out of keeping with the more moderate portraits painted by other novelists. I include Fern's portrait simply to underline the point that novelists did occasionally show self-employed women—even if the portraits are not always as favorable a one would expect after having read Virginia Penny.

Penny mentions with great enthusiasm small businesses that sell "smallwares" (tape, pins, wool, thread, cording, ribbons, and so forth) and those that sell china and common ware (dinner service for everyday use). Penny notes that "the number of women" selling smallwares "is legion" because very little capital is required to get started and simple facilities—only a room "well-located in town" with no direct competition—to make a success of the business. Penny explains how a woman can enter the business: "Many a poor woman, unable to purchase the articles required, has obtained them to sell on commission, and by industry and economy, earned sufficient, in the course of time, to purchase a stock of her own."[56]

Warner's character Mrs. Vawse, described as a "not more independent woman breathing," peddles wool, knitted goods, and other wares around the neighborhood when she is not practicing nursing or tailoring.[57] Though she never sets up her own notions shop as Penny suggests such a woman might, she is highly respected in the neighborhood for her independence and desire to support herself—all the more admirable, Warner suggests indirectly, because she is not a "real" American—she immigrated thirty years earlier from Switzerland.

The business of china seller, Penny feels, is like smallwares because the stock is familiar to women—china and dishes. Though she does insist that "it takes time to learn the business well" (6 to 8 months), she points out that it is lucrative. Even the salesladies get a salary of between $5 and $8 a week; in fact, Penny suggests that being a saleslady is a good way to get started. She can learn the business by observation and experience over a period of years and then set up her own store. When opening a shop of one's own, Penny suggests, it is better to sell primarily common ware than to start out immediately with fine china. Common ware is more profitable, she notes, because it is less subject to changes in fashion, there is a bigger volume of turnover, and there are more customers.[58]

The subject of independent businesswomen raises yet another possibility for employment, one suggested even by advice writers who give few details like Arthur and Weaver: working as a private bookkeeper either sporadically here and there or employed full time by a particular business. Millinery, dress shops, and yard goods shops are three that Penny particularly mentions. One does not simply announce oneself as a bookkeeper and start working. As Penny and Weaver point out, bookkeepers need training in the subject, either at a "mercantile college" or privately. Training takes approximately a month and a half and costs approximately $15 for twenty lessons. The rewards could be better than average. According to Penny, a female bookkeeper who writes a clear hand can earn between $4 and $8 a week and occasionally more. The work is steady, and the woman can set her own variable hours, a boon to those with children.[59]

Bookkeeping, perhaps even more than professional sewing, offers the flexibility in employment encouraged by the Ideal of Real Womanhood. In several stories and exempla which advice writers offer, the heroine takes such bookkeeping skills back into the sphere of domestic employment. Sarah Sherman, for example, takes over the bookkeeping for her husband when he has to cut down on his expenses, and Lewis's formerly "selfish daughters" make use of the skill in their father's store. Other women, like Aunt Fortune in *Wide, Wide World*, save money by doing their own bookkeeping. Though no heroines practice bookkeeping as a living, it is obvious that money can be saved by doing it oneself—surely a measure of worth, especially in the sphere of domestic employment.

One other form of independent business enterprise is farming. As Thomas Cochran points out, despite the rise in commerce and industry, 4.5 million farms still existed in 1890, in contrast to approximately 1.5 million other forms of organized business firms. Nearly two-thirds of Americans, Cochran adds, lived in rural areas. Although, according to Penny's surveys, few women started out independently running farms, some inherited them as widows or as only children. Warner's Aunt Fortune Emerson in *Wide, Wide World* runs the farm by herself, with a hired man to do the heavy work; she inherited the farm from her father. She makes a good living as an independent farmer, but the strain of such work seems, from the portrait Warner paints, to take its toll on her "female nature." Significantly, she eventually marries the hired man and they run the farm together, though not before Fortune has shown her ability both to take care of herself and to make the farm self-sufficient

and profitable. The enormous physical labor involved in farming probably made it a less attractive option than other avenues of business.
Fortune Emerson is able to make farming pay primarily because she has
someone to do the hard manual labor. A parallel character, elderly Mrs.
Vawse, who inherits her house and bit of land as a widow, barely
scratches out a living and is reduced to peddling her handwork for additional money while relying on her feckless granddaughter Nancy for
such labor as splitting kindling.[60]

In other domestic novels farming is regarded as impracticable for
women. In Holmes's *Meadowbrook* and *'Lena Rivers*, for example, the
heroines must leave the home farm after the death of the father or
grandfather. In the first case, Rosa Lee goes to work as a governess and
sends money home because the farm has been lost through foreclosure;
in *'Lena Rivers*, 'Lena and her grandmother have to move in with
wealthier family members when the grandfather dies because they are
unable to make the farm a successful enterprise by themselves.

Holmes, however, provides one character who makes a go of it as a
widow—though not with any degree of comfort. Widow Simms in *Rosa
Mather* manages her own little piece of land, but she has the help of her
three sons. She barely scrapes by, even with their help, and when her
sons join the Union army, she is devastated.

In both Warner's and Holmes's novels, the women who farm alone
are either single or have grown male children who can help them; as
Fortune Emerson illustrates, when a woman runs a farm without sons
she ceases to be an effective or nurturing mother, as is highlighted by the
arrival of her orphan niece, Ellen Montgomery, whom she treats
brusquely. Ellen soon spends as much of her time as possible with the
Humphreys family and especially Miss Alice Humphreys, a young
woman sufficiently well off to be able to devote herself to nurturance
and philanthropic projects such as Ellen, a difference Aunt Fortune is
quick to point out sarcastically.

More common, even in Penny's tome, is the farm woman who becomes independent by selling extra produce or prepared food. Marion
Harland's character Agnes Sloane, selling eggs and jelly to the railroad,
is an example. This form of entrepreneurship was commonly practiced,
not merely suggested in advice books, as Susan Strasser points out.[61]
Obviously, such a business sideline fits in with family needs much more
easily than does running the entire farming enterprise alone. Once

again, it illustrates the advice book and domestic novel prejudice in favor of "helping out" in times of crisis rather than practicing a profession when one is also a wife and mother.

Other fields of opportunity opened in the 1850s, among them employment with the federal bureaucracy. This became an option not in the Civil War years as one would expect but almost a decade earlier, when the U.S. Patent Office began hiring women as copyists or secretaries. In the days before the typewriter (which did not emerge as a standard piece of office equipment until the late 1870s[62]), the government needed people who could write a "fair hand" and had an adequate grasp of spelling to copy important legal documents and, later, resolutions, bills, speeches, and laws. Clara Barton, better known for organizing both American nursing and the American Red Cross, worked for the Patent Office between 1854 and 1857, earning ten cents per hundred words. She was said to be able to copy up to ten thousand words a day—making the (then) enormous sum of $10 a day.[63]

During the Civil War, many other government departments enlisted the aid of female copyists, including the Quartermaster General's Office (1862), the Treasury Department (1862), and Congress itself, for which women would copy bills, resolutions, and correspondence. Pay varied, but the figure given in the quartermaster general's payroll books indicates that $600 a year was an average salary, though male clerks generally earned twice as much.[64] It is no wonder, then, that Penny strenuously urged women to become copyists. As she points out, not only could women copy documents for the government, but they could expand their endeavors and copy speeches for congressmen or work for lawyers and museums. Between winter work (when Congress was in session) and summer work with law firms and museums, a copyist could make as much as $1,200 a year, and she could often do the work at home.[65] All that was required to qualify for such a job was a "common school education," adequate spelling skills, punctuality, reliability, and neat penmanship—all virtues supposedly taught in public schools.

Officialdom also provided places for females who, even if they could not write a fair hand, could supervise, though such jobs were not as esteemed by advice writers. State and local governments provided jobs for women who would agree to supervise or run houses of female correction (jails) and orphanages, asylums, and charity hospitals. Penny, however, makes almost no mention of such employment beyond noting that it existed and paid a salary. Her neglect may be because of the punitive nature of the work or, in the case of asylums and jails, the nature of the society with which a woman would be forced to have contact. Certainly in domestic novels women who hold these jobs emerge the worse for it: harsh, cruel, and "unwomanly," they function fictionally as villainesses who steal from and mistreat their charges. Fern's arch-villainess, Mrs. Markham, the vicious matron of the charity school asylum where the orphaned Rose Clark is placed, allows children to die from neglect and is eventually fired for abusing the children under her charge.[66]

Employment as a matron or the head of a charity asylum apes a professional position in a slightly sordid way. Interestingly, Penny and others openly approve of women being in professions, though they suggest that fewer professions are appropriate for women than for men, and again, these tend to be ones that can be taken up and put down or reentered after a period of absence. Teaching and medicine are the ones most often suggested, perhaps because they extend a domestic or "natural" skill into a means of earning a living.

Indeed, when one thinks of the nineteenth-century working woman, one of the first images that leaps to mind is that of the teacher. There are historical as well as philosophical reasons for the popularity of teaching. As Keith Melder points out, around 1841 American educational leaders discovered the reservoir of well-educated single young women in the country and recruited as many as possible to further their vision of mass education. As usual, however, young women were paid only from one-third to one-half the salaries of male teachers, and it was a buyer's market because there were many candidates among which to choose. Women teachers were employed in record numbers because, as Melder explains scathingly, they were the best bargain for the price: "All agreed that by employing one male teacher to every four female teachers, they could purchase more schooling for the same cost, given the fact that women earned half or less than half the pay of men."[67]

In addition to active recruitment, other forces contributed to the large numbers of women who entered teaching, not least of which was Real Womanhood's vision of woman's God-given duty to be employed, to use her talents, and to improve the community. Melder points especially to the pressures exerted by evangelical and mainline Protestant churches, which continually urged "the Christian duty of rearing new generations in the paths of virtue and righteousness," as well as the example set by the female principals and teachers in the multitudes of female seminaries which young women attended. Such women as Almira Phelps, Emma Willard, Mary Lyon, and Catharine Beecher "encouraged their students" to consider teaching an acceptable, noble alternative to immediate motherhood and wifely duties.[68] Teaching also provided a way to use academic skills in a profession that women could reenter after a lapse of time.

Graves's principal at Oakwood School, the saintly Mrs. Norville, provides just such a model. Having been a teacher earlier in her life, Mrs. Norville sets up her own school after the death of her husband and makes a living as its headmistress by taking boarding pupils, of which Graves is one. Hentz's heroine, Linda, finds a model in the person of Mrs. Reveire, the headmistress of Rose Bower, her own boarding school, and it is partly because of this vision (as well as Robert's sadistic nature) that Linda argues with her father so strenuously against going back home to get married without finishing school.[69]

Obviously, the vision of the single woman employed as a schoolteacher was not a shocking one, though the writers understood that such employment would not be at the secondary level with "mixed" (that is, coeducational) classes, but in elementary schools. Women, as Melder explains, were thought to be more adept than men at communicating with young children, whereas men with their greater size and strength, as well as advanced training in regular universities (rather than through academies or home study), could deal more appropriately with adolescent boys. Thanks to such a division of interests—and the large number of women willing to enter the profession—mass education in America became a reality, as Melder points out: "By their willingness to answer the demand for teachers and their belief in the capacity of schools to bring about cultural progress, the young women who entered the teaching profession in these years [1830–60] literally made possible a comprehensive system of public schools."[70]

Though some argue that teaching was one of the few alternatives to domestic service open to women during the nineteenth century,[71] it is clear that the Ideal of Real Womanhood encouraged a variety of work beyond teaching and a variety within the field of teaching. Work in private schools—either as a teacher, principal, or headmistress—offered different experience than teaching in public schools (which is where most critics suggest the bulk of women taught) or being a governess or tutor in a private home. Governesses were better paid than public school teachers, though governessing as an occupation receives much less attention in both fiction and advice books than it does in similar English sources, perhaps because of the greater number of other employment possibilities. Teaching and running schools are more often mentioned. Penny points out in 1862 that a public school female principal was paid no more than $800 a year, about half as much as male principals; governesses in the United States (and especially in the South) received between $600 and $800 a year plus room and board.[72]

Domestic novelists often repeat this pattern of employment in their novels. After working in the wretched Massachusetts public school system, Holmes's heroine Rosa Lee becomes a governess in the South for $600 a year—almost twice the salary she made before. Jessie Hampton, Arthur's self-sacrificing heroine, is another who earns her living as a governess; though her salary is only $400 a year, she receives room and board as well. Technically, public school teachers received room and board—boarding with the families of their students—but, as Penny explained, this was hardly an ideal situation. Food tended to be scanty and bedroom accommodations crowded, and privacy in one's personal life was an unheard-of luxury, whether one were a public or private school teacher or a governess.

A brief examination of actual conditions of board and room at the time shows that Penny is accurate about the less than optimal conditions of the boarding teacher. Anna Howard Shaw, who eventually earned both M.D. and D.D. degrees at Boston College and in 1904 became president of the National American Woman's Suffrage Association, began teaching school at fifteen in Michigan, the same year Penny did her survey. She was paid $2 a week plus board to teach fourteen pupils of varying ages, sizes, and dispositions. Although in her autobiography, *The Story of a Pioneer*, Shaw dwells colorfully on the oppressive conditions under which she taught, her disgust is strikingly reserved for the realities of both board and room: "In 'boarding round' I often found myself in one-room cabins, with bunks at the end and the sole partition a sheet or blanket, behind which I slept with one or two of the children . . . the meals [were] so badly cooked I could not eat them." Shaw adds that her "boarding schedule" required that she change her residence and move in with another pupil's family every two weeks.[73]

Despite its great popularity in novels as a means of employment for the heroine, teaching, perhaps because of experiences like Shaw's, is not one of the professions Penny urges strenuously. She explains, "There is no employment more uncertain than that of a teacher," and she cites the low wages, the fluctuating conditions at country schools from passably comfortable to intolerable depending on the weather, the cranky dissatisfaction of the parents or the school board, and the "anti-education bias" of the populace in general. Once again, novels tend to reflect this view. Rosa Lee loses her job because a school board member's daughter spreads lies about her; other heroines, like Jessie Hampton or Edna Earl, are gratefully released from teaching by marriage. Penny's final suggestion is that a lady run her own school rather than teach in one; that way "she will be far more likely to succeed."[74]

Success—or at least a measure of sanity as well as a salary—is the point. One description of the schoolteacher's daily job of discipline and the strain most lived under pops up in Warner's *Wide, Wide World* in an aside at a party; it illustrates the hectic, even sanity-sapping conditions under which many public school teachers worked. At the quilting bee, Ellen Montgomery's friend Jenny tells her about the local schoolteacher, Mr. Starks, a man apparently driven to the limit, whose methods of punishment include regularly swinging children around the room by their legs and arms until they are dizzy and tying children under the table. If these methods of discipline fail, Mr. Starks uses an ingenious method of disciplining boys who have been fighting: Jenny says, "Sometimes when he wanted to punish two boys at a time he would set them to spit in each other's faces." This, Jenny tells the astonished Ellen (and the astonished reader), stops fisticuffs; no one wants to repeat the punishment.[75] Significantly, the teacher in this case is male, and even he has been driven into bizarre forms of discipline. How much worse must it have been for the female teacher, who was probably smaller than at least a third of her class and could hardly resort to physical restraint or punishment in every case? It is not surprising, then, that Penny and others suggest many other forms of employment than teaching.

One favored profession was medicine, which, as Penny explains, pays better than teaching. Though we today tend to think of nineteenth-century women more often as nurses than doctors, the advice books and articles urge women to get formal medical training as physicians much more often than they urge them to become nurses. Advice writers con-

Harper's Weekly, January 27, 1866

sider nursing one of many domestic employments, and it is presented fictionally in that context. Professional female medical training, however, had its loud and insistent champions in both the periodicals and advice books. Both P. Thorne and "M.W.-F." loudly proclaim the advantages of women becoming physicians, as does Samuel Gregory, founder of the New England Female Medical College, the first women's medical college in the United States. Trumpets Gregory unequivocally, "The medical profession is incomplete and ineffective without female co-workers in promoting health and relieving sickness and suffering. While the doctor cannot be dispensed with, the doctoress is no less essential to the physical well-being of society."[76]

Dr. Dio Lewis also waves the banner of female medical training, exclaiming that "all but such as live in darkness welcome women to the medical profession" and pointing out that nursing, which women already do at home, requires much "intelligent" decision making and that women would need no more intelligence than that learned at home to assign drugs as a doctor would. This vision of doctors as primarily dispensers of drugs is, however, biased by Lewis's formal training in homeopathy at Harvard Medical College (1849). He does not consider medicine a profession that necessarily includes surgery—something even he would feel women would be unable to do.[77]

The exhaustive Virginia Penny has more than a few words to say on the subject of female medical training, especially as an alternative to teaching. Penny explains that, thanks to institutions such as Gregory's New England Female Medical College, the Female Medical College of Pennsylvania, and others, more than two hundred female physicians had graduated from medical schools by 1862, and "the idea of female practice has become more familiar to the public mind, and the custom is becoming gradually established." Female physicians, especially those in midwifery, diseases of women and children, and general practice, have a "broad field" and a good chance of success "in all of the cities and large villages of the country." With training requiring only three years of formal study, including a year in residence at a hospital, and tuition (in 1862) costing approximately $60 to $80 a term with $30 for books, it is possible for women to attend medical school, Penny insists. She explains as well that many of the female colleges have scholarships for needy students, citing Gregory's college as one example. She exhorts her female readers to consider the profession seriously: "I know of no pursuit that offers a more inviting field for educated women than the practice of medicine." It pays twice to three times the salary that teaching does, even when one first starts a practice.[78]

A modern social historian, Mary Walsh, points out that Penny perhaps paints an overly rosy picture and notes that females were never allowed into "regular" medical schools such as Harvard Medical College but only "sectarian" schools like Gregory's, which specialized in homeopathy, Thompsonianism, phrenology, and general practice. These, however, were "legitimate medicine," as William Rothstein points out in his study *American Physicians of the Nineteenth Century*, before the formation and widespread influence of the doctors of the "heroic medicine" school through the American Medical Association. Walsh agrees, noting that in the nineteenth century, "with few medically valid theories available, no one had a monopoly on medical truth." She adds that the lack of standardized licensing enabled women to train with established doctors under the apprenticeship system rather than attending medical school. She cites the case of Harriot K. Hunt, who, when denied admission to Harvard Medical College twice (in 1847 and 1850), apprenticed herself to two "sectarian" doctors, Mr. and Mrs. Mott (authors of the *Ladies' Medical Oracle*). She had a "silver wedding anniversary" celebration after twenty-five years of practice, having received an honorary medical degree from the Female Medical College of Pennsylvania in 1853.[79] Despite Walsh's informal reservations, the injunctions of nineteenth-century writers such as Penny, Lewis, and "M.W.-F." to young women—especially single women—to study medicine were entirely realistic.

Nursing as a profession, rather than a domestic skill, was organized and to a degree popularized by Clara Barton on the Nightingalean model during the Civil War, but it receives much less mention in the advice literature than becoming a physician for quite some time, perhaps in part because it was professionalized later—the first American school of nursing opened in 1873 in New York City. In the 1870s, near the end of Real Womanhood's reign as a popular ideal, magazines began to praise the efforts of professional nurses and urged women to enroll in schools such as the Bellevue Training School for Nurses in New York City. One article, for example, explains that "ladies of a high grade of intelligence and character" can see in nursing "an opportunity for honorable usefulness" and an "appropriate sphere for their activity and devotion"; the article does not suggest that women become physicians. Perhaps it is important that, by the late 1870s, doctoring had begun to solidify into the "heroic" model of surgery and purgatives taught at male medical schools and advertised as "true" and "regular" medicine by the American Medical Association whereas homeopathy and other less violent (and more nutritionally and pharmacologically oriented) forms of medicine were fast on their way to being declared "quackery."[80]

Certainly during the midcentury reign of the Ideal of Real Womanhood advice writers continued to urge single women to attempt medicine as viable, lucrative, and self-supporting professional employment and to regard nursing as only one of many domestic skills handy to the wife, mother, or daughter for use in her own or her extended family. Though Gregory suggests that a woman trained as a doctor could stay out, have children, and return to the profession and that her professional training would prove a positive boon to her family,[81] few other advice writers suggest such a route. The years of training and the single-minded dedication evident in the case of Dr. Harriot Hunt with her silver anniversary (complete with gown and ring) in active medical practice suggest the necessity of making a choice. Medicine could not be picked up after a twenty-year gap; patients did not wait around for a married woman to raise a family—they went to another doctor. Once again, the basic crisis orientation of Real Womanhood's injunctions to salaried employment peep through in what they do not say as well as what they do. More significantly, although the heroines of domestic novels are often crack nurses privately within the family or with a beloved suitor, they never appear as doctors. That profession would not fit in with the marriage that usually occurs at the end of the novel, after a stint of self-supporting employment. Even Louisa May Alcott's tomboy heroine Nan in *Little Men* and *Jo's Boys* accepts the fact that if she chooses to be a doctor, she will also have to choose a solitary life. And we must remember that though Real Womanhood did not insist that marriage was necessary for all women, it did accept it as the norm for the majority of them and aimed most of its advice at that majority.

Two other professions that women might choose were law and missionary work. Like medicine, law required both dedicated study and apprenticeship, though (again like medicine) it did not acquire standardized professional requirements set by its association until the late 1870s.[82] Women could and, according to some writers, did apprentice themselves to lawyers to learn the trade. Lewis claims that law would be better if more women practiced it, noting that women would "cleanse and elevate the profession." Unfortunately, his vision of what they might do smacks more of law clerking than of practicing before the bar, but he does suggest that they would prove to be successful advocates in court. "M.W.-F." agrees strenuously and cites the historical case of Lavinia Goodell, who was admitted to the bar after "having passed a brilliant examination" but was denied the right to argue before the Supreme Court simply because of her sex. According to the article's author, Goodell argued everywhere else very successfully and even squelched Supreme Court Chief Justice Ryan in a series of closely reasoned, slashing arguments in the *Legal News*. Nor did "M.W.-F." see any loss of femininity in Lavinia's acquisition of a legal education and skills, describing her as "a shrewd, quick-witted girl, fond of humor, studious and argumentative. In person she was of medium height, but looking tall from her slender erect figure, blue-eyed, and with light-brown curling hair." Lavinia Goodell is obviously a heroine to the author, not only because of her splendid career before the bar but because of her sturdy rejection of a purely domestic life, as she herself makes evident when she describes her early decision about what to do with her life: "I was quite clear that I would not spend my time washing dishes and making over my old dresses."[83]

Perhaps the reason so few novelists suggest law as a career is again the need to choose between career and marriage. Certainly there is something disjunctive in the vision of the mid-nineteenth-century mother of three getting the two oldest off to school, arranging with a neighbor to take the baby, and then, with her husband's permission, going to argue the case of a rapist before the district court. Such a profession would be faintly conceivable for a single woman; for a married woman it would be not feasible to the Real Womanhood writers, who undoubtedly objected as well to the clients (or associates) a lady lawyer would be forced to endure: robbers, murderers, rapists, thugs, burglars, crooked politicians, and card sharks, to name a few. Though single women could, it seemed, endure such shocking sights as dead bodies in the field of medicine and rapists in court, the "softer," more feminine woman with a family—and, more important, a married name to protect—either could not or (more likely) should not.

A much more womanly occupation, again one in which single women predominated (though married women occasionally were employed with their husbands) was that of medical or educational missionary, either at "home" in the inner cities or more often abroad in "heathen lands." Missionary work combined a number of skills—teacher, nurse, evangelical church worker, and pamphleteer—while serving the greater glory of the Lord. The *Illustrated Christian Weekly* calls it "this important form of woman's work" and lauds the appearance of good Christian women among the heathen, noting that in distant lands "the Christian woman finds an open door for her when she labors to spread the truths of the common salvation."[84]

Though the article mentions the reservations shared initially by "those who had long and successfully conducted our great Missionary Associations," it points out that women's success as missionaries eventually swept aside such reservations. The author of the article explains that the pioneering Women's Union Missionary Society and the women's boards of missions served as innovators and agencies for women who wished to minister to the benighted either at home or abroad. After all, women (as everyone knew) were more spiritually sensitive and generally of a finer character than men—a basic difference even writers of Real Womanhood acknowledged; therefore, women's natural propensities could find fertile soil in missionary work. Nor did it take years of preparation, as Penny explains: "Piety and good common education are all that are necessary. [The missionaries] learn the language after arriving at their place of destination. None go without a certificate from a physician saying they are free from organic disease." Real Womanhood's insistence on a sound physique and general good health as well as solid schooling and a desire to work at productive occupations prepared its ideal women admirably for running church schools in remote areas of the Congo or Samoa or China. Teaching little brown or black or olive faces the Scripture could earn such women not only passage to exotic lands but a slender stipend (in 1862) in excess of $350 a year (the figure Penny gives for a "city missionary"); the more remote the area to which the woman was sent, the higher the salary.[85]

Although work overseas frequently involved great dangers as well as the risk of disease and a pitifully small salary, the lure of foreign lands and purposeful work had an obvious appeal for educated, self-reliant women. Even in 1862, well before the formation of the women's boards of missions, Penny states that 451 "lady missionaries" were out in the field and being supported by their various denominational boards. There were, in fact, more applications from women than there were positions for them to fill. If such activity demanded a further stamp of popular approval, the well-known doyen of women's affairs, Sarah J. Hale, editor of *Godey's Ladies' Book*, offered an imprimatur on the project by making herself the "contact" person for medical female missionaries.[86]

In addition to foreign missionary work, many churchmen and boards of missions saw the German and Irish ghettos of large cities in America in need of missionary attention. The advice literature makes passing mention of domestic missionary work as a form of salaried employment, but it generally relegates such work to women practicing philanthropic employment or to clergymen performing their parish duties. Lewis's rich girls ministering soap, food, and uplifting tracts to the local Irish leap to mind, as does the charitable work at home done by Warner's Alice Humphreys and, of course, Harland's Frank Berry. One recalls as well Marmee's visits to the German family in *Little Women* and all the pure and angelic little girl heroines in midcentury juvenile fiction who personally minister to the less fortunate and the benighted. To advice writers such work seems, at least earlier in the period, to have been viewed as a natural and unpaid part of domestic and communal duties, rather than a way to earn a living.

Whereas missionary work led to fulfillment in meeting the needs of others, the arts were suggested by some advice writers as a way to fulfill the needs of the self and earn money in the process. The arts are "glamour" professions generally restricted to single women in domestic novels, and Penny mentions them approvingly.

One such profession, writing, handily combined art and family life, as is shown by the example of authors of domestic novels, such as Lydia Child, many of whom had children and other family members or sometimes a husband dependent on their income. Authors of magazine articles, novels, advice books, and even textbooks made good money, though not as much as other professions, as Penny is quick to point out: "The labor of authors is not rewarded as well as other kinds of intellectual labor of the same extent: for instance, a physician or lawyer, with the same abilities, amount of learning and application, would derive a greater reward pecuniarily." Although it did not assure the substantial regular salary that medicine or law did, Penny lists it as a field wide open to women and one in which they experienced great success. "The success of women in works of fiction is unquestioned," she notes, and writing creatively carries other benefits, including a smaller (and more flexible) time commitment, no apprenticeship or required advanced training, exercise of intellect, and the chance for reasonable profit. As examples, she points to Susan Warner and Fanny Fern, noting that Warner's two latest novels brought her from $12,000 to $15,000 and that Fern "received not less than $6,000 for the duodecimo volume published . . . six months since."[87]

Indeed, regardless of the question of salary, an occasional advice author points to the patriotic benefit in women writing fiction about American heroines and American concerns. Graves especially sees a need in literature and belle lettres for the female American voice: "There is even in this [English literature] a great deal that is unsuited to us as republicans, and which operates unfavorably upon our national character. We need a literature truly and properly our own—one in conformity with our government and social institutions: a literature exposing the folly and the inconsistency of the anti-republican fashions, tastes, and opinions which we have derived from the literature and manners of the

Old World." She goes on to explain that the English models of ideal women and men are "faded and worn-out copies of foreign pictures" that fail to provide heroines of real virtue, a virtue shown by, among other things, employment. Graves, never one to hide her opinions under a bushel, explains exactly the kinds of heroines and themes American women writers should develop for the good of the nation. They should write about "some humble seamstress, whose daylight and midnight task it has been, perhaps, to prepare the habiliments in which [a] butterfly devotee of idle pleasure is arrayed . . . we could learn from her [the "humble seamstress" not the "butterfly"] the instructive history of the vicissitudes she has experienced. The trials of life have taught her wisdom, and its sufferings have given depth and intensity to her feelings . . . [they suggest] the experiences of the solitary female orphan, thrown upon the world to struggle unaided amid its difficulties and temptations, and triumphing over them all by her unconquerable rectitude and energy." Such portraits, Graves insists, will provide readers with "healthful and invigorating literature, adapted to their condition as the daughters of this great and free nation."[88]

Patriotic questions aside, Penny points out that magazine contributors especially make a decent living. Big magazines such as *Harper's* and *Atlantic Monthly* or journals such as the *North American Review* and *Knickerbocker* all pay "better prices" to women than they do to men, according to the editors responding to Penny's survey. *Harper's* claims to pay between $7.50 and $10 a page for articles, *Atlantic Monthly*, $6 to $10, and *Knickerbocker*, $3. Penny adds, however, that such figures probably have been somewhat "exaggerated" and are "the exception, not the rule."[89]

For those without the creative fire to concoct fictional heroines and cozy worlds, money could be made, Penny argued, from writing textbooks and books of advice. The uplifting example of Penny herself and hundreds like her undoubtedly made such employment seem feasible to female readers. Perhaps Penny whetted their appetite for such work when she suggested that Eliza Leslie (of advice book fame) had made a grand total of $12,000 from the sales of her recipe and cooking books. School texts in subjects such as geography, history, and mathematics, she advised, could make almost as much money as a novel.[90]

Penny's advice was probably good. Both Carl Bode and Frank L. Mott indicate the enormous market and wildly popular publication history from 1820 to 1870 of advice and etiquette books, manuals, cookbooks, and home texts. The market was obviously there for the woman willing to write the books. Bode explains that any how-to-do-it books such as cookbooks and "conduct of life" books sold extremely well. Another noted historian, Arthur Schlesinger, Sr., estimated that by the 1840s and 1850s, there were between thirty-six and thirty-eight different etiquette books on the market in any one year, and an average of three new ones appeared each year before the Civil War.[91]

For a woman with a good education such as Real Womanhood suggests is necessary, writing as a career might seem more advantageous than the other normal option, teaching. We should not be surprised, then, to notice that both careers are sometimes combined in the domestic fiction of the period. Redoubtable Edna Earl, for example, though a scholar of the first order, takes time out from her task of compiling scholarly treatises to become a governess—and a highly successful one—before she returns to the world of philosophy and languages. Certainly writing was to many mid-nineteenth-century women a form of teaching, or at least of educating mass opinion, as Graves indicates.

Teaching and "art" were not an unknown combination in employment. As the Reverend Daniel Wise, T. S. Arthur, and Penny all suggest, those with "artistic skills" could always make a slender but definite income teaching their art. Penny, as usual, lists specific advantages from teaching art. She suggests that art teachers must have both talent and fondness for art; that they must seek out a clientele that can afford to pay for lessons in the more lucrative intricacies of oil painting rather than drawing; and that the woman offering lessons should charge standard fees in all mediums, though Penny prefers oil painting to charcoal sketching. She adds that art teachers can work at home and have their clients come there rather than taking on the expense of setting up a business establishment. Moreover, the lessons can be arranged at times that coincide with the teacher's schedule of obligations. With a flexibility in working hours, no overhead, and standard fees, a woman can make a small but decent supplement and still care for her family. According to Penny, the fee for art lessons should be no lower than fifty cents an hour and no higher than $2, depending on the medium.[92]

Drawing and painting were not the only artistic subjects one could teach. Fancy work also had a potential for making money. Crocheting, embroidery, leather working, molding wax fruit and flowers, making hair jewelry, doing beadwork, arranging mosses and grasses artistically,

Harper's Weekly, August 24, 1878

and teaching fancy knitting could also yield a small sum. Leather work, making wax fruit and flowers, and beadwork paid the best because they were skills not normally taught to well-brought-up girls. Penny explains that most teachers charge $1 a lesson or $6 for a set of five long lessons. Knitting, crocheting, and moss arrangements pay less (twenty-five or fifty cents an hour depending on local competitive prices), but teaching these skills can supplement pay earned from the more highly priced lessons. Overall, Penny suggests that an enterprising woman with skillful fingers and a certain knack can make $3 to $4 a week if she has a good clientele. By comparison, this is the salary of an average saleslady in a department store and much more than that of a domestic.[93] Certainly the work was less grueling physically, and the woman was her own employer, setting her own schedule and taking on only as much work as she chose.

Strangely, such teaching does not dominate in the domestic fiction, though the heroines are always well-versed in artistic and musical skills, which they bring to domestic employment, beautifying the home, entertaining loved ones, and making gifts. When they teach art or music in domestic novels, it is most often as governesses or in a school rather than as free-lance art teachers. All of Graves's "good" heroines in *Girlhood and Womanhood* beautify their surroundings; Rosa Lee in *Meadowbrook* is a good sketch artist, but it remains a private outlet, not a skill she teaches.

Domestic fiction demands a more dramatic employment, one that requires the heroine to enter the world rather than conduct lessons at home. Certainly there would be little scope for romance, dramatic confrontation, or victory by a fireside teaching pupils the elements of color-washing or moss-arranging. Even schoolteaching has more dramatic overtones—either through the daily confrontations with recalcitrant older boys or the vagaries and injustices of school boards and inspectors. Governessing, of course, holds even more dramatic potential for fiction with its usually attendant handsome widower, gallant grown-up brother of the charge, and evil or demanding mistress over whom the heroine can triumph. Rosa Lee, Jessie Hampton, and Edna Earl leap to mind as examples of this sort of heroine.

Painting as a profession, in place of the pale, ladylike teaching of lessons, is not urged by many advice writers. Perhaps women artists were not well enough accepted by the public to make a secure living; perhaps, like medicine and law, opera singing, playing an instrument professionally, or acting, painting as a career required a lifetime commitment and did not fit the lifestyle of the majority of married women. Penny does discuss the possibility of such a career, but she limits the scope of the endeavor to art forms that are small in size and can be done at home, rather than Butleresque war scenes or seascapes. She is encouraging about the future, however, noting that "the prospect to lady artists in the United States is very encouraging. Ladies are allowed the privilege, on proper application, to copy paintings in the Academy of Fine Arts, Philadelphia, the Dusseldorf, and the Bryant galleries, New York."[94]

Copying models was, of course, a time-honored nineteenth-century method of learning the craft, so such permission (even limited by the need for "proper application") was an important step forward. Penny, however, suggests that the most lucrative work for lady artists lay not in copying seascapes, generals on horseback, or crucifixions but in pastel or crayon portraits of mothers and children or in painting miniatures. Some portrait artists such as Mrs. Hildreth of Boston, Penny claims, have been "very successful" with crayon portraits and have charged as much as $40 a portrait. Miniature painters, over the ages, have frequently been women; because they are publicly accepted, such women artists fetch large sums for their well-executed miniatures. Mrs. Hill is one example Penny cites of a successful woman miniaturist. She receives "regularly" between $75 and $100 per miniature, and the successful Ann Hall of New York City receives as much as $500 per commission.[95]

Needless to say, women artists only rarely make their way into domestic novels, and when they do, they do not seem to win public acceptance. Fern's ill-fated novel *Rose Clark* contains perhaps one of the most vivid depictions of a female artist in mid-nineteenth-century domestic fiction. The heroine, Rose's friend Gertrude Dean, is an independent "bohemian" artist, despising men, supporting herself with her art, and sneering at marriage. She is also a successful artist in oil with her own studio and a clientele large enough that she can turn down commissions when she finds the subject unappealing. Though initially married happily to a clergyman, Gertrude suffers widowhood and then is forced into marriage with the brutal Mr. Stahle, a sadistic drunkard and wife-beater. Gertrude's response to this horrible situation is to find a career for herself and leave the beast, later obtaining a divorce. Her spirit is evident (if somewhat threatening to certain male midcentury values) in her explanation to Rose of how her career in art began: "I weighed every faculty God had given me, measured every power with a view to its marketable use . . . [then] I seized my pencil and I triumphed!"[96]

Later, when her brother John (who eventually marries Rose) remonstrates with Gertrude over her solitary, single life and urges her to exert her "attractive power" to obtain a husband, Gertrude brings him up short: " 'I have no desire to exert it,' replied Gertrude; 'there are undoubtably men in want of housekeepers, and plenty of widowers in want of nurses for their children. My desires do not point that way.' " She adds scathingly, "I have no very exalted opinion of the sex to which you belong. Men are so gross and unspiritual, John, so wedded to making money and promiscuous love, so selfish and unchivalric; of course there are occasionally glorious exceptions, but who would be foolish enough to wade through the leagues of brambles, and briars, to find perchance one flower?"[97]

Rose Clark—and Gertrude—did not sell well; the *National Union Catalogue* shows only two years of publication, and the 1876 *American Catalogue* does not list it. It is significant that Gertrude and the values she espouses overshadow the much more traditional heroine of the novel, Rose Clark. One wonders if employment to the point of an independent career, combined with the openly expressed contempt for males, had something to do with the novel's lack of popularity. Certainly its portrait of woman-as-artist, though vivid and endearing to modern female ears, must have raised a few alarms even to Real Womanhood writers, steeped as they were in a much more shadowy, less openly defiant independence.

The character Gertrude Dean poses interesting questions about the direction in which Real Womanhood was developing. Like the advice writers' heroines and model women, she refuses to take ill treatment and cruelty from a man the author describes as a "hypocrite, and a gross sensualist," to whom marriage "was only the stepping stone to an else impossible gratification," as Fern puts it delicately.[98] She does take a God-given talent and parlay it into self-support, just as Real Women were supposed to do. This self-support allows her to leave an intolerable situation, and this, too, is a course suggested by advice writers. One suspects that had Gertrude Dean made a living giving art lessons instead of becoming an artist, the book might have sold better. The belligerent choice of a "male" career, the open scorn for husbands, families, and males in general—and her stunning success—suggest that women need not simply supplement a family's income or merely support themselves; they can have full-fledged careers and enjoy them without enduring familial or wifely duties. Real Womanhood stops short of suggesting such a course. Its vision of the spinster career woman always places her in a somewhat drab context of sturdy self-support and sometimes as the breadwinner of an extended family but never living zestfully for herself alone and being successful in the process. This veers too close to feminism—and the Real Womanhood writers denied strenuously that they were feminists. Although Miss Craydocke, the spinster botanist in Mrs. A. D. T. Whitney's book, is happy and busy, she only suggests that misery need not necessarily accompany a single life; she does not make a single life look seductively attractive. Gertrude Dean does. Her lack of popularity as a character in a poorly selling novel once more highlights the difference between Real Womanhood and either feminism or True Womanhood, especially concerning the uses of, the reasons for, and the rationales behind employment.

Epilogue: *The "Lost" Ideal*

When I started my research and first identified the Ideal of Real Womanhood, I called it by another name—the "Lost" Ideal. Not only was Real Womanhood as an articulated, independent, but coherent set of ethics and values lost to modern researchers up to this point, but it was lost as a system of belief to women readers at the end of the last century as well. The Ideal of Real Womanhood vanished as an identifiable entity sometime after 1880 and has never been seen again, except in fragments. What happened to it? That question continues to plague anyone studying the primary sources, especially in light of Real Womanhood's obvious earlier vitality and popularity. It is, however, a question that demands a separate, full-length treatment taking into account such factors as the growth of professionalism and the devaluation of amateur work; the influence of science and its cadre of experts, including especially "nerve specialists," "sex doctors," and, later, psychiatrists; and finally, the nation's growing nervousness about its own mature identity and its gradual orientation, near the turn of the century, to European, and especially British, standards of gentility, particularly for women.

Although future scholarship must delve deeper for more complete answers, I can offer one tentative hypothesis suggested by my research: the Ideal of Real Womanhood trembled, then dissolved, because it could no longer resist the contradictory tensions pulling it toward resolution either into the conservative camp of True Womanhood or into the growing tide of turn-of-the-century feminism.

Initial evidence suggests that the Ideal of Real Womanhood gave inadvertent rise to the "New Woman" of the 1880s and 1890s and that that ideology eventually merged with turn-of-the-century feminism, thus losing its popular and widespread base of support. This loss of support might have resulted in a vulnerability to the more conservative continuing ideal of True Womanhood, which, being less dynamic, continued to survive fully articulated and clearly defined as a popular alternative that was ostentatiously "feminine" in its values.

Unlike the Real Woman, the New Woman was particularly vulnerable on this "feminine" issue. Instead of viewing work inside the careful confines of financial necessity (the boundary set by Real Womanhood), the New Woman insisted on her right to a career, irrespective of the financial needs of her family or her marital status. The similarity to the employment ideals of Real Womanhood is obvious, but the differences are dangerously distinct. Real Womanhood heroines often did work outside the home both as married and as single women, but they did so, according to their authors, with the understanding that it was only because it was necessary, not because it was personally fulfilling. The line is a fine but important one, since Real Womanhood authors could continue to soothe public nervousness about female employment with the well-known and approved nostrum of woman's "natural" duty to take care of her family or herself in times of crisis so that neither would be a burden on society. However close an Edna Earl or a Rosa Lee came to claiming a career for herself, eventually she married and resumed a more "normal" life, though she was prepared for any future economic contingency requiring her to go back to work temporarily.

The New Woman refused to consider such a sporadic work history. As Rosalind Rosenberg defines her, the New Woman's primary distinguishing characteristics included both an independent spirit and commitment to a lifetime career. The thin shell of "female" rationales for work cracked under the press of New Woman attitudes, which indicated a distressing disinterest in the female domestic sphere—especially an overt disgust with housework, the approved wearing of more sensible (less feminine) clothing, sweaty athleticism, and a shocking desire for "fellowship" with men.[1]

Conversely, though Real Womanhood writers had claimed loudly that women were not "made" to be men's slaves or skivvies, they did believe women were men's spiritual and emotional superiors—the species in human history best suited to maintain civilized values and common decency in the world and the species whose moral duty it was to reform and uplift society by female taste and the influence of a quiet feminine example. For writers of Real Womanhood, this effort was best and most successfully practiced inside the separate sphere of female influence—the home and interpersonal relations.

The New Woman, however, rejected the concept of separate spheres and claimed her portion in one united human sphere in which every human being, male and female, had the right to exercise his or her talents and the right to fulfilling and challenging work, even if that work existed in man's sphere. This shift from work because of necessity to work for fulfillment, from improving the world indirectly through improving society's moral tone by influencing fathers, husbands, and brothers, to one of direct action, professional accomplishment, and individual effort, finally broke the frail surface tension of the vastly and dangerously extended bubble of Real Womanhood's version of the separate sphere. Strained to the limit by Real Womanhood's need to accommodate the frequent reality of financial exigency, higher education, vocational education, and physical fitness, the soap-film boundaries could no longer stand the strain of the overt demands of the New Woman. Those demands seemed to necessitate the jettisoning of some important values, which the public saw itself in danger of losing if it followed the New Woman: the loss of a society characterized by the "gentler" values of moral decency and grace and the loss of love for women with careers.

A quick sampling of periodical fiction and articles after 1880 suggests that the public, in reaction to these perceived losses, attached a growing value to an ideology that was clearly feminine. As Helen Woodward has pointed out in her work on nineteenth-century ladies' magazines, the sharp bifurcation between "feminine" and "other" was part of a larger reaction. As she explains, "The downgrading of the man of the family and the upgrading of the woman had gone so far that women became frightened and began to rebel against their power."[2]

Certainly reactions such as those expressed in Caroline Ticknor's 1901 *Atlantic Monthly* article "The Steel-Engraving Lady and the Gibson Girl" support Woodward's contention and suggest that the New Woman had gone too far in her insistence on only one human sphere rather than clearly separate ones for men and women. Doubt and nervousness about the losses to civilization reverberate through the pages of the article. The home, the last middle-class refuge to which a man could retreat from the soul-destroying horrors of the marketplace, Ticknor's article suggests strongly, would be destroyed when women were made "unfit" for that refuge by education and career. With women joined in the crass and ignoble jungle battle for economic advantage, the home without its guiding spirit and votary would cease to be anything but a structure. As the New Woman closed the door on a life of dedicated and primary domesticity and took her place in the single human sphere of work, she would close the door as well, Ticknor mourns, on such necessary societal virtues as grace, gentleness, beauty, courtesy, and piety. If women abandoned these virtues, men (being men) would be either unable or unwilling to pick them up and promulgate them.[3]

Not only worry about the deformation of society but fears for the emotional life of the New Woman herself plagued the reading public and the popular writers. The New Woman, it seemed, might want to have both a career and a marriage, but popular perception gradually began to insist that, from any practical standpoint, the two would prove mutually exclusive. As Caroline Forrey points out in her survey of popular images of the New Women at the end of the 1880s and into the 1890s, the choice between career and love became more and more marked. Forrey points to novels such as Sarah Orne Jewett's *A Country Doctor* (1884) and Constance Cary Harrison's *A Bachelor Maid* (1894) as proof of this growing dilemma. Both novels portray the independent woman of self-reliance and meaningful career, although Harrison's later heroine, Marion Irving, eventually quits her "lark" of independence and decides she cannot live without love and marriage. Jewett's earlier heroine, Nan Price, equitably chooses to be a spinster and a doctor rather than to marry, obviously feeling that meaningful work and relationships such as friendships are enough to fill the emotional void. What becomes increasingly obvious as the decades progress, Forrey suggests, is the solidifying belief that there is no "real" love outside of marriage and that emotional fulfillment occurs only through heterosexual love. As Forrey explains, "Rejecting marriage for most of these heroines means rejecting love as well, for they have no social framework for sexual love outside of marriage. . . . Thus the New Woman is essentially a lonely figure."[4]

Some might argue this, citing Carroll Smith-Rosenberg's work to refute the public perception of the inevitability of loneliness if a woman chose a career. In her study of female friendships in nineteenth-century America, Smith-Rosenberg points out that women commonly and naturally maintained passionate friendships throughout their lives even if they were married. Whether these friendships were "passionate" in a genital sense or merely emotionally intense, she asserts, does not detract from their centrality in women's lives; ultimately, the sexual question does not matter when viewed within the larger context of shared experiences, perceptions, conversations, aid to one another during crises, and emotional support.[5] Until late in the century, no one considered such relationships deviant. There was, therefore, an emotional alternative, such critics would claim, for the career woman that did not lead her back irreducibly to heterosexual love and marriage.

Although Smith-Rosenberg's evidence about the widespread phenomenon of passionate female friendships is both overwhelming and convincing, she also points out that the public's perception of emotional alternatives to heterosexual love and marriage started to change radically during the late 1880s and 1890s, finally culminating after World War I and in the 1920s in psychiatric prohibitions against any nonfecund, nonheterosexual close emotional alliance. As she says of the period during which the New Woman reigned: "To both women and men, the 'intermediate sex' symbolized the New Woman's demand for a role beyond conventional gender restraints; the 'Mannish Lesbian' embodied *her* demand to exercise male rights and powers—to act, that is, as if she were a man! To male physicians, politicians, even modernist writers, the New Woman/Mannish Lesbian symbolized disorder in a world gone mad."[6] Although a heroine like Jewett's Nan Price in the 1880s might find nothing either unhealthy or remarkable about female friendships (nor would her audience), by the time of Harrison's Marion Irving in the 1890s, a growing uneasiness existed about close same-sex relationships, especially as sources of emotional fulfillment. This growing popular distaste expressed itself in stories by having the heroine ultimately give up the career-oriented life and enfold herself within the "normal" bonds of matrimony and male love. The New Woman, if she were to remain normal in the popular mind, ultimately had to give up being the New Woman. With the polarities between New Woman/feminism and True Woman so strongly expressed and defined, it seems likely that Real Womanhood writers, facing these dilemmas, split among themselves, joining the forces of either True Womanhood or New Woman/feminism, depending on whether they valued more highly the separate sphere and woman's moral duties to have a family and indirectly refine society or the individual need for education, self-reliance, self-determination, and self-support. Real Womanhood, then, simply ceased to exist as a compromise position.

Anyone interested in the peculiar record of women's rights in the United States would find a fruitful area of inquiry in determining the exact dynamics of Real Womanhood's disappearance. Its demise has something important to say about the way American women saw—and perhaps still do see—themselves, their abilities, their duties, and their purpose. Why did American women get the vote, for example, so much later than Australian women, who had a cultural inheritance in many ways similar to our own? Why did American women fail to press their claims for legal rights as violently as their British sisters? Anyone studying the disappearance of Real Womanhood may very well find answers to those questions because they might suggest a particular psychological and cultural reason for a vestigial influence still active today. This may explain the slackening of momentum for the Equal Rights Amendment (ERA) in the last decade and the reappearance of an aggressive modern version of True Womanhood under the auspices of writers and lecturers such as Phyllis Schlafley and Maribel Morgan. What part might organized religion have played in championing and proselytizing for the virtues of True Womanhood and rejecting the ERA as "nonwomanly"?

Finally, what could answers to the disappearance of Real Womanhood tell us about the new "superwoman" phenomenon—the frantic attempt simultaneously to have a full-blown career, raise a family, have a fulfilling marriage, and support social causes? Is the modern answer to "feminism" versus "female" to try to comprehend both extremes and do both rather than be forced to a choice when no ideological middle position is available? A book such as Betty Friedan's *Second Stage* seems to suggest the need for such a middle position, and her directives seem very much a revisitation of Real Womanhood's familiar ground. Her stress on the need for an integration of roles—home, career, family, friends, causes— in a realistically achievable context lends itself to a popular rather than a revolutionary feminist position and sounds "traditional" to those of us familiar with Real Womanhood.

A reexamination of the rationales and goals espoused by the Ideal of Real Womanhood between 1840 and 1880—in physical fitness, education, employment, and marriage—might suggest not only what American women have historically valued intrinsically but how the resulting, seemingly inevitable, political and social polarization can be avoided the next time around.

Notes

Introduction

1. Lois W. Banner, *American Beauty* (New York: Knopf, 1983), p. 45.

2. See, for example, Carroll Smith-Rosenberg, *Disorderly Conduct: Visions of Gender in Victorian America* (New York: Oxford University Press, 1985), pp. 13, 300 n. 6; Catherine Clinton, *The Other Civil War: American Women in the Nineteenth Century* (New York: Hill and Wang, 1984), p. 22; Banner, *American Beauty*, p. 304 n. 21.

3. Banner, *American Beauty*, pp. 40–42.

4. Ibid., p. 88.

5. Dr. Dio Lewis, *Our Girls* (New York: Harper and Brothers, 1871), pp. 66–67.

6. Nora Perry, "Rosalind Newcomb," *Harper's New Monthly Magazine* 20 (May 1860): 780.

7. "A Revolutionary Girl's Pluck," *Illustrated Christian Weekly* 6 (July 15, 1876): 343.

8. Banner, *American Beauty*, p. 91.

9. See, for example, Keith Melder, "Woman's High Calling: The Teaching Profession in America, 1830–1860," *American Studies* 13, no. 2 (1972): 19–32; Richard M. Bernard and Maris A. Vinovskis, "The Female School Teacher in Ante-Bellum Massachusetts," *Journal of Social History* 10 (Mar. 1977): 332–45; Bernice M. Deutrich, "Propriety and Pay," *Prologue: The Journal of the National Archives* 3, no. 2 (1971): 67–72; David M. Katzman, *Seven Days a Week: Women and Domestic Service in Industrializing America* (New York: Oxford University Press, 1978).

10. Smith-Rosenberg, *Disorderly Conduct*, p. 17.

11. Jill Ker Conway, however, in a recent article, "Utopian Dream or Dystopian Nightmare? Nineteenth Century Feminist Ideas about Equality," *Proceedings of the American Antiquarian Society* 96, pt. 2 (1987): 285–94, suggests that "feminist" is too monolithic a term to reflect the many divisions within the ranks of those supporting an "improvement" of "women's position" (285). She would classify my advocates of "Real Womanhood," in part, as "conservative sentimental" rather than "utopian-radical," with the first represented by Harriet Beecher Stowe and Dorothea Dix and the latter by Frances Wright and John Humphrey Noyes (285–86). Certainly

her point is well taken that an obvious continuum existed within feminist ranks, but I question her use of the term for women who not only rejected suffrage but who also held grimly to a theory of separate spheres. This to me is a case of calling any writer with enlightened views on education or employment a prima facie "feminist." Feminists *then* did not agree, nor generally do they now. Her article, however, is valuable because it does suggest the existence of a broad spectrum from the most passive examples of True Womanhood to the most radical feminists of the day; this sense of various possible positions along a continuum tends to be lost in the polarization I discussed earlier. My point is that Real Womanhood, though occupying the middle of this continuum, attempted to draw boundaries between itself and feminism, utterly rejecting any uniting likenesses.

12. See Nina Baym's classic study *Woman's Fiction: A Guide to Novels by and about Women in America, 1820–1870* (Ithaca: Cornell University Press, 1978).

13. Gerda Lerner, *The Majority Finds Its Past: Placing Women in History* (Oxford: Oxford University Press, 1979), p. 18.

14. Thomas C. Cochran, *200 Years of American Business* (New York: Basic Books, 1977), pp. 51–54.

15. Burton J. Bledstein, *The Culture of Professionalism: The Middle Class and the Development of Higher Ed-*

ucation in America (New York: Norton, 1976), p. 6.

16. Rev. George W. Burnap, *Lectures on the Sphere and Duties of Woman and Other Subjects* (Baltimore: John Murray, 1841), p. 144; Mrs. L. G. Abell, *Woman in Her Various Relations* (New York: William Holdredge, 1851), p. 26; Rev. George Sumner Weaver, *Aims and Aids for Girls and Young Women on the Various Duties of Life* (New York: Fowler and Wells, 1856), p. 20; see also ibid., "Lecture Eight," pp. 122–35.

17. Lerner, *Majority Finds Its Past,* pp. 25, 18, 135.

18. Helen Woodward, *The Lady Persuaders* (New York: Ivan Obolensky, 1960), p. 1; Mrs. A. J. Graves, *Woman in America: Being an Examination into the Moral and Intellectual Condition of American Female Society* (New York: Harper and Brothers, 1843), pp. 177–78; "Working-Women in New York," *Harper's New Monthly Magazine* 61 (1880): 25–37; Barbara Ehrenreich and Deirdre English, *For Her Own Good: 150 Years of the Experts' Advice to Women* (Garden City, N. Y.: Doubleday Anchor Press, 1978), p. 24.

19. Carl Bode, *The Anatomy of American Popular Culture, 1840–1861* (Berkeley and Los Angeles: University of California Press, 1959), pp. 120, 128; Carl Degler, *At Odds: Women and the Family in America from the Revolution to the Present* (New York: Oxford University Press, 1980), p. 82.

20. See, for example, Lerner's con-

tention that after 1840 women grew acutely frustrated with the "failed promises of Jacksonian optimism" (*Majority Finds Its Past*, p. 27).

21. Baym, *Woman's Fiction*, pp. 36–38; Baym, "Portrayal of Women in American Literature, 1790–1870," in Marlene Springer, ed., *What Manner of Woman: Essays on English and American Life and Literature* (New York: New York University Press, 1977), p. 229; Ehrenreich and English, *For Her Own Good*, p. 24; Frances B. Cogan, "Weak Fathers and Other Beasts: An Examination of the American Male in Domestic Novels, 1850–1870," *American Studies* 25 (Fall 1984): 5–20.

22. Barbara Leslie Epstein, *The Politics of Domesticity: Women, Evangelism, and Temperance in Nineteenth Century America* (Middletown, Conn.: Wesleyan University Press, 1981); Karen Halttunen, *Confidence Men and Painted Women: A Study of Middle-Class Culture in America, 1830–1870* (New Haven: Yale University Press, 1982).

23. Page Smith, *Daughters of the Promised Land: Women in American History* (Boston: Little, Brown, 1970); Ernest Earnest, *The American Eve in Fact and Fiction, 1775–1914* (Chicago: University of Chicago Press, 1974); Erna Olafson Hellerstein, Leslie Parker Hume, and Karen Offen, eds., *Victorian Women: A Documentary Account of Women's Lives in Nineteenth Century England, France, and the United States* (Stanford: Stanford University Press, 1981); Rosalind Rosenberg, *Beyond Separate Spheres: Intellectual Roots of Modern Feminism* (New Haven: Yale University Press, 1982); Conway, "Utopian Dream," p. 4.

24. Burton J. Bledstein, *The Culture of Professionalism: The Middle Class and Development of Higher Education in America* (New York: Norton, 1976), pp. 123–24.

25. Mary Walsh, *"Doctors Wanted: No Women Need Apply": Sexual Barriers in the Medical Profession, 1835–1975* (New Haven: Yale University Press, 1977), p. viii.

Chapter 1: *Muscles Like Harp-Strings: Physical Fitness, Health, and the Real Woman*

1. Carroll Smith-Rosenberg and Charles Rosenberg, "The Female Animal: Medical and Biological Views of Woman and Her Role in Nineteenth Century America," *Journal of American History* 60 (Sept. 1973): 334–35.

2. Carroll Smith-Rosenberg, "Puberty to Menopause: The Cycle of

Femininity in Nineteenth Century America," in Mary S. Hartman and Lois Banner, eds., *Clio's Consciousness Raised* (New York: Harper & Row, 1974), pp. 26–27.

3. See chapter 3, below, for a fuller discussion of the opposing medical positions regarding the biological

nature and limitations of women and the theories behind such positions, as well as the peculiar critical use of both British and American sources.

4. Lewis, *Our Girls,* pp. 66–67, 72.

5. Emily Thornwell, *The Lady's Guide to Perfect Gentility in Manners, Dress, and Conversation* . . . (New York: Derby and Jackson, 1856), p. 19.

6. William A. Alcott, *The Young Woman's Book of Health* (Boston: Tappan, Whittemore and Mason, 1850), pp. 15–16.

7. Mary J. Holmes, *'Lena Rivers* (New York: G. W. Dillingham, 1856), p. 167.

8. Edwin Hubbell Chapin, *Duties of Young Women* (Boston: G. W. Briggs, 1848), pp. 35, 38–48.

9. T. S. Arthur, *Advice to Young Ladies on Their Duties and Conduct in Life* (Boston: G. W. Cottrell, 1851), pp. 105–6.

10. "Winifred's Vow," *Harper's New Monthly Magazine* 12 (Dec. 1855): 81–83.

11. Virginia Penny, "Poor Health of American Women," *Ladies' Repository* 25 (Mar. 1865): 155.

12. Mrs. H. C. Gardner, "Invalid Women," *Ladies' Repository* 25 (Dec. 1865): 724.

13. "Crofut on Skates," *Harper's Weekly* 4 (Feb. 11, 1860): 91.

14. William Blaikie, *How to Get Strong and How to Stay So* (New York: Harper and Brothers, 1879), pp. 20–21; Catharine E. Beecher, *A Treatise on Domestic Economy for the Use of Young Ladies at Home and at School,*

ed., rev. (New York: Harper and Brothers, 1855), p. 5.

15. Abell, *Woman in Her Various Relations,* p. 269.

16. Mary J. Holmes, *Meadowbrook* (Chicago: Donahue Brothers, n.d. [1857]), p. 5.

17. "Benefit of Household Care," *Ladies' Repository* 25 (Apr. 1865): 246; "Editorial Chitchat," *Peterson's Magazine* 3 (Mar. 1858): 248.

18. Abell, *Woman in Her Various Relations,* pp. 11, 255–58.

19. Blaikie, *How to Get Strong,* pp. 42–43.

20. Eleanor Wolf Thompson, *Education for Ladies, 1830–1860: Ideas on Education in Magazines for Women* (New York: King's Crown Press, 1947), p. 51. See, for example, advertisements for girls' boarding schools such as that for Riverside Seminary in Wellsville, Allegany County, New York, in 1876 issues of the *Illustrated Christian Weekly*; Calvin Cutter, M.D., *The Female Guide* . . . (West Brookfield [Mass.?]: Charles A. Mirick, 1844), pp. 14–15; Cutter, *First Book on Anatomy, Physiology, and Hygiene for Grammar Schools and Families,* rev. stereotype ed. (Philadelphia: J. B. Lippincott, 1854), pp. 24–26.

21. Cutter, *Female Guide,* p. 20.

22. Thornwell, *Lady's Guide,* pp. 18–19.

23. Emily Huntington Miller, "A Summer's Adventures," *Ladies' Repository* 25 (Feb. 1865): 74–78; ibid. (Mar. 1865): 139.

24. "Sister Anne," *Harper's New Monthly Magazine* 12 (Dec. 1855): 92–93.

25. Blaikie, *How to Get Strong,* pp. 68–72.

26. Dr. Dio Lewis, *New Gymnastics for Men, Women and Children,* 4th ed. (Boston: Ticknor and Fields, 1863), pp. 69, 16–60.

27. Ibid., pp. 169, 256–58, quoting from (and translating) with additions, D. G. M. Schreber, *The Pangymnastikon* (N.p.: n.d.) [Leipzig].

28. Ibid., p. 99.

29. Marion Harland, *Ruby's Husband* (New York: Sheldon and Co., 1869), pp. 288–90.

30. Diana Reep, *The Rescue and Romance: Popular Novels before World War I* (Bowling Green: Bowling Green State University Popular Press, 1982), pp. 10, 89.

31. Holmes, *'Lena Rivers,* p. 40.

32. Ibid., pp. 134, 196.

33. Richard Osborn Cummings, *The American and His Food,* 2d ed. (New York: Arno Press, 1970), pp. 53–57.

34. *Ladies' Indispensable Assistant, Being a Companion for the Sister, Mother and Wife* . . . (New York: Nassau-Street, 1852), p. 40.

35. Alcott, *Young Woman's Book of Health,* pp. 86–89.

36. Ibid., pp. 90–92, 33–36.

37. Thornwell, *Lady's Guide,* pp. 24–25; "Rules for Health," *Illustrated Christian Weekly* 6 (Oct. 28, 1876): 521; "14 Ways by Which People Get Sick," *Ladies' Repository* 25 (July 1865): 438.

38. Thornwell, *Lady's Guide,* pp. 12–16.

39. *Ladies' Indispensable Assistant,* p. 121; *Ladies' Repository* 25 (July 1865): 438.

40. Abell, *Woman in Her Various Relations,* pp. 265–266.

41. Thornwell, *Lady's Guide,* p. 21.

42. Alcott, *Young Woman's Book of Health,* p. 60.

43. Ibid., pp. 60–63.

44. Florence Hartley, *The Ladies' Book of Etiquette and Manual of Politeness: A Complete Handbook for the Use of the Lady in Polite Society* (Boston: G. W. Cottrell, 1860), pp. 34–37.

45. Arthur, *Advice,* pp. 101–2; "14 Ways by Which People Get Sick," p. 438; "Rules for Health," p. 521.

46. Harland, *Ruby's Husband,* pp. 230ff.

47. Rev. Daniel Wise, *The Young Lady's Counsellor; or Outlines and Illustrations of the Sphere, the Duties, and the Dangers of Young Women* (New York: Carlton and Phillips, 1854), pp. 185–86.

48. "Addressed to Wise Women," *Ladies' Repository* 25 (Apr. 1865): 245.

49. "A Warning to Lady Skaters," *Harper's Weekly* 4 (Feb. 11, 1860): 87; Blaikie, *How to Get Strong,* pp. 42–43.

50. Miller, "Summer's Adventures," pp. 75–77.

51. Abell, *Woman in Her Various Relations,* pp. 262–63; see also Cutter, *Female Guide,* pp. 16–17, regarding loose yet healthily appropriate clothing.

52. *Ladies' Indispensable Assistant* on corseting p. 122; *Ladies' Repository* 25 (July 1865): 438; Rev. Bernard O'Reilly, *The Mirror of True Woman-*

hood: A Book of Instruction for Women in the World, 14th ed. (New York: Peter F. Collier, 1880), p. 247.

53. Thornwell, *Lady's Guide,* pp. 133–37.

54. Ibid.

55. Blaikie, *How to Get Strong,* p. 52.

Chapter 2: *Education and Real Womanhood*

1. Barbara Welter, *Dimity Convictions: The American Woman in the Nineteenth Century* (Athens: Ohio University Press, 1976), p. 21; Smith-Rosenberg and Rosenberg, "Female Animal," pp. 334–35.

2. See, for example, Carroll Smith-Rosenberg, "Puberty to Menopause: The Cycle of Femininity in Nineteenth Century America," in Hartman and Banner, eds., *Clio's Consciousness Raised,* pp. 30–31; see also pp. 26, 35, n. 4, 336, n. 7.

3. *Appleton's Cyclopaedia of American Biography* (1888), 2:48, 1:41, 3: 702.

4. Walsh, *"Doctors Wanted,"* p. 35.

5. Thompson, *Education for Ladies,* pp. 24–28.

6. Catharine E. Beecher and Harriet Beecher Stowe, *The New Housekeeper's Manual: . . . Together with the Handy Cook Book by Catharine Beecher* (New York: Fords, Howard and Hubert, 1873), p. 15.

7. Blaikie, *How to Get Strong,* pp. 49–50; Lewis, *New Gymnastics;* see also Alcott, *Young Woman's Book of Health,* pp. 104–5; Abell, *Woman in Her Various Relations,* p. 273.

8. Thompson, *Education for Ladies,* pp. 32–33.

9. Allen quoted in "The Other Side of the Question," *Nation* 5 (Oct. 17, 1867): 316; Edward H. Clarke, M.D., *Sex in Education; or A Fair Chance for the Girls* (Boston: James R. Osgood & Co., late Ticknor and Fields and Fields, Osgood and Co., 1873), pp. 13, 112, 15–18.

10. Clarke, *Sex in Education,* pp. 18–19, 128.

11. Ibid., pp. 133, 75–104.

12. Ely Van De Warker, M.D., "The Genesis of Woman," *Popular Science Monthly* 5 (July 1874): 269–77.

13. Samuel Gregory, "Female Physicians," *Littell's Living Age* 73 (May 3, 1862): 243.

14. Ibid., pp. 245–46.

15. Alcott, *Young Woman's Book of Health,* pp. 104–5, 107–8; Lewis, *Our Girls,* pp. 213–25.

16. Baym, *Woman's Fiction,* pp. 18–20.

17. Ibid., p. 18.

18. Arthur, *Advice,* pp. 162–63, 166–67; Abell, *Woman in Her Various Relations,* p. 209.

19. Augusta J. Evans, *St. Elmo* (New York: G. W. Carleton, 1866), pp. 102–33, 328–29ff.

20. Susan Warner, *The Wide, Wide World* (New York: Grosset and Dunlap,

n.d. [1851]), pp. 164–83, 468–69, 526–29.

21. Holmes, *'Lena Rivers,* pp. 408ff.; Holmes, *Meadowbrook,* pp. 79–89ff.

22. T. S. Arthur, "Engaged at Sixteen," in *The Angel of the Household and Other Tales* (Philadelphia: John E. Potter, n.d. [1854]), pp. 177, 189.

23. Lewis, *Our Girls,* pp. 194–95.

24. Burnap, *Lectures,* pp. 151–53. On the romantic value of education for a woman, see also "Taxes on Bachelors," *Harper's Weekly* 4 (Jan. 28, 1860): 50.

25. "What Everybody Said," *Harper's Weekly* 4 (Feb. 4, 1860): 76; "Olive West," *Harper's New Monthly Magazine* 32 (Apr. 1866): 655–57; "The School-Teacher at Bottle-Flat," *Frank Leslie's Popular Monthly,* Feb. 1876, pp. 162–67.

26. O'Reilly, *Mirror of True Womanhood,* pp. 65, 57–59, 248–49.

27. "Husbands and Wives," *Illustrated Christian Weekly* 6 (Sept. 9, 1876): 440; see also "Marriage a la Mode," *Harper's New Monthly Magazine* 32 (May 1866): 760–61.

28. Marion Harland, "What Shall We Do with Our Daughters?" *Illustrated Christian Weekly* 6 (Apr. 1, 1876): 158; Lewis, *Our Girls,* pp. 200–201, 213–26.

29. Alcott, *Young Woman's Book of Health,* pp. 110–18; Burnap, *Lectures,* pp. 154–57.

30. For the opposing point of view, see Welter, *Dimity Convictions,* pp. 4–21; Mary P. Ryan, *Womanhood in America: From Colonial Times to the* Present (New York: New Viewpoints, 1975), pp. 148–49; Smith, *Daughters of the Promised Land,* p. 208; Madonna Kolbenschlag, *Kiss Sleeping Beauty Good-Bye: Breaking the Spell of Feminine Myths and Models* (Garden City, N.Y.: Doubleday, 1979), p. 14.

31. Thompson, *Education for Ladies,* pp. 35–38.

32. Marion Harland, *Common Sense in the Household: A Manual of Practical Housewifery* (New York: Charles Scribner's Sons, 1871), pp. 16–18; "How Shall Our Daughters be Educated," *Peterson's Magazine* 33 (May 1858): 169.

33. Beecher, *Treatise on Domestic Economy,* p. 5.

34. Mary Jane Holmes, *Rose Mather: A Tale* (New York: Carleton, 1868), pp. 63–64, 1–60.

35. Mrs. A. D. T. Whitney, *A Summer in Leslie Goldthwaite's Life* (Boston: Houghton Mifflin, 1891).

36. Beecher and Stowe, *New Housekeeper's Manual,* pp. 13–22.

37. Beecher, *Treatise on Domestic Economy,* pp. 11–24.

38. Beecher and Stowe, *New Housekeeper's Manual,* pp. 14–17ff.

39. Ibid., pp. 44–56.

40. Cutter, *First Book on Anatomy,* p. v; Cutter, *Female Guide,* p. 164.

41. Cutter, *First Book on Anatomy,* pp. 11, 30–35, 14.

42. Anne Douglas, *The Feminization of American Culture* (New York: Knopf, 1977), pp. 8–9.

43. Harriet Beecher Stowe, *Pink and White Tyranny: A Society Novel,* in *The Writings of Harriet Beecher Stowe,*

Riverside ed. (Boston: Houghton Mifflin, 1899), 11: 267–523.

44. Burnap, *Lectures*, p. 31. For the comments of the critics, see, for example, Earnest, *American Eve;* Susan Phinney Conrad, *Perish the Thought: Intellectual Women in Romantic America, 1830–1860* (New York: Oxford University Press, 1976), pp. 8–11; Bode, *Anatomy of American Popular Culture*, pp. 169–73; Baym, *Woman's Fiction*, pp. 22–25, 35, 47–49.

45. Abell, *Woman in Her Various Relations*, pp. 298–99; Burnap, *Lectures*, p. 42.

46. Abell, *Woman in Her Various Relations*, p. 153; Baym, *Woman's Fiction*, p. 20.

47. T. S. Arthur, "Taking Boarders," in *Woman's Trials; or Tales and Sketches from the Life around Us* (New York: James B. Millar, 1885), pp. 40–122; "Olive West," pp. 655–56; "Winifred's Vow," pp. 81–85.

48. Earnest, *American Eve*, p. 62, citing Brown's *The Sentimental Novel in America, 1789–1860;* Welter, *Dimity Convictions*, p. 17; on ideal submission and passivity, see Kolbenschlag, *Kiss Sleeping Beauty Good-Bye*, p. 14; Ryan, *Womanhood in America*, p. 148; Smith, *Daughters of the Promised Land*, p. 210.

49. Lewis, *Our Girls*, pp. 102–3, 132–41; for a fuller discussion of possible employment, see ibid., chap. 11.

50. Wise, *Young Lady's Counsellor*, pp. 168–71.

51. Smith-Rosenberg, "Puberty to Menopause," pp. 24–31; Welter, *Dimity Convictions*, p. 25; Anne Douglas Wood, " 'The Fashionable Diseases':

Women's Complaints and Their Treatment in Nineteenth Century America," in Hartman and Banner, eds., *Clio's Consciousness Raised*, pp. 1–2, 17.

52. See, for example, Lewis, *Our Girls*, pp. 66–72; Alcott, *Young Woman's Book of Health*, pp. 23–27; Abell, *Woman in Her Various Relations*, pp. 265–67.

53. Abell, *Woman in Her Various Relations*, 274–75, 270; see also p. 276 regarding the effects of ennui; Thomas Wentworth Higginson, "Essay II," in Julia Ward Howe, ed., *Sex and Education: A Reply to Dr. E. H. Clarke's "Sex in Education"* (1874; rpt. New York: Arno Press, 1972, ed. Annette K. Baxter and Leon Stein), p. 42.

54. Clarke, *Sex in Education*, 103; Ada Shepard Badger, "Essay IV," in Howe, ed., *Sex and Education*, pp. 75–77.

55. Burnap, *Lectures*, pp. 151–52, 42.

56. Arthur, *Advice*, pp. 73, 61–62; see also, in regard to the deleterious effects of "light" reading, Abell, *Woman in Her Various Relations*, p. 274; Lewis, *Our Girls*, pp. 213–23; "Marriage a la Mode," p. 760; Alcott, *Young Woman's Book of Health*, pp. 104–8.

57. Abell, *Woman in Her Various Relations*, pp. 28–38, 118, 198.

58. Wise, *Young Lady's Counsellor*, pp. 181–84; Alcott, *Young Woman's Book of Health*, pp. 20–22; Arthur, *Advice*, pp. 58–60.

59. P. Thorne, "The Coming Woman," *Lippincott's Magazine* 5 (May 1870): 529.

60. Harland, *Common Sense,* pp. 13–14.

61. Ibid., p. 19.

Chapter 3: *Preparation for the Marriage Choice*

1. See Robert L. Griswold, "Law, Sex, Cruelty, and Divorce in Victorian America, 1840–1900," *American Quarterly* 38 (Winter 1986): 721–45. Though Griswold explores the slowly growing trend of courts to grant divorces based on physical and sexual cruelty, divorce was still comparatively rare until after 1886 (p. 722).

2. John Cawelti, "Pornography, Catastrophe, and Vengeance: Shifting Narrative Structures in a Changing American Culture," in Sam B. Girgus, ed., *The American Self: Myth, Ideology, and Popular Culture* (Albuquerque: University of New Mexico Press, 1981), p. 184.

3. Mary Kelley, "The Sentimentalists: Promise and Betrayal in the Home," *Signs: Journal of Women in Culture and Society* 4 (Spring 1979): 436–37. See, by contrast, Henry Nash Smith, "Fiction and the American Ideology: The Genesis of Howell's Early Realism," in Girgus, ed., *American Self,* p. 45.

4. See Cogan, "Weak Fathers and Other Beasts," p. 8; Kelley, "Sentimentalists," p. 443.

5. See, for example, "Honorable Often to Be an Old Maid," *Peterson's Magazine* 33 (May 1858): 395; Emma Willard, *Morals for the Young; or Good Principles Instilling Wisdom* (New York: A. S. Barnes, 1857), p. 83; Artemus

Bowers Muzzey, *The Young Maiden,* 3d ed. (Boston: W. Crosby, 1842), pp. 153–55; see also the highly favorable portrait of Miss Craydocke in Whitney, *A Summer in Leslie Goldthwaite's Life,* pp. 91–101.

6. Chapin, *Duties of Young Women,* p. 132.

7. Weaver, *Aims and Aids,* p. 163.

8. Arthur, *Advice,* pp. 161–263; Weaver, *Aims and Aids,* p. 171; see also Muzzey, *Young Maiden,* p. 204; Chapin, *Duties of Young Women,* pp. 57–58; Sarah Josepha Hale, as quoted by Ola Winslow, "Books for the Lady Reader, 1820–1860," in George Boas, ed., *Romanticism in America* (Baltimore: Johns Hopkins Press, 1940), p. 105. The age of heroine Edna Earl in Evans, *St. Elmo,* supports this point.

9. See Welter's description of the True Woman as "a lady in the tower, weaving her tapestry," in *Dimity Convictions,* pp. 16–17; see also Ryan, *Womanhood in America,* pp. 148–49; Kolbenschlag, *Kiss Sleeping Beauty Good-Bye;* Kelley, "Sentimentalists."

10. See Virginia Penny, *The Employments of Women: A Cyclopaedia of Woman's Work* (titled *500 Employments for Women* in later editions) (Boston: Walker, Wise, 1863), pp. v–ix; see also Lewis, *Our Girls,* pp. 131–41; "At Home and Abroad," *Illustrated*

Christian Weekly 6 (Dec. 30, 1876): 645; Thorne, "Coming Woman."

11. "Honorable Often to Be an Old Maid," p. 395; for similar expressions of censure, see Willard, *Morals for the Young*, pp. 82–83.

12. See, for example, T. S. Arthur's "Engaged at Sixteen," in *Angel of the Household*, pp. 175–89; Mrs. A. J. Graves, *Girlhood and Womanhood; or Sketches of My Schoolmates* (Boston: T. H. Carter and Co., and Benjamin B. Mussey, 1844), pp. 133–45; see also the portrait of Dr. Clayton in Holmes, *Meadowbrook*.

13. E. D. E. N. Southworth, *Ishmael; or In the Depths* (Philadelphia: T. B. Peterson & Bros., 1876).

14. Graves, *Girlhood and Womanhood*, pp. 145, 133, 138, 140–45.

15. Ibid., pp. 135–37.

16. Ibid., pp. 147–48.

17. Ibid., pp. 149, 151.

18. Muzzey, *Young Maiden*, p. 171.

19. Ibid., pp. 171–72, 170; Willard, *Morals for the Young*, p. 83.

20. Mrs. Caroline Lee Hentz, *Linda; or the Young Pilot of the Belle Creole* (Philadelphia: T. B. Peterson & Brothers, 1869), p. 104.

21. Holmes, *'Lena Rivers*, pp. 308, 312, 321–22.

22. Baym, "Portrayal of Women," p. 230.

23. Kelley, "Sentimentalists," p. 438; Baym, *Woman's Fiction*, pp. 44, 16; Baym, "Portrayal of Women," p. 234 n. 9.

24. Muzzey, *Young Maiden*, pp. 179–80.

25. Graves, *Girlhood and Womanhood*, pp. 59–60.

26. Ibid., pp. 53, 57–58, 60–61.

27. Ibid., pp. 60–63.

28. Ibid., p. 64.

29. Chapin, *Duties of Young Women*, p. 130; Rev. George Sumner Weaver, *Hopes and Helps for the Young of Both Sexes* (New York: Fowler and Wells, 1857), p. 216; Muzzey, *Young Maiden*, p. 215; Arthur, *Advice*, pp. 168–74.

30. Southworth, *Ishmael*, pp. 28, 31, 39, 40.

31. Ibid., p. 72.

32. Ibid., pp. 72–74.

33. See, for example, T. S. Arthur, "Taking in Boarders," in *Woman's Trials*, pp. 40–122; see also more general warnings regarding "secret" courtship in Muzzey, *Young Maiden*, pp. 194–95, 232; Halttunen, *Confidence Men and Painted Women*, pp. 33–60.

34. Welter, *Dimity Convictions*, pp. 4–6.

35. Ibid., p. 11.

36. Southworth, *Ishmael*, p. 80.

37. Ibid., pp. 117, 116.

38. Ibid., p. 102.

39. Ibid., pp. 162–67.

40. Muzzey, *Young Maiden*, pp. 172–73; Chapin, *Duties of Young Women*, p. 130.

41. Muzzey, *Young Maidens*, p. 177. See also Weaver, *Hopes and Helps*, p. 216; Abell, *Woman in Her Various Relations*, pp. 202–3.

42. Baym, *Woman's Fiction*, p. 18.

43. Halttunen, *Confidence Men and Painted Women*, p. 57; Augusta Evans, *Vashti; or "Until Death Us Do Part"* (New York: G. W. Carleton, 1869).

44. Edward B. Foote is not listed in *Appleton's Cyclopaedia of American Biography* (1888) as are other writers

I have cited, including Dr. Dio Lewis, Dr. Calvin Cutter, and William Blaikie. Perhaps Foote was not prominent enough to be listed, rather than being omitted because he was not a doctor. The *National Union Catalog: Pre-1956 Imprints* (Chicago: Mansell, 1968) indicates that his book, though initially published by the author in 1858, was reprinted in an enlarged edition and reissued until 1870—some proof of its public acceptance.

45. Dr. Edward B. Foote, *Medical Common Sense; Applied to the Causes, Prevention and Cure of Chronic Diseases and Unhappiness in Marriage*, Rev. and enlarged ed. (New York: Published by the Author, 1867), pp. 310–15.

46. Ibid., pp. 315, 310–13.

47. Muzzey, *Young Maiden*, p. 178;

Weaver, *Hopes and Helps*, pp. 211–13.

48. Muzzey, *Young Maiden*, pp. 175–76.

49. Arthur, "Taking Boarders," in *Woman's Trials*, pp. 90–93.

50. Burnap, *Lectures*, p. 143.

51. "M. Carlier on Marriage in America," *Nation* 4 (May 2, 1867): 351; Muzzey, *Young Maiden*, pp. 209–10, 207, 211.

52. Esther B. Aresty, *The Best Behavior: The Course of Good Manners—from Antiquity to the Present—as Seen through Courtesy and Etiquette Books* (New York: Simon and Schuster, 1970), pp. 246, 244–45.

53. Halttunen, *Confidence Men and Painted Women*, p. 92.

54. Graves, *Girlhood and Womanhood*, pp. 51–52.

Chapter 4: *Courtship and the Winnowing Process*

1. Muzzey, *Young Maiden*, pp. 185, 188.

2. Baym, *Woman's Fiction*, pp. 24–26.

3. Aresty, *Best Behavior*, p. 200; Reep, *Rescue and Romance*, pp. 7–8.

4. Weaver, *Aims and Aids*, pp. 154–55.

5. Holmes, *Meadowbrook*, pp. 110–30.

6. Arthur, "Taking Boarders," in *Woman's Trials*, p. 46.

7. Arthur, "New Year's Gift," in ibid., p. 160.

8. Weaver, *Hopes and Helps*, pp. 224–26, 244.

9. Muzzey, *Young Maiden*, pp. 200–

201. See also T. S. Arthur, "Engaged at Sixteen," in *Angel of the Household*, pp. 175–89; Abell, *Woman in Her Various Relations*, pp. 209, 202; Weaver, *Hopes and Helps*, p. 244.

10. Aresty, *Best Behavior*, p. 201.

11. Muzzey, *Young Maiden*, p. 180.

12. Miss Eliza Leslie, *Behaviour Book: A Guide and Manual for Ladies as Regards Their Conversation, Manners, Dress . . . etc.* (Philadelphia: T. B. Peterson and Brothers, 1859), p. 89. See also Aresty, *Best Behavior*, p. 200; Weaver, *Aims and Aids*, pp. 13–14.

13. Weaver, *Hopes and Helps*, p. 227; Muzzey, *Young Maiden*, pp. 198–99.

14. See Dr. Edward B. Foote's section on birth control in *Medical Common Sense,* pp. 310–15. See also the somewhat opaque references of another marriage manual author, Frederick Hollick, M.D., to religious strictures against birth control and abortion in *The Marriage Guide; or Natural History of Generation. A Private Instructor for Married Persons and Those about to Marry, Both Male and Female* (New York: T. W. Strong, n.d. [1859]), pp. 333–36.

15. Warner, *Wide, Wide World,* pp. 521–22.

16. Abell, *Woman in Her Various Relations,* pp. 199–209; see also Muzzey, *Young Maiden,* pp. 211, 171.

17. Muzzey, *Young Maiden,* pp. 194–96. See also Abell's injunction against marrying contrary to judgment and feeling (*Woman in Her Various Relations,* p. 209) and her recommendation to stay single. Weaver, *Aims and Aids,* p. 164.

18. Graves, *Girlhood and Womanhood,* pp. 183–85.

19. Halttunen, *Confidence Men and Painted Women,* pp. 111–13; see also the complicated rules of ballroom acquaintanceship suggested by Hartley in *Ladies' Book of Etiquette,* pp. 166–67.

20. Graves, *Girlhood and Womanhood,* pp. 51–52; Weaver, *Aims and Aids,* p. 164; Muzzey, *Young Maiden,* p. 165.

21. Muzzey, *Young Maiden,* p. 203; see also Weaver, *Hopes and Helps,* p. 224.

22. Holmes, *'Lena Rivers,* pp. 308–20.

23. Muzzey, *Young Maiden,* p. 202; see also Weaver's injunctions about "physical constitution," in *Hopes and Helps,* p. 243.

24. Graves, *Girlhood and Womanhood,* p. 140.

25. Halttunen, *Confidence Men and Painted Women,* pp. 51, 35.

26. Evans, *St. Elmo,* pp. 56–57.

27. Muzzey, *Young Maiden,* p. 228; Weaver, *Hopes and Helps,* pp. 211–15.

28. "The Doctor," "Hints to Lovers; or Courtship Reduced to Rule: With Observations upon the Symptoms and Treatment of Desperate Cases," *Knickerbocker* 25 (Apr. 1845): 342.

29. Ibid.

30. Hentz, *Linda,* pp. 106–37; Evans, *St. Elmo,* pp. 75–78; Southworth, *Ishmael,* pp. 159–60; Willard, *Morals for the Young,* p. 53.

31. "The Doctor," "Hints to Lovers," pp. 342–43.

32. Muzzey, *Young Maiden,* p. 208.

33. Ibid., pp. 208–9; Thornwell, *Lady's Guide,* pp. 146–47; Chapin, *Duties of Young Women,* pp. 89–90; Hartley, *Ladies' Book of Etiquette,* pp. 17, 13.

34. Thornwell, *Lady's Guide,* pp. 146–48, 153.

35. Lewis, *Our Girls,* pp. 194–96.

36. Holmes, *Meadowbrook,* pp. 103, 110, 112.

37. Harland, *Ruby's Husband,* p. 100.

38. Ibid., pp. 99–109.

39. Holmes, *'Lena Rivers,* pp. 401–11.

40. "What Everybody Said," p. 76.

41. Weaver, *Aims and Aids,* pp. 13–14.

42. Weaver, *Hopes and Helps,* pp. 217, 225. See also Muzzey, *Young Maiden,* pp. 196–201; Chapin, *Duties of Young Women,* pp. 131–39, on the nature of marriage and what to seek; Sarah J. Hale, *Manners; or Happy Homes and Good Society All the Year Round* (1868; rpt. New York: Arno Press, 1972), pp. 125–26.

43. Thornwell, *Lady's Guide,* p. 157.

44. Muzzey, *Young Maiden,* pp. 228–29.

45. Leslie, *Behaviour Book,* p. 164; see, for comparison, historically documented couples in Ellen K. Rothman, *Hands and Hearts: A History of Courtship in America* (New York: Basic Books, 1984), pp. 97–99.

46. Graves, *Girlhood and Womanhood,* pp. 69–72.

47. Muzzey, *Young Maiden,* pp. 215, 139; see also Arthur, *Advice,* pp. 172–73.

48. Graves, *Girlhood and Womanhood,* p. 72.

49. Willard, *Morals for the Young,* p. 51; Weaver, *Hopes and Helps,* p. 226.

50. Weaver, *Hopes and Helps,* pp. 224–26; see also Muzzey's warning about overaccommodation in a man, *Young Maiden,* p. 183.

51. Graves, *Girlhood and Womanhood,* p. 70.

52. T. S. Arthur, *Alice Melville; or The Indiscretion* and *Mary Ellis* (Philadelphia: Henry F. Anners, 1850), pp. 1–90.

53. Muzzey, *Young Maiden,* p. 218; see also Esther Aresty's overview of the initiative taken by American girls in courtship, especially in regard to "encouraging" a particular suitor to propose (*Best Behavior,* pp. 244–45).

54. Muzzey, *Young Maiden,* p. 221.

55. Ibid., p. 154.

56. Ibid., pp. 152, 165; see also Willard, *Morals for the Young,* p. 83, on the advisability and honor of a single life, along with Abell, *Woman in Her Various Relations,* p. 209, and Weaver, *Hopes and Helps,* p. 237.

57. Baym, *Woman's Fiction,* pp. 38–39; Whitney, *A Summer in Leslie Goldthwaite's Life,* pp. 92–93.

58. Whitney, *A Summer in Leslie Goldthwaite's Life,* pp. 107, 100–101.

59. Evans, *St. Elmo,* p. 186.

60. "Why Is Single Life Becoming More General?" *Nation* 6 (Mar. 5, 1868): 190–92.

61. Ibid., p. 191.

Chapter 5: *Engagement and Aftermath*

1. Muzzey, *Young Maiden,* pp. 234–35; this argument is advanced by Hale (*Manners,* pp. 121–22) as sufficient reason for *early* marriage, but her arguments are the same as those offered by Muzzey and others for *brief* engagements.

2. Muzzey, *Young Maiden,* p. 222.

3. Weaver, *Hopes and Helps,* pp. 226–27. See also Muzzey, *Young Maiden,* pp. 224–28.

4. Weaver, *Hopes and Helps,* p. 227; Weaver, *Aims and Aids,* pp. 174–75. See also Chapin, *Duties of Young*

Women, pp. 131–32; Abell, *Woman in Her Various Relations,* pp. 202–4.

5. Hale, *Manners,* pp. 226–27; Epstein, *Politics of Domesticity,* p. 78; Weaver, *Aims and Aids,* p. 175; Muzzey, *Young Maiden,* p. 197; Graves, *Girlhood and Womanhood,* pp. 183–205.

6. Graves, *Girlhood and Womanhood,* pp. 187–92.

7. Degler, *At Odds,* pp. 63–65.

8. Graves, *Girlhood and Womanhood,* pp. 195–96.

9. Ibid., p. 196.

10. Ibid., pp. 197–98.

11. Ibid., p. 201.

12. Ibid., pp. 201–5.

13. Welter, *Dimity Convictions,* pp. 27–29.

14. Chapin, *Duties of Young Women,* pp. 133–34; Muzzey, *Young Maiden,* pp. 196–97.

15. Muzzey, *Young Maiden,* pp. 197–98; see also Weaver, *Aims and Aids,* pp. 174–75; Abell, *Woman in Her Various Relations,* p. 209.

16. Abell, *Woman in Her Various Relations,* p. 207.

17. Graves, *Girlhood and Womanhood,* pp. 69, 70, 75.

18. Ibid., p. 75.

19. Ibid., pp. 79–82.

20. Weaver, *Aims and Aids,* p. 174;

Weaver, *Hopes and Helps,* p. 243.

21. Muzzey, *Young Maiden,* p. 226; see also Weaver, *Hopes and Helps,* pp. 226–27; Chapin, *Duties of Young Women,* p. 132.

22. Muzzey, *Young Maiden,* p. 232.

23. Leslie, *Behaviour Book,* p. 113.

24. Hollick, *Marriage Guide,* p. vi.

25. See listings for Hollick's *Marriage Guide* in *National Union Catalogue,* 251:523–26.

26. Carl Degler, "What Ought to Be and What Was: Women's Sexuality in the Nineteenth Century," *American Historical Review* 79 (Dec. 1974): 1473.

27. Chapin, *Duties of Young Women,* p. 133.

28. Thornwell, *Lady's Guide,* pp. 176, 175, 167.

29. Chapin, *Duties of Young Women,* pp. 131–32; Muzzey, *Young Maiden,* p. 223; "Society and Marriage," *Nation* 10 (May 26, 1870): 332–33. On the McFarland controversy see a series of letters in the *Nation* from May 26, 1870, to June 23, 1870, especially "Mr. Henry James on Marriage," pp. 366–68, and "Reply of Mr. James," pp. 404–5.

30. "Society and Marriage," p. 333.

Chapter 6: *Employment and the Real Woman*

1. Ehrenrich and English, *For Her Own Good,* p. 22; Kolbenschlag, *Kiss Sleeping Beauty Good-Bye,* p. 14.

2. William G. Webster and William

A. Wheeler, *A Common-School Dictionary of the English Language* (New York: Ivison, Blakeman; Springfield, Mass.: G. & C. Merriam, 1867), p. 117.

3. Weaver, *Aims and Aids*, pp. 124–25; Lewis, *Our Girls*, p. 103.

4. Warner, *Wide, Wide World*, p. 142.

5. Lewis, *Our Girls*, pp. 114, 120.

6. Alcott, *Young Woman's Book of Health*, pp. 48–49.

7. Arthur, *Advice*, pp. 29–35.

8. Lewis, *Our Girls*, p. 102.

9. Weaver, *Aims and Aids*, pp. 130–32.

10. Mrs. H. C. Gardner, "Labor; or Striking for Higher Wages," *Ladies' Repository* 19 (Jan. 1859): 7–11.

11. Ibid., *Ladies' Repository* 19 (Feb. 1859): 82–85.

12. Holmes, *'Lena Rivers*, pp. 105–6.

13. Ibid., p. 127.

14. Graves, *Girlhood and Womanhood*, pp. 183–85, 194–97.

15. Fanny Fern, *Rose Clark* (New York: Mason Brothers, 1856).

16. Gerda Lerner, *The Female Experience: An American Documentary* (Indianapolis: Bobbs-Merrill, 1977), p. 124.

17. Ibid., pp. 125–36.

18. Ehrenreich and English, *For Her Own Good*, p. 23.

19. Weaver, *Aims and Aids*, p. 128.

20. Evans, *Vashti*, p. 10.

21. Whitney, *A Summer in Leslie Goldthwaite's Life*, pp. 90–108.

22. Graves, *Woman in America*, pp. 178–79.

23. Ibid., p. 178.

24. "Working-Women in New York," *Harper's New Monthly Magazine* 61 (Dec. 1880): 25.

25. Virginia Penny, *How Women Make Money, Married or Single in All Branches of the Arts and Sciences, Professions, Trades, Agricultural and Mechanical Pursuits* (Philadelphia: John E. Potter, 1862), p. 294.

26. Penny, *Employments of Women*, p. 291 (this is an updated version of Penny's 1862 book); Penny, *How Women Make Money*, pp. 291–92; *Nation* 120 (Oct. 17, 1867): 324.

27. "Working-Women in New York," p. 26.

28. Ibid., pp. 25–31.

29. Graves, *Girlhood and Womanhood*, pp. 149–51, 145.

30. Susan Strasser, *Never Done: A History of American Housework* (New York: Pantheon Books, 1982), p. 146.

31. Penny, *How Women Make Money*, pp. 183, 120.

32. Ibid., pp. 425–26.

33. Strasser, *Never Done*, p. 163.

34. Bledstein, *Culture of Professionalism*, pp. 4–5.

35. "Working-Women in New York," pp. 30–33.

36. Caroline Dall, *Women's Rights to Labor, or Low Wages and Hard Work* (Boston: Walker, Wise, 1860) as quoted by Lerner, *Female Experience*, pp. 273–74.

37. Ibid., p. 274.

38. Penny, *How Women Make Money*, pp. 238–44.

39. Ibid., pp. 221, 178–80.

40. Ibid., p. 180.

41. Judith A. McGaw, " 'A Good Place to Work': Industrial Workers and Occupational Choice, The Case of Berkshire Women," *Journal of Interdisciplinary History* 10 (Autumn

1979): 228; Dall, as quoted by Lerner, *Female Experience*, p. 273.

42. McGaw, " 'A Good Place to Work,' " pp. 230, 243; Penny, *How Women Make Money*, pp. 172–77, 183.

43. Penny, *How Women Make Money*, pp. 181, 173–74, 293–94.

44. Wise, *Young Lady's Counsellor*, pp. 168–69; Lewis, *Our Girls*, p. 102; "How Shall Our Daughters Be Educated?" p. 169; Arthur, *Advice*, pp. 24–28; Penny, *How Women Make Money*, pp. 110–11, 113.

45. Penny, *How Women Make Money*, pp. 237, 52–54, 103, 476; see also "Working-Women in New York," pp. 31–32.

46. Penny, *How Women Make Money*, pp. 103–4, 53–54.

47. Ibid., pp. 139–41.

48. Marion Harland, *Ruby's Husband*, pp. 214–26.

49. Penny, *How Women Make Money*, pp. 278–79.

50. Ibid., pp. 100–102.

51. *Illustrated Christian Weekly* 6 (June 17, 1876): 299; *Harper's Weekly* 4 (Apr. 14, 1860): 239.

52. Penny, *Employments of Women*, pp. 289–90; Penny, *How Women Make Money*, pp. 289–90.

53. Penny, *How Women Make Money*, p. 167.

54. Harland, *Ruby's Husband*, pp. 3–80.

55. Fern, *Rose Clark*, pp. 20–135.

56. Penny, *How Women Make Money*, p. 124.

57. Warner, *Wide, Wide World*, p. 196.

58. Penny, *How Women Make Money*, p. 109.

59. Ibid., pp. 40–41.

60. Cochran, *200 Years of American Business*, p. 70; Warner, *Wide, Wide World*, pp. 120–25, 142–45, 196–97.

61. Strasser, *Never Done*, p. 18.

62. Cochran, *200 Years of American Business*, p. 79.

63. Deutrich, "Propriety and Pay," pp. 67–71.

64. Ibid., pp. 68–71.

65. Penny, *How Women Make Money*, pp. 10–11.

66. Fern, *Rose Clark*, pp. 40–42, 342–43.

67. Melder, "Woman's High Calling," pp. 23–24.

68. Ibid., p. 24.

69. Graves, *Girlhood and Womanhood*, pp. 9–10, 13–16; Hentz, *Linda*, pp. 80–82, 110–14.

70. Melder, "Woman's High Calling," pp. 22–23, 19.

71. See especially Bernard and Vinovskis, "Female School Teacher," pp. 332–45.

72. Penny, *How Women Make Money*, pp. 38–39.

73. Anna Howard Shaw, *The Story of a Pioneer* (New York: Harper Bros., 1915), as quoted by Lerner, *Female Experience*, pp. 231–32.

74. Holmes, *Meadowbrook*, pp. 168–69; Arthur, "Jessie Hampton," in *Woman's Trials*, p. 139; Penny, *How Women Make Money*, pp. 36–37.

75. Warner, *Wide, Wide World*, p. 259.

76. Gregory, "Female Physicians," p. 243; see also Thorne, "Coming

Woman," pp. 530–31; "M.W.-F.," "Women as Lawyers," *Lippincott's Magazine* 5 (Mar. 1879), in which the author uses the "fitness and success of women as doctors" as an argument for admitting them to the bar (p. 386).

77. Lewis, *Our Girls*, pp. 139–41.

78. Penny, *How Women Make Money*, pp. 25–27.

79. Mary Roth Walsh, *"Doctors Wanted,"* pp. 23–26, viii, 28–32.

80. *Illustrated Christian Weekly* 6 (Feb. 12, 1876): 82; Bledstein, *Culture of Professionalism*, pp. 84–85; William G. Rothstein, *American Physicians in the Nineteenth Century* (Baltimore: Johns Hopkins University Press, 1972).

81. Gregory, "Female Physicians," p. 246.

82. Bledstein, *Culture of Professionalism*, pp. 81–84.

83. Lewis, *Our Girls*, p. 136; "M.W.-F.," "Women as Lawyers," p. 387.

84. "Woman's Missionary Work," *Illustrated Christian Weekly* 6 (Oct. 28, 1876): 525.

85. Ibid.; Penny, *How Women Make Money*, pp. 22–23.

86. Penny, *How Women Make Money*, p. 23; see also "At Home and Abroad," *Illustrated Christian Weekly* 6 (Dec. 30, 1876): 643.

87. Penny, *How Women Make Money*, pp. 3–4.

88. Graves, *Woman in America*, pp. 189, 191–92, 190.

89. Penny, *How Women Make Money*, p. 21.

90. Ibid., pp. 3–4.

91. Bode, *Anatomy of American Popular Culture*, pp. 120–28; Frank Luther Mott, *Golden Multitudes: The Story of Best Sellers in the United States* (New York: Macmillan, 1947), pp. 9–10; Arthur M. Schlesinger, Sr., *Learning How to Behave: A Historical Study of American Etiquette Books* (New York: Macmillan, 1946), p. 18.

92. Wise, *Young Lady's Counsellor*, pp. 168–69; Arthur, *Advice*, pp. 24–26; Penny, *How Women Make Money*, p. 42.

93. Penny, *How Women Make Money*, pp. 126, 404; see also Strasser, *Never Done*, pp. 163–66.

94. Penny, *How Women Make Money*, p. 80.

95. Ibid., pp. 80–83.

96. Fern, *Rose Clark*, pp. 219–55.

97. Ibid., pp. 283–84.

98. Ibid., p. 235.

Epilogue: *The "Lost" Ideal*

1. Rosenberg, *Beyond Separate Spheres*, p. 54.

2. Woodward, *Lady Persuaders*, p. 3.

3. Caroline Ticknor, "The Steel-Engraving Lady and the Gibson Girl," *Atlantic Monthly* 88 (July 1901): 107–8.

4. Carolyn Forrey, "The New Woman Revisited," *Women's Studies* 2, no. 1 (1974): 42–54.

5. Smith-Rosenberg, *Disorderly Conduct,* pp. 58–59.

6. Ibid., p. 40.

Bibliography

Square brackets [] indicate original date of publication for primary sources if known and different from the one cited.

Primary Sources

Abell, Mrs. L. G. *Woman in Her Various Relations.* New York: William Holdredge, 1851.

"Addressed to Wise Women," *Ladies' Repository* 25 (Apr. 1865): 245.

Alcott, Dr. William A. *The Young Woman's Book of Health.* Boston: Tappan, Whittemore and Mason, 1850.

Arthur, T. S. *Advice to Young Ladies on Their Duties and Conduct in Life.* Boston: G. W. Cottrell, 1851 [1847].

———. *Alice Melville; or The Indiscretion,* and *Mary Ellis,* bound together. Philadelphia: Henry F. Anners, 1850.

———. *The Angel of the Household and Other Tales.* Philadelphia: John E. Potter, n.d. [1854].

———. *Woman's Trials; or Tales and Sketches from the Life around Us.* New York: James B. Millar, 1885 [1851].

"At Home and Abroad." *Illustrated Christian Weekly* 6 (Dec. 30, 1876): 645.

Badger, Ada Shepard. "Essay IV." In Julia Ward Howe, ed., *Sex and Education: A Reply to Dr. E. H. Clarke's "Sex in Education."* 1874. Reprint. New York: Arno Press, 1972, pp. 72–86.

Beecher, Catharine E. *A Treatise on Domestic Economy for the Use of Young Ladies at Home and at School.* 3d ed., rev. New York: Harper and Brothers, 1855 [1842].

———, and Harriet Beecher Stowe. *The New Housekeeper's Manual: . . . Together with the Handy Cook Book by Catharine Beecher.* New York: Fords, Howard and Hubert, 1873.

"Benefit of Household Care." *Ladies' Repository* 25 (Apr. 1865): 246.

Blaikie, William. *How to Get Strong and How to Stay So.* New York: Harper and Brothers, 1879.

Burnap, Rev. George W. *Lectures on the Sphere and Duties of Woman, and Other Subjects.* Baltimore: John Murray, 1841.

Carlier, M. "M. Carlier on Marriage in America." *Nation* 4, no. 96 (1867): 351.

Chapin, Edwin Hubbell. *Duties of Young Women.* Boston: G. W. Briggs, 1848.

Clarke, Edward H., M.D. *Sex in Education; or A Fair Chance for the Girls.* 1873. Reprint. New York: Arno Press and the New York Times, 1972.

"Crofut on Skates." *Harper's Weekly* 4 (Feb. 11, 1860): 91–92.

Cutter, Calvin, M.D. *The Female Guide: Containing Facts and Information upon the Effects of Masturbation, and the Causes, Prevention, Treatment, and Cure of Hernia or Rupture, Costiveness.* . . . West Brookfield, [Mass.?]: Charles A. Mirick, 1844.

————. *First Book on Anatomy, Physiology and Hygiene for Grammar Schools and Families.* Rev. stereotype ed. Philadelphia: J. B. Lippincott, 1854 [1852].

"The Doctor." "Hints to Lovers; or Courtship Reduced to Rule: With Observations upon the Symptoms and Treatment of Desperate Cases." *Knickerbocker* 25 (Apr. 1845): 341–45.

"Editorial Chitchat." *Peterson's Magazine* 3 (Mar. 1858): 248.

Evans, Augusta J. *St. Elmo.* New York: G. W. Charleton, 1866.

————. *Vashti; or "Until Death Us Do Part."* New York: G. W. Carleton, 1869.

Fern, Fanny. *Rose Clark.* New York: Mason Brothers, 1856 [1855].

Foote, Dr. Edward B. *Medical Common Sense; Applied to the Causes, Prevention and Cure of Chronic Diseases and Unhappiness in Marriage.* Rev. and enlarged ed. New York: Published by the Author, 1867 [1858].

"14 Ways by Which People Get Sick." *Ladies' Repository* 25 (July 1865): 438.

Gardner, Mrs. H. C. "Invalid Women." *Ladies' Repository* 25 (Dec. 1865): 724.

————. "Labor; or Striking for Higher Wages." *Ladies' Repository* 19 (Jan. 1859): 7–11 and (Feb. 1859): 82–85.

Graves, Mrs. A. J. *Girlhood and Womanhood; or Sketches of My Schoolmates.* Boston: T. H. Carter & Co., and Benjamin B. Mussey, 1844.

————. *Woman in America: Being an Examination into the Moral and Intellectual Condition of American Female Society.* New York: Harper and Brothers, 1843 [1841].

Gregory, Samuel. "Female Physicians." *Littell's Living Age* 73 (May 3, 1862): 243–49.

Hale, Sarah J. *Manners; or Happy Homes and Good Society All the Year Round.* 1867. Reprint. New York: Arno Press, 1972.

Harland, Marion. *Alone.* New York: J. C. Derby, 1856 [1854].

————. *Common Sense in the Household: A Manual of Practical Housewifery.* New York: Charles Scribner's Sons, 1871.

————. *Ruby's Husband.* New York: Sheldon and Co., 1869 [1868].

_____. "What Shall We Do with Our Daughters?" *Illustrated Christian Weekly* 6 (Apr. 1, 1876): 158–59.

Hartley, Florence. *The Ladies' Book of Etiquette and Manual of Politeness: A Complete Hand Book for the Use of the Lady in Polite Society*. Boston: G. W. Cottrell, 1860.

Hentz, Mrs. Caroline Lee. *Linda; or The Young Pilot of the Belle Creole*. Philadelphia: T. B. Peterson & Brothers, 1869 [1848].

Higginson, Thomas Wentworth. "Essay II." In Julia Ward Howe, ed., *Sex and Education: A Reply to Dr. E. H. Clarke's "Sex in Education."* 1874. Reprint. New York: Arno Press, 1972, pp. 32–52.

Hollick, Frederick, M.D. *The Marriage Guide; or Natural History of Generation. A Private Instructor for Married Persons and Those about to Marry, Both Male and Female*. 196th edition. New York: T. W. Strong, n.d. [1859].

Holmes, Mary J. *'Lena Rivers*. New York: G. W. Dillingham, 1856.

_____. *Meadowbrook*. Chicago: Donohue Brothers, n.d. [1857].

_____. *Rose Mather: A Tale*. New York: Carleton, 1868.

"Honorable Often to Be an Old Maid." *Peterson's Magazine* 33 (May 1858): 395–96.

"How Shall Our Daughters Be Educated." *Peterson's Magazine* 33 (May 1858): 169.

Howe, Julia Ward, ed. *Sex and Education: A Reply to Dr. E. H. Clarke's "Sex in Education."* 1874. Reprint. New York: Arno Press, 1972.

"Husbands and Wives." *Illustrated Christian Weekly* 6 (Sept. 9, 1876): 440.

Ladies' Indispensable Assistant, Being a Companion for the Sister, Mother and Wife. . . . New York: Nassau Street, 1852 [1851].

Leslie, Miss Eliza. *Behaviour Book: A Guide and Manual for Ladies as Regards Their Conversation, Manners, Dress . . . etc*. Philadelphia: T. B. Peterson and Brothers, 1859.

Lewis, Dr. Dio. *New Gymnastics for Men, Women and Children*. 4th ed. Boston: Ticknor and Fields, 1863.

_____. *Our Girls*. New York: Harper and Brothers, 1871.

"Marriage a la Mode." *Harper's New Monthly Magazine* 32 (May 1866): 760–61.

Meigs, Charles D., M.D. *Females and Their Diseases: A Series of Letters. . . .* Philadelphia: Lea and Blanchard, 1848.

Miller, Emily Huntington. "A Summer's Adventures." *Ladies' Repository* 25 (Feb. 1865): 74–78 and (Mar. 1865): 139.

"Mr. Henry James on Marriage." *Nation* 10 (June 9, 1870): 366–68.

Muzzey, Artemus Bowers. *The Young Maiden*. 3d ed. Boston: W. Crosby, 1842 [1840].

"M.W.-F." "Women as Lawyers." *Lippincott's Magazine* 5 (Mar. 1879): 386–88.

Newcomb, Harvey. *How to Be a Lady: A Book for Girls.* 6th ed. Boston: Gould, Kendall, and Lincoln, 1849 [1846].

"Olive West." *Harper's New Monthly Magazine* 32 (Apr. 1866): 655–57.

O'Reilly, Rev. Bernard, L.D. *The Mirror of True Womanhood; A Book of Instruction for Women in the World.* 14th ed. New York: Peter F. Collier, 1880 [1877].

"The Other Side of the Question." *Nation* 5 (Oct. 17, 1867): 316.

Parley, Peter. *What to Do and How to Do It; or Morals and Manners Taught by Examples.* New York: Sheldon, 1859 [1843].

Penny, Virginia. *The Employments of Women: A Cyclopaedia of Woman's Work.* Boston: Walker, Wise, 1863.

————. *How Women Make Money, Married or Single in All Branches of the Arts and Sciences, Professions, Trades, Agricultural and Mechanical Pursuits.* Philadelphia: John E. Potter, 1862.

————. "Poor Health of American Women." *Ladies' Repository* 25 (Mar. 1865): 155.

Perry, Nora. "Rosalind Newcomb." *Harper's New Monthly Magazine* 20 (May 1860): 778–93.

Phelps, Elizabeth Stuart. *The Gates Ajar.* Boston: Fields, Osgood (formerly Ticknor and Fields), 1869 [1868].

Porter, Rev. James. *The Operative's Friend, and Defence; or Hints to Young Ladies, Who Are Dependent on Their Own Exertions.* 3d ed. Boston: C. H. Peirce, 1850.

"Reply to Mr. James." *Nation* 10 (June 23, 1870): 404–5.

"A Revolutionary Girl's Pluck." *Illustrated Christian Weekly* 6 (July 15, 1876): 343.

"Rules for Health." *Illustrated Christian Weekly* 6 (Oct. 28, 1876): 521.

"The School-Teacher at Bottle Flat." *Frank Leslie's Popular Monthly,* Feb. 1876, pp. 162–67.

"Sister Anne." *Harper's New Monthly Magazine* 12 (Dec. 1855): 92–93.

Skating on the Ladies' Skating Rink in the Central Park, New York. Engraving in *Harper's Weekly* 4 (Jan. 28, 1860): 56–57.

"Society and Marriage." *Nation* 10 (May 26, 1870): 332–33.

Southworth, E. D. E. N. *Ishmael; or In the Depths.* Philadelphia: T. B. Peterson & Bros., 1876 [1864].

Stowe, Harriet Beecher. *Pink and White Tyranny: A Society Novel.* In *The Writings of Harriet Beecher Stowe,* Riverside ed., 11:267–523. Boston: Houghton, Mifflin, 1899 [1878].

"Taxes on Bachelors." *Harper's Weekly* 4 (Jan. 28, 1860): 50.

Thorne, P. "The Coming Woman." *Lippincott's Magazine* 5 (May 1870): 529–32.

Thornwell, Emily. *The Lady's Guide to Perfect Gentility in Manners, Dress, and Conversation.* . . . New York: Derby and Jackson, 1856.

Ticknor, Caroline. "The Steel-Engraving Lady and the Gibson Girl." *Atlantic Monthly* 88 (July 1901): 105–8.

Van De Warker, Dr. Ely, M.D. "The Genesis of Woman." *Popular Science Monthly* 5 (July 1874): 269–77.

Warner, Susan. *The Wide, Wide World.* New York: Grosset and Dunlap, n.d. [1851].

"A Warning to Lady Skaters." *Harper's Weekly* 4 (Feb. 11, 1860): 87.

Weaver, Rev. George Sumner. *Aims and Aids for Girls and Young Women on the Various Duties of Life.* New York: Fowler and Wells, 1856 [1855].

————. *Hopes and Helps for the Young of Both Sexes.* New York: Fowler and Wells, 1857 [1852].

Webster, William G., and William A. Wheeler. *A Common-School Dictionary of the English Language.* New York: Ivison, Blakeman; Springfield, Mass.: G. & C. Merriam, 1867.

"What Everybody Said." *Harper's Weekly* 4 (Feb. 4, 1860): 76.

Whitney, Mrs. A. D. T. *A Summer in Leslie Goldthwaite's Life.* Boston: Houghton Mifflin, 1891 [1866].

"Why Is Single Life Becoming More General?" *Nation* 6 (Mar. 5, 1868): 190–91.

Willard, Emma. *Morals for the Young; or Good Principles Instilling Wisdom.* New York: A. S. Barnes, 1857.

"Winifred's Vow." *Harper's New Monthly Magazine* 12 (Dec. 1855): 81–85.

Wise, Rev. Daniel. *The Young Lady's Counsellor; or Outlines and Illustrations of the Sphere, the Duties, and the Dangers of Young Women.* . . . New York: Carlton and Phillips, 1854 [1851].

"Women as Politicians." *Nation* 6 (Dec. 1868): 475–76.

"A Working Woman's Statement." *Nation* 4 (Feb. 21, 1867): 155–56.

"Working-Women in New York." *Harper's New Monthly Magazine* 61 (Dec. 1880): 25–37.

Secondary Sources

Aresty, Esther B. *The Best Behavior: The Course of Good Manners—from Antiquity to the Present—as Seen through Courtesy and Etiquette Books.* New York: Simon and Schuster, 1970.

Armitage, Shelley. "Rawhide Heroines: The Evolution of the Cowgirl and the Myth of America." In Sam B. Girgus, ed., *The American Self,* pp. 166–81. Albuquerque: University of New Mexico Press, 1981.

Banner, Lois W. *American Beauty.* New York: Knopf, 1983.

Baym, Nina. "Portrayal of Women in American Literature, 1790–1870." In Marlene Springer, ed., *What Manner of Woman: Essays on English and American Life and Literature,* pp. 211–34. New York: New York University Press, 1977.

————. *Woman's Fiction: A Guide to Novels by and about Women in America, 1820–1870.* Ithaca: Cornell University Press, 1978.

Berg, Barbara J. *The Remembered Gate: Origins of American Feminism; The Woman and the City, 1800–1860.* New York: Oxford University Press, 1978.

Bernard, Richard M., and Maris A. Vinovskis. "The Female School Teacher in Ante-Bellum Massachusetts." *Journal of Social History* 10 (Mar. 1977): 332–45.

Bledstein, Burton J. *The Culture of Professionalism: The Middle Class and the Development of Higher Education in America.* New York: Norton, 1976.

Boas, George, ed. *Romanticism in America: Papers Contributed to a Symposium Held at the Baltimore Museum of Art, May 13–15, 1940.* Baltimore: Johns Hopkins Press, 1940.

Bode, Carl. *The Anatomy of American Popular Culture, 1840–1861.* Berkeley and Los Angeles: University of California Press, 1959.

Cawelti, John. "Pornography, Catastrophe, and Vengeance: Shifting Narrative Structures in a Changing American Culture." In Sam B. Girgus, ed., *The American Self: Myth, Ideology, and Popular Culture,* pp. 182–92. Albuquerque: University of New Mexico Press, 1981.

Clinton, Catherine. *The Other Civil War: American Women in the Nineteenth Century.* New York: Hill and Wang, 1984.

Cochran, Thomas C. *200 Years of American Business.* New York: Basic Books, 1977.

Cogan, Frances B. "Weak Fathers and Other Beasts: An Examination of the American Male in Domestic Novels, 1850–1870." *American Studies* 25 (Fall 1984): 5–20.

Conrad, Susan Phinney. *Perish the Thought: Intellectual Women in Romantic America, 1830–1860.* New York: Oxford University Press, 1976.

Conway, Jill Ker. "Utopian Dream or Dystopian Nightmare? Nineteenth Century Feminist Ideas about Equality." *Proceedings of the American Antiquarian Society* 96, pt. 2 (1987): 285–94.

Cummings, Richard Osborn. *The American and His Food.* 2d ed. New York: Arno Press, 1970.

Degler, Carl. *At Odds: Women and the Family in America from the Revolution to the Present.* New York: Oxford University Press, 1980.

————. "What Ought to Be and What Was: Women's Sexuality in the Nineteenth Century." *American Historical Review* 79 (Dec. 1979): 1467–90.

Deutrich, Bernice M. "Propriety and Pay." *Prologue: The Journal of the National Archives* 3, no. 2 (1971): 67–72.

Douglas, Anne. *The Feminization of American Culture*. New York: Knopf, 1977.

Eakin, Paul John. *The New England Girl: Cultural Ideas in Hawthorne, Stowe, Howells and James*. Athens: University of Georgia Press, 1976.

Earnest, Ernest. *The American Eve in Fact and Fiction, 1775–1914*. Chicago: University of Chicago Press, 1974.

Ehrenreich, Barbara, and Deirdre English. *For Her Own Good: 150 Years of the Experts' Advice to Women*. Garden City, N.Y.: Doubleday Anchor Press, 1978.

Epstein, Barbara Leslie. *The Politics of Domesticity: Women, Evangelism, and Temperance in Nineteenth Century America*. Middletown, Conn.: Wesleyan University Press, 1981.

Fishburn, Katherine. *Women in Popular Culture: A Reference Guide*. Westport, Conn.: Greenwood Press, 1981.

Forrey, Carolyn. "The New Woman Revisited." *Woman's Studies* 2 (1974): 37–56.

Freedman, Estelle B. "The New Woman: Changing Views of Women in the 1920's." *Journal of American History* 61 (Sept. 1974): 372–93.

Friedman, Jean E., and William E. Shade, eds. *Our American Sisters: Women in American Life and Thought*. 2d ed. Boston: Allyn and Bacon, 1976.

Girgus, Sam B., ed. *The American Self: Myth, Ideology and Popular Culture*. Albuquerque: University of New Mexico Press, 1981.

Griswold, Robert L. "Law, Sex, Cruelty, and Divorce in Victorian America, 1840–1900." *American Quarterly* 38 (Winter 1986): 721–45.

Habegger, Alfred. *Gender, Fantasy and Realism in American Literature*. New York: Columbia University Press, 1982.

Halttunen, Karen. *Confidence Men and Painted Women: A Study of Middle-Class Culture in America, 1830–1870*. New Haven: Yale University Press, 1982.

Hartman, Mary S., and Lois Banner, eds. *Clio's Consciousness Raised*. New York: Harper & Row, 1974.

Hellerstein, Erna Olafson, Leslie Parker Hume, and Karen M. Offen, eds. *Victorian Women: A Documentary Account of Women's Lives in Nineteenth Century England, France, and the United States*. Stanford: Stanford University Press, 1981.

Howe, Daniel Walker, ed. *Victorian America*. Philadelphia: University of Pennsylvania Press, 1976.

Irwin, Inez Haynes. *Angels and Amazons: A Hundred Years of American Women*. New York: Doubleday, Doran, 1933.

Jones, Betty H., and Alberta Arthurs. "The American Eve: A New Look at American Heroines and Their Critics." *International Journal of Women's Studies* 1 (1978): 1–12.

Katzman, David M. *Seven Days a Week: Women and Domestic Service in Industrializing America.* New York: Oxford University Press, 1978.

Kelley, Mary. "The Sentimentalists: Promise and Betrayal in the Home." *Signs: Journal of Women in Culture and Society* 4 (Spring 1979): 434–46.

Kolbenschlag, Madonna. *Kiss Sleeping Beauty Good-Bye: Breaking the Spell of Feminine Myths and Models.* Garden City, N.Y.: Doubleday, 1979.

Lerner, Gerda. *The Female Experience: An American Documentary.* Indianapolis: Bobbs-Merrill, 1977.

––––––. *The Majority Finds Its Past: Placing Women in History.* Oxford: Oxford University Press, 1979.

Lynes, Russell. *The Domesticated Americans.* New York: Harper & Row, 1963.

McGaw, Judith A. " 'A Good Place to Work': Industrial Workers and Occupational Choice, The Case of Berkshire Women." *Journal of Interdisciplinary History* 10 (Autumn 1979): 227–48.

Melder, Keith. "Woman's High Calling: The Teaching Profession in America, 1830–1860." *American Studies* 13, no. 2 (1972): 19–32.

Mott, Frank Luther. *Golden Multitudes: The Story of Best Sellers in the United States.* New York: Macmillan, 1947.

––––––. *A History of American Magazines. Vol. 2: 1850–1865.* Cambridge, Mass: Harvard University Press, 1957 [1938].

Reep, Diana. *The Rescue and Romance: Popular Novels before World War I.* Bowling Green: Bowling Green State University Popular Press, 1982.

Riegel, Robert E. *American Women: A Story of Social Change.* Madison, N.J.: Fairleigh Dickinson University Press, 1970.

Rosenberg, Charles E. "Sexuality, Class and Role in 19th Century America." *American Quarterly* 25 (May 1973): 131–54.

Rosenberg, Rosalind. *Beyond Separate Spheres: Intellectual Roots of Modern Feminism.* New Haven: Yale University Press, 1982.

Rothman, Ellen K. *Hands and Hearts: A History of Courtship in America.* New York: Basic Books, 1984.

Rothstein, William G. *American Physicians in the Nineteenth Century.* Baltimore: Johns Hopkins University Press, 1972.

Ryan, Mary P. *Womanhood in America: From Colonial Times to the Present.* New York: New Viewpoints, 1975.

Schlesinger, Arthur M., Sr. *Learning How to Behave: A Historical Study of American Etiquette Books.* New York: Macmillan, 1946.

Smith, Henry Nash. "Fiction and the American Ideology: The Genesis of Howell's Early Realism." In Sam B. Girgus, ed., *The American Self: Myth, Ideology and Popular Culture,* pp. 43–57. Albuquerque: University of New Mexico Press, 1981.

Smith, Page. *Daughters of the Promised Land: Women in American History.* Boston: Little, Brown, 1970.

Smith-Rosenberg, Carroll. *Disorderly Conduct: Visions of Gender in Victorian America.* New York: Oxford University Press, 1985.

————. "Puberty to Menopause: The Cycle of Femininity in Nineteenth-Century America." In Mary S. Hartman and Lois Banner, eds., *Clio's Consciousness Raised,* pp. 23–37. New York: Harper & Row, 1974.

Smith-Rosenberg, Carroll, and Charles Rosenberg. "The Female Animal: Medical and Biological Views of Woman and Her Role in Nineteenth-Century America." *Journal of American History* 60 (Sept. 1973): 332–56.

Strasser, Susan. *Never Done: A History of American Housework.* New York: Pantheon, 1982.

Taylor, William R. *Cavalier and Yankee: The Old South and American National Character.* New York: Braziller, 1961.

Thompson, Eleanor Wolf. *Education for Ladies, 1830–1860: Ideas on Education in Magazines for Women.* New York: King's Crown Press, 1947.

Walsh, Mary Roth. *"Doctors Wanted: No Women Need Apply": Sexual Barriers in the Medical Profession, 1835–1975.* New Haven: Yale University Press, 1977.

Welter, Barbara. *Dimity Convictions: The American Woman in the Nineteenth Century.* Athens: Ohio University Press, 1976.

Westling, Louise. *Sacred Groves and Ravaged Gardens: The Fiction of Eudora Welty, Carson McCullers, and Flannery O'Connor.* Athens: University of Georgia Press, 1985.

Winslow, Ola Elizabeth. "Books for the Lady Reader, 1820–1860." In George Boas, ed., *Romanticism in America: Papers Contributed to a Symposium Held at the Baltimore Museum of Art, May 13–15, 1940,* pp. 89–109. Baltimore: Johns Hopkins Press, 1940.

Wood, Anne Douglas. " 'The Fashionable Diseases': Women's Complaints and Their Treatment in Nineteenth Century America." In Mary S. Hartman and Lois Banner, eds., *Clio's Consciousness Raised,* pp. 1–22. New York: Harper & Row, 1974.

Woodward, Helen, *The Lady Persuaders.* New York: Ivan Obolensky, 1960.

Reference Works

The American Catalogue. Compiled by Lyns E. Jones. New York: A. C. Armstrong, 1880.

Appleton's Cyclopaedia of American Biography. Edited by J. G. Wilson and John Fiske. New York: Appleton, 1886, 1887, 1888, 1889.

Bobbitt, Mary Reed. *A Bibliography of Etiquette Books Published in America before 1900.* New York: N.p., 1947.

National Union Catalog: Pre-1856 Imprints. Chicago: Mansill, 1968.

Poole's Index to Periodical Literature, 1815–1899 (Abridged). Boston: James R. Osgood, 1901.

Schlesinger, Arthur M., Jr., general ed. *The Almanac of American History.* John S. Bowman, executive ed. New York: Putnam, 1983.

Who Was Who in America: Historical Volume, 1607–1896; A Component Volume of Who's Who in American History. Chicago: A. N. Marquis, 1963.

Willard, Frances E., and Mary A. Livermore, eds. *American Women: A Comprehensive Encyclopedia of the Lives and Achievements of American Women during the Nineteenth Century.* Rev. ed. New York: Mast, Crowell, and Kirkpatrick, 1897 [1893].

Index